Narrative and the Cultural Construction of Illness and Healing

Narrative and the Cultural Construction of Illness and Healing

Edited by

Cheryl Mattingly
and Linda C. Garro

UNIVERSITY OF CALIFORNIA PRESS
Berkeley · Los Angeles · London

University of California Press
Berkeley and Los Angeles, California

University of California Press, Ltd.
London, England

© 2000 by the Regents of the University of California

Library of Congress Cataloging-in-Publication Data

Narrative and the cultural construction of illness
and healing / edited by Cheryl Mattingly and
Linda C. Garro.
    p.   cm.
  Includes bibliographical references and index.
  ISBN 0-520-21824-8 (cloth : alk. paper)—
  ISBN 0-520-21825-6 (pbk. : alk paper)
    1. Social medicine.   2. Medical anthropology.
3. Discourse analysis, Narrative.   4. Medicine and
psychology.   I. Mattingly, Cheryl.   II. Garro,
Linda C.
RA418 .N36 2000
306.4'61—dc21   00-031629

Manufactured in the United States of America

09 08 07 06 05 04 03 02 01 00

     9 8 7 6 5 4 3 2 1

The paper used in this publication meets the mini-
mum requirements of ANSI/NISO Z39.48-1992 (R
1997) (Permanence of Paper). ♾

For Bill and Robert

Contents

Acknowledgments

We are indebted to Arthur Kleinman, Byron Good, and Mary-Jo Del-Vecchio Good for bringing us together through the Harvard Friday Morning Seminar in medical anthropology. This seminar provided the intellectual environment in which our collaborative work on narrative first took root and flourished.

We would like to express our sincere thanks to the two anonymous reviewers of this volume and the board member from the University of California Press. All three provided strong encouragement and useful suggestions for revision. The guidance they provided greatly assisted us in completing this volume. Partial support was provided by Maternal and Child Health, Department of Health and Human Services (MC5-060745) for Cheryl Mattingly. Robert Whitmore generously provided assistance in reading through and commenting on several earlier drafts of our chapters. We also thank Bill Roubal and Robert Whitmore for all their support through the entire project.

ONE

Narrative as Construct and Construction

LINDA C. GARRO and CHERYL MATTINGLY

Narrative is a fundamental human way of giving meaning to experience. In both telling and interpreting experiences, narrative mediates between an inner world of thought-feeling and an outer world of observable actions and states of affairs (J. Bruner 1986; Carrithers 1992; Mattingly and Garro 1994; Mattingly 1998a). Creating a narrative, as well as attending to one, is an active and constructive process—one that depends on both personal and cultural resources. Stories can provide a powerful medium for learning and gaining understanding about others by affording a context for insights into what one has not personally experienced. By reading, for example, Laura Bohannon's (1966) account of the lively interchange that occurred when she was cajoled into telling a story to a group of Tiv men in West Africa during her field research, we come to share, albeit vicariously and partially, in this experience and the understanding that it engendered. Initially she is confident that Shakespeare's *Hamlet* has "only one possible interpretation" as "the general plot and motivation of the greater tragedies would always be clear—everywhere—although some details of custom might have to be explained and difficulties of translation might produce other slight changes" (1966:28). She views this storytelling occasion as her "chance to prove *Hamlet* universally intelligible" (29). Instead, her telling brings about numerous opportunities for Tiv elders to present alternative interpretations of why the story unfolds as it does, thereby instructing her about its "true meaning" (for, as they tell Bohannon as she nears the end of the story, "it is clear that the elders of your country have never told you what the story really means" [33]). One of many such instances occurs when Bohannon explains that Hamlet seeks to kill his uncle, who is also his father's murderer, and by this act to avenge his father's death. She recounts:

> This time I had shocked my audience seriously. "For a man to raise his hand against his father's brother and the one who has become his father—that is a terrible thing. The elders ought to let such a man be bewitched."
>
> I nibbled at my kola nut in some perplexity, then pointed out that after all the man had killed Hamlet's father.
>
> "No," pronounced the old man, speaking less to me than to the young men sitting behind the elders. "If your father's brother has killed your father, you must appeal to your father's age mates; *they* may avenge him. No man may use violence against his senior relatives." Another thought struck him. "But if his father's brother had indeed been wicked enough to bewitch Hamlet and make him mad that would be a good story indeed, for it would be his fault that Hamlet, being mad, no longer had any sense and thus was ready to kill his father's brother."
>
> There was a murmur of applause. *Hamlet* was again a good story to them, but it no longer seemed quite the same story to me. (Bohannon 1966:32)

For the listeners, hearing the story sets in motion a search for meaning among possible meanings (Iser 1978). By the end of Bohannon's article, the key events have remained the same, but alternative interpretations of these events have been put forward, recastings consistent with Tiv understandings of the social and moral order. A co-constructed narrative emerges through the push and pull between Bohannon's telling of a story world and the world where the story is told.

Exploring narrative as a theoretical construct provides a broader context for considering what happened in this particular telling, in this particular co-construction of *Hamlet*. The claim that narrative is a fundamental mode of thought has been eloquently put forward by Jerome Bruner. He contends that narrative offers a way of "ordering experience, of constructing reality" (1986:11) that deals in "intention and action and the vicissitudes and consequences that mark their course" (13). Bruner follows literary critic Algirdas Julien Greimas in arguing that a story constructs two landscapes, one of action and another of consciousness. The landscape of action focuses on what actors do in particular situations. The landscape of consciousness concerns "what those involved in the action know, think, or feel, or do not know, think, or feel. The two landscapes are essential and distinct: it is the difference between Oedipus sharing Jocasta's bed before and after he learns from the messenger that she is his mother" (J. Bruner 1986:14). Comprehending the plot of a story means "therefore to have some notion of the changes in an inner landscape of thought in the participants as well as the outer landscape of events" (Carrithers 1992:84). The meaning one attributes to emplotted events reflects expectations and understandings gained through participating in a specific social and moral world. The Tiv elders make sense of the events recounted in the story of *Hamlet* by filling in what they perceive as gaps and reframing what the main actors must have thought and felt in order to act the way they did. Even though *Hamlet* is a story from another cultural world, it is understood by the listeners with reference to their own involvements with the world. And through Bohannon's interactions with the elders, she comes to better understand the emotional, moral, and social grounding of the Tiv through the version of the story they construct. As a "powerful means of socializing values and world views to children and other intimates" (Capps and Ochs 1995:13), narrative mediates emergent constructions of reality. And, finally, narrative is open to alternative readings, as can be seen in the elder's deliberations quoted earlier, as it traffics in "human possibilities rather than settled certainties" (J. Bruner 1986:26).

From his studies of storytelling among urban youths in the United States, William Labov tells us that the most important narrative question a storyteller must answer (and answer so well that the question is never explicitly raised) is "So what?" (Labov 1972, 1981; Labov and Waletzky 1967). The interventions by the Tiv elders serve to keep Bohannon's rendition of *Hamlet* on track so that ultimately it is judged "a very good story" (Bohannon 1966:33). In contrast, a failed story is one that leaves the audience wondering why anyone bothered to tell it. A story may be well formed from a purely structural perspective, and it may have a clear "point," but if the audience doesn't know why the point matters to them, if the events in the story never touch them, then the story doesn't work.

EMERGENCE OF NARRATIVE
THEORY IN ANTHROPOLOGY

This implicit "So what?" narrative question can be leveled at the recent proliferation of narrative studies in anthropology. What is suddenly so appealing about stories, about narrative? After all, there is nothing recent about the entrance of stories into anthropology. Anthropologists are quite accustomed to overhearing, eliciting, and analyzing stories told by their interlocutors as a standard part of their cultural investigations. They have studied myths, folktales, and proverbs, a culture's repertoire of well-known tales. They have long been interested in stories of personal experience in the form of life histories (e.g., Radin [1926] 1983; Peacock and Holland 1993; Crapanzano 1977, 1984; G. Frank 1996, 2000; Langness and Frank 1981). Linguistic anthropologists and folklorists have also studied naturally occurring personal stories, such as gossip or the "tall tale," which emerge as a casual part of everyday social discourse (e.g., Baumann 1986; Briggs 1996). Although social and cultural anthropologists have always dealt in stories (their own and those of their informants), they have not always explicitly heeded the fact that so much of their data has come in narrative form. With the notable exception of studies influenced by linguistics (e.g., Hymes 1981; Brenneis 1984, 1996; C. Goodwin 1984; M. H. Goodwin 1990; Haviland 1977, 1996; Ochs, Smith, and Taylor 1996; Brenneis and Lein, 1977; Capps and Ochs 1995; Ochs and Capps in press), this neglect has been especially marked when it comes to personal tales through which a teller might couch an experience or recount to an audience important events in the social world. Even when anthropologists have been highly cognizant of the aesthetic qualities of a culture's enduring myths and folktales, they have not always been so keenly aware that the personal stories they were hearing might be more than transparent mediums for communicating significant social facts.

Lately, however, things have changed. Anthropologists are noticing stories everywhere. Furthermore, they are paying increasing attention to the complex relation between narrative form, narrative performance, and referential content. While interest in narrative cannot be described as new, what characterizes the recent surge of attention among a wide range of scholars is the pronounced concern to take stories seriously. With regard to the life history tradition, for example, critiques pointing to the neglect of the life story as text or as oral performance (Crapanzano 1980; Peacock and Holland 1993; Agar 1980; Chamberlain and Thompson 1998) have contributed to a renewed interest and an enhanced appreciation of the complexities involved in representing and analyzing life stories. Overall, anthropologists are less content to treat stories as the accidental form in which the data come—a critical attentiveness that extends to work in medical anthropology. A more extended discussion of this critical attentiveness is offered in the closing chapter.

As part of their exploration of narrative, anthropologists have introduced constructs drawn from a range of disciplines—linguistics, literary theory, history, cognitive psychology, philosophy—to investigate relations between narrative form and narrative content, between an individual's stories of personal experience and cultural knowledge, or narrative as communicative act. There has been a concern for the pragmatics of narrative, how interlocutors are "doing things with stories," and how, therefore, narratives carry rhetorical weight. Increased awareness about narrative as form and rhetorical practice has also added a critical dimension to anthropological discourse. At the same time, anthropologists have begun to wonder what is and what is not useful in the efflorescence of narrative theorizing that pervades the writing of so many contemporary anthropologists.

This volume has been inspired by the possibilities of narrative, that is, how narratives from healers and patients serve to illuminate aspects of practices and experiences that surround illness but might not otherwise be recognized. It has also been inspired by the possibilities of increased theoretical consciousness with regard to the elicitation and analysis of narratives of illness and healing. What can be learned by taking a comparative look at the range of narrative theories and styles of narrative analysis being used by anthropologists to make sense of their ethnographic data? Do divergent strategies of narrative analysis offer different ways to understand illness and healing? Does the focus on narrative detract from or conceal other, more fruitful, avenues for exploring the experiences of illness and the practices of healing? The essays in this collection, taken together, explore just these kinds of questions and do so by offering a range of answers.

The idea for this volume developed gradually. Our initial collaboration—a symposium organized for the 1990 American Anthropological Association (AAA) meetings—was sparked by our mutual curiosity about the quite different perspectives we each bring to our work on narrative. While we each consider problems relevant to medical anthropology, one of us (Mattingly) is primarily concerned with the relation between narrative and lived experience, drawing extensively on literary and philosophical perspectives, while the other (Garro) is concerned with narrative as a way to relate the study of culture to the study of mind. Many of the papers from this first symposium later appeared in a special issue of *Social Science and Medicine* entitled *Narrative Representations of Illness and Healing* (Garro and Mattingly 1994).

Our enduring interest in exploring alternative modes of narrative analysis germane to medical anthropology led to a second AAA symposium and subsequently to the essays in this book. Chapters by anthropologists predominate, but there are also contributions from individuals trained in sociology, psychiatry, and psychology. In narrative studies it makes little sense to band together in exclusionary disciplinary tribes. There is too much to be gained from cross-fertilizations that draw widely upon the social sciences, as well as literature, history, and philosophy. And, indeed, the essays in this book rely upon a broad range of analytic approaches: phenomenological, literary, critical, cognitive, linguistic, constructivist, hermeneutic, and autobiographical. While these approaches do not represent stable or mutually exclusive systems of thought, they have emerged from various home disciplines that often define narrative in distinct ways.

In forming this collection, we also encouraged contributions from scholars with a skepticism about the recent enthusiasm for narrative. Several of the chapters raise questions about prevailing trends in narrative theory or widespread assumptions about narrative. Some ask how adequately narrative models capture cultural life, social action, or personal experience and wonder what is likely to be neglected by a reliance on a narrative model of social life. We believe these critical voices are essential if narrative analysis is to offer an enduring contribution to medical anthropology and not merely a fashionable gloss on interpretations that gain no analytic depth from being dressed up as narrative theory.

This introductory chapter serves as a backdrop situating these papers within broader trends, trends confined neither to medical anthropology nor to cultural anthropology more generally, but extending into diverse disciplines. The recent emphasis on narrative in cultural studies of illness and healing is part of a very deep and broad contemporary current. One may reasonably claim, as Jerome Bruner does in *Acts of Meaning* (1990, also 1996), that there is now a narrative turn on the horizon of the human sciences. This turn has had a powerful influence in cross-cultural studies of illness and healing.

NARRATIVE IN MEDICINE

The centrality of narrative to some forms of therapeutic practice dates at least to the end of the nineteenth century in the writings of Sigmund Freud. A primary assumption of Freud's psychoanalytic theory is that "the symptom carries a meaning and is connected with the experience of the patient" (Freud 1920:221). Freud is portrayed by Donald Spence (1982:21) as a "master" of "the narrative tradition" who had the ability to take "pieces of the patient's associations, dreams, and memories" and to weave them into a coherent pattern that integrates and makes sense of "previously random happenings" and memories.

> Freud made us aware of the persuasive power of the coherent narrative—in particular, of the way in which an aptly chosen reconstruction can fill the gap between two apparently unrelated events, and in the process, make sense out of nonsense. There seems no doubt but that a well-constructed story possesses a kind of narrative truth that is real and immediate and carries an important significance for the process of therapeutic change. (Spence 1982:21)

Contemporary psychotherapeutic practices continue to stress the role of narrative in decoding and reframing the past to make sense of the present and provide an orientation for the future. Young (1995) studied a Veterans Administration psychiatric facility specializing in the diagnosis and treatment of war-related posttraumatic stress disorder (PTSD). A basic assumption of the treatment program is that in order for a patient to recover, the traumatic memory must be recalled and told to others: "The memory/narrative is the Rosetta stone of his disorder. The patient's postwar histories are generally saturated with misfortune and failure. . . . A properly decoded traumatic memory gives the chaotic surface a coherent subtext" (Young 1995:185).[1] Waitzkin and Magaña, writing about their therapeutic work with Central American refugees who have experienced severe trauma, point to "the importance of a patient's enunciating a coherent narrative . . . as a critical component of the healing process" (Waitzkin and Magaña 1997:822).

Taking a somewhat broader sweep, Eisenberg has suggested that the co-construction of a tenable account between the patient and healer is an important part of clinical care and psychiatric practice:

> The decision to seek medical consultation is a request for interpretation. . . . Patient and doctor together reconstruct the meanings of events in a shared mythopoesis. . . . Once things fall into place; once experience and interpretation appear to coincide, once the patient has a coherent "explanation" which leaves him no longer feeling the victim of the inexplicable and the uncontrollable, the symptoms are, usually, exorcised. (Eisenberg 1981:245)

Writing about narrative processes in psychotherapeutic interactions, Capps and Ochs (1995:176) maintain that "telling and retelling experiences" provide the opportunity for collaborations between therapist and client in developing "alternative versions of stories" that "create new understandings" while also conveying "a revised view of self and others that not only reshapes the past but creates new paths for the future."

In recent years there has been increased attention to the processual and hermeneutic nature of psychotherapeutic practices (e.g., Kirmayer

1994; Schafer 1981, 1992; Spence 1982). For example, concern with how a therapist "functions more as a pattern maker than a pattern finder" (Spence 1982:293) has led to research illuminating how the therapist works to shape an emerging narrative with the patient to be compatible with the narrative expectations of preexisting theories or ideologies. Situations in which patients and therapists converge on a co-constructed account, as well those in which they do not, shed light on the interactive dynamics and structural relationships in clinical encounters (e.g., Kirmayer this volume; Waitzkin and Britt 1993; Young 1995).

Despite this recognition of the role of narrative in the clinical specialty of psychiatry, a specialty that is "regarded as marginal by the rest of biomedicine" (Kleinman 1995:2), much of Western medicine can be described as traditionally hostile to connotative discourse. But this legacy is eroding. As Good (1994) points out, a crisis of representation has found its way into the world of the clinic. Narrative has constituted an alternative mode of representation that is somehow more appropriate to certain aspects of clinical experience (M. Good 1995; M. Good et al. 1992; Hunter 1991; Mattingly 1998b; Brody 1987). Clinicians themselves have also recognized the narrative qualities of their work (e.g., Coles 1989; Eisenberg 1981; Sacks 1987b, 1995; Luria 1968, 1972; Zimmerman and Dickerson 1994).

What has drawn the clinical community to narrative? One reason is that narrative foregrounds the human dramas surrounding illness. This is wonderfully expressed by the neurologist Oliver Sacks. Speaking critically of authorized medical discourse, he distinguishes the traditional medical history from narrative proper in which the "human subject" rather than the pathology is the central character. "Such [medical] histories," he writes,

> are a form of natural history—but they tell us nothing about the individual and his history; they convey nothing of the person, and the experience of the person, as he faces, and struggles to survive, his disease. There is no "subject" in a narrow case history; modern case histories allude to the subject in a cursory phrase ("a trisomic albino female of 21") which could as well apply to a rat as a human being. (1987b:viii)

Sacks advocates narrative discourse as a way to bring persons, with their particular experiences of illness, into focus:

> To restore the human subject at the center—the suffering, afflicted, fighting, human subject—we must deepen a case history to a narrative or tale; only then do we have a "who" as well as a "what," a real person, a patient, in relation to disease—in relation to the physical. (1987b:viii)

Through his writings and his therapeutic practices, Sacks, like Luria before him, envisions the possibilities of a "romantic science" that "treats analytic science and synthetic biography of the individual case as essentially complementary" (Cole 1996:346) and can be portrayed as "the dream of a novelist and a scientist combined" (Sacks 1987a:xii).[2]

Much recent work argues the need to get at illness experience through illness narratives (e.g., Kleinman 1988, 1995; Broyard 1992; Frank 1995). Physicians have published accounts of their own afflictions and encounters with the medical profession, typically conveying their hard-won realization that there is more to the story of being a patient than can be captured by a medical synopsis or charted medical history. Such "wounded healers" have written about how their experiences have significantly affected or transformed the way they think about their broader lives as well their understanding of the medical profession and its practices (Hahn 1995:254; for an insightful review of a number of accounts written by physicians, see Hahn 1995:ch. 9; for a case example of a "wounded healer," see Kleinman 1988:211–13). An important thread in the literature which has emerged from or is directed toward the clinical community and aspires to reorient medical practices in society, is the need to distinguish disease, as phenomena seen from the practitioner's perspective (from the outside), from illness, as phenomena seen from the perspective of the sufferer. Writing as both physician and anthropologist, Kleinman (1988:3) turns to illness narratives to impart "the innately human experience of symptoms and suffering."

WHAT IS A STORY?

Before looking more closely at the implications of this narrative shift in medical anthropology, we attempt to come to grips with what is meant by a story and then to explore some of the different uses of the narrative form. In ordinary speech and in much scholarly writing, there is a certain tendency to treat a story as a "natural" object that needs no explaining, which one can somehow just point to. Yet it is plagued by a kind of pervasiveness, an unboundedness. It is as common as air. When are we not telling or hearing stories? More diffusely, if identity itself is essentially a narrative matter, as many have suggested (e.g., MacIntyre 1981; Polkinghorne 1991; Gergen and Gergen 1997), is there anything in human life that is *not* a story? Are we always living out stories? Some would argue that even science itself is essentially a storytelling enterprise (Landau 1997; MacIntyre 1980). Provocative as these claims are, the far reach of narrative means that rather than having any stable meaning, this term is flung far and wide.

Without attempting to offer anything too precise, we propose a few remarks about the nature of stories that hold generally true across cultures and analytic traditions and turn out to be significant when we try to understand why narrative analysis has become so powerful in studies of illness and healing. If we begin, very simply, by noting that stories seem to offer some fundamental way to make sense of experience, this already suggests that there is some basic form which we call "a story," that underneath the extreme variability of kinds of stories, functions of stories, and situations of telling, there exists a shared core, a fundamental "storyness" belonging to all particular stories. French structuralists, following the Russian formalists (notably Propp 1968) who studied fairy tales, have been energetic advocates and explorers in the search for fundamental narrative form. This exploration has come under serious attack, even by its own early enthusiasts. Roland Barthes, one of those early narratologists, later offered one of the most succinct criticisms in literary theory of the whole enterprise. He opens *S/Z* with this:

> There are said to be certain Buddhists whose ascetic practices enable them to see a whole landscape in a bean. Precisely what the first analysts of narrative were attempting: to see all the world's stories (and there have been ever so many) within a single structure: we shall, they thought, extract from each tale its model, then out of these models we shall make a great narrative structure, which we shall reapply (for verification) to any one narrative: a task as exhausting (ninety-nine percent perspiration, as the saying goes) as it is ultimately undesirable, for the text thereby loses its difference. (1974:3)

No tight formal model of story may actually exist, or, if it can be constructed, it may turn out to be a foolishly empty category, a useless abstraction, as Barthes suggests. Although there may well be no fundamental narrative structure to uncover, nor any simple and consistent notion of "story," this does not mean that less ambitious structural endeavors are fruitless or that creating a language in aid of such an enterprise is foolish. And, as it happens, a few things about the nature of stories can reliably be noted. Most basic, stories concern action, more specifically human or humanlike action, even more specifically, social interaction. They offer us "dramatistic" forays into social life (Burke 1945), exploring the meaning of events by linking motive, act, and consequence. Some would even claim that in this chaining they offer causal explanations of events (Fisher 1997; Mattingly 1991a, 1998b), a claim made compellingly by Aristotle (1970), for whom narrative plot was a form of moral argument.

Stories also concern events as experienced and suffered through by quite specific actors. They allow us (the audience) to infer something about what it *feels like* to be in that story world, that is, they give form to feeling (Langer 1953). Telling a story is a "relational act" that necessarily implicates the audience (Linde 1993:112–13). Stories are intended to be evocative and provocative. Story language is very often image-dense, connotative rather than denotative (Jakobson 1960). Furthermore, following a story, especially one rich in metaphor and featuring highly charged human dramas, provokes an experience in the audience. Put another way, following a compelling story is no mere abstract matter; it involves an imaginative journey into a story world.

A story, an effective one at least, not only is about something but also *does* something. This is what John Austin (1962) designates the perlocutionary and illocutionary functions of language. Austin speaks of two ways in which words do things. One, much more thoroughly discussed by anthropologists, he labels the "illocutionary function." This involves saying something in a conventional situation (say, a ritual), in which the saying is a performance of a cultural act, for instance, baptizing a child or marrying a couple. Inefficacy of an illocutionary act is a public matter, a matter of infraction of some socially agreed upon conventions. But a perlocutionary act is much less clear or predictable in its outcome. Because efficacy depends upon the rhetorical power of words to persuade and influence the listener, the audience plays an active role in the creation of meaning. It works, as an action, if it can engender certain effects in the listener. In telling stories narrators moralize the events they recount and seek to convince others to see some part of reality in a particular way. But whether this occurs depends upon what sort of contract the listener is willing to make. Stories are very often acts of this particularly vulnerable kind.[3] If they have power as actions, this only comes through developing a particular kind of relationship between teller (or text) and audience, one in which the listener comes to care about the events recounted.

Telling stories allows narrators to communicate what is significant in their lives, how things matter to them (Rosaldo 1986:98). Narratives offer a powerful way to shape conduct because they have something to say about what gives life meaning, what is inspiring in our lives, what is dangerous and worth taking risks for. Compelling stories move us to see life (and to act out life) in one way rather than another. Interestingly, this is not because stories tell us about the usual round of affairs. As Rosaldo (1986:98) points out: "Narratives often reveal more about what can make life worth living than about how it is routinely lived." This very focus on the singular can reveal what is worth risk and struggle, what situations matter enough that actors are "in suspense" about what will happen next.

THE NARRATIVE CONSTRUCT: TERMINOLOGICAL MATTERS (AND MUDDLES)

Some, like Wikan in this volume, question whether anything at all is added by the construct of narrative that is not already contained in "story." And indeed, when one begins to examine narrative studies, the welter of confusing categories can prove daunting and even obfuscating. For something that starts out to be such an intuitively obvious act (telling a story), the specialized vocabulary that has grown up around it can appear to mask more than it illuminates. In this chapter and throughout this volume, narrative and story are often used interchangeably. In some schools of narrative analysis, however, the terms have come to designate two quite distinct phenomena—though what these entities are depends upon which school of analysis one turns to. As well, other terms have been advanced either to be consistent with preexisting positions or to stake out new terrain. Despite such semantic confusion, there are several specific theoretical grounds for elaborating terminology which make it possible to distinguish different sorts of narrative phenomena.

   In much of literary theory, maintaining a narrative construct that is separate from story serves to mark the artifice of the text where *narrative* or *discourse* refers to the discursive rendering and 'story' (or 'fabula' or 'histoire') to the underlying events that the narrative recounts. Scholars draw upon this distinction to portray the aesthetic reworkings of sequential time, which are an integral part of creating a compelling plot. The literary critic Culler notes the importance and prevalence of this convention within structuralist literary theory, stating that "if these theorists agree on anything it is this: that the theory of narrative requires a distinction between what I shall call 'story'—a sequence of actions or events, conceived as independent of their manifestation in discourse—and what I shall call 'discourse,' the discursive presentation of events" (1981:169–70). This convention underscores that any narrative that as told (or written) necessarily changes the structure of the original events, which literary critics often take to be a simple chronology (Bal 1985). In literary circles, this differentiation expresses a view not only that there is a gap between narrative discourse and life as lived but also that any narrative text (whether purportedly true or not) is a "distortion" of the events recounted (Gennette 1982; Forster 1927; White 1980). Thus the convention belongs to a literary movement associated with both modernism and postmodernism in which representation itself becomes an object of study and one is never allowed to forget that any representation colors our view of the world portrayed.

Others, working within linguistic traditions, may follow Roman Jakobson's (1971) work and distinguish "narrated events" from "narrative events." The folklorist Richard Bauman argues that both narrated events and narrative events emerge in the process of performance itself: "The narrated event, as one dimension of the story's meaning, evoked by formal verbal means in the narrative text, is in this respect emergent in performance, whatever the external status of the narrated event may be, whether it in some sense 'actually occurred' or is narratively constructed by participants out of cultural knowledge of how events are— or are not, or may be—constituted in social life" (1986:6). In this differentiation, there is no prior chronology of events that exist in some way outside the story performance. There is nothing "out there" waiting to be narrated.

Along quite different lines, scholars have differentiated between individual stories and their underlying hypothesized organizational principles, structures, or patterns. For instance, a prevailing construct in cognitive theories across various disciplines is that of a schema (D'Andrade 1992). Schemas are interpretive processes, integral to the constructive nature of cognition, which mediate our understanding of the world. For both teller and audience, schemas organize the hearing, telling, and remembering of stories. Schemas are involved in conveying the specifics of a given story but also supply the narrative structures that characterize stories more generally. General-level story schemas or story grammars have been proposed by cognitive psychologists (e.g., Johnson and Mandler 1980, Mandler 1984, Mancuso 1986; for an anthropological application, see Mathews 1992). From such a perspective, it thus becomes possible to explore how any given oral story or text is "shaped by implicit theories of narrative and narration" (Neisser 1994:9).[4]

That these implicit narrative theories are culturally constituted is explicitly acknowledged by some psychologists. Bruner and Feldman note that the "facts" of the past, by themselves, "do not supply the patterning or schematic structure of narrated reports." They maintain that such narrated reports "must be constructed of cultural material." To shape one's past experiences, for example, "meaningfully into a public and communicable form," it is necessary to draw upon "narrative properties like genre and plot type that are widely shared within a culture, shared in a way that permits others to construe meaning the way the narrator has" (1996:293).

Within a culture, this two-level distinction—with particular instances of storytelling differentiated from but also linked with more general culturally based narrative patterns or properties—provides a way to theorize about what is shared across stories without disregarding the uniqueness of individual accounts. Holland and Kipnis (1994), in their analysis of stories of embarrassment in American culture, found that over 90 percent of the stories they collected were consistent with a four-step "prototypic event sequence" for embarrassment.

Along somewhat similar lines, Arthur Frank, a medical sociologist, uses *story* when "referring to the actual tales people tell" and *narrative* when discussing the general structural types that comprise various stories" (A. Frank 1995:188 n. 5). According to Frank: "A narrative type is the most general storyline that can be recognized underlying the plot and tensions of particular stories. People tell their own unique stories, but they compose these stories by adapting and combining narrative types that cultures make available" (A. Frank 1995:75; cf. Schank 1990; Bruner and Feldman 1996). Drawing on stories of illness in principally North American settings, Frank points to three underlying thematic types—"restitution," "chaos," and "quest" narratives—and explains that different narrative types can be present in the same story.

A final illustration of the value of differentiating between underlying narrative structure and the particularities of an individual story comes from research carried out by Allan Young at a U.S. Veterans Administration psychiatric unit specializing in the treatment of service-related PTSD. Young (1995) examines how treatment staff (referred to as "presenters") relate case histories at diagnostic sessions for discussion with other staff members. In analyzing the presenter's opening accounts about individual patients and the applicability of the PTSD diagnosis, Young found that while the *content* of the narrated accounts changes from case to case, the *structure* remains constant. He notes:

> Listening to a presenter's opening account, it is easy to get the impression that narrative structure is intrinsic to the details provided by the interviewees, and that the structure of a presenter's narrative is also the structure of his inter-

viewee's life. In practice, the structure of these narratives exists prior to their content. Even before an interviewer has begun to collect his statements, the organization of this account is already in place, embedded in the composition and clustering of the questions making up his protocols. Even before his audience has heard all the details, they know, in a general way, what is coming next and how it all fits together: the structure of the account is presupposed in their knowledge of the account of PTSD provided in the American Psychiatric Association's *Diagnostic and Statistical Manual of Mental Disorders (DSM-III)*. (Young 1995:169–70)

Young's findings suggest that attending to underlying narrative structure may allow a researcher to see more clearly the imprint of institutionalized practices and ideology.

Yet another slant and terminology have been developed by scholars wishing to describe narrative patterning across stories told by the same individual at temporally discontinuous occasions or within extended discourse, for example, in research interviews, where what comes to be referred to as the individual's story is not necessarily bounded as a unit. The heterogeneous literature on self-narrative life history, or life story (see discussion in Peacock and Holland 1993 and Mishler 1995:95–96) brings together groupings of stories told by the same person, usually at different points in time. According to Linde (1993), the life story is a "particularly important" type of everyday discourse (3) as "every normal adult in this [American] culture engages in telling a life story in a more or less elaborated form" (43). A life story consists of "a set of stories that are retold in various forms over a long period of time and that are subject to revision and change as the speaker drops some old meanings and adds new meanings to portions of the life story" (219–20; cf. Fitzgerald 1996:369; Barclay and DeCooke 1988:120; Capps and Ochs 1995:14–15; Price 1995). Linde examines the variety of ways coherence is created and how the life story relates to the "internal, subjective sense of having a private life story that organizes our understanding of our past life, our current situation, and our imagined future" (11). According to Peacock and Holland (1993:374), life stories are "likely important in self-formation and self-expression, though not perhaps in all cultures."

As intimated in this last statement from Peacock and Holland, questions concerning the comparability of narrative forms or underlying narrative structures across cultural settings are likely to remain the subject of debate for some time to come. Linde, who provides an assessment of life histories in anthropology (1993:47–48), concludes that "the notion of a life story itself is not universal, but is the product of a particular

culture" (220). When Renato Rosaldo began his attempt to elicit a life
history from Tukbaw, an Ilongot man, he shared in what he considered
to be a common anthropological assumption that "the life history is a
natural and universal narrative form" (Rosaldo 1976:145). A useful
summary of what transpired between Rosaldo and Tukbaw is provided
by Linde (1993:47–48). She informs us that Rosaldo:

> found that his expectations that Tukbaw, his intelligent and introspective sub-
> ject, would produce a deep and intricate life story were not fulfilled. Rather,
> Tukbaw's account focused on his public self and public actions, but hardly
> touched on what Rosaldo considered a necessary description of his private
> self. To obtain such material, Rosaldo found himself eliciting narratives that
> his informant never would have produced on his own. Life story narratives
> were not familiar discourse types in his informant's culture. Narratives were
> familiar; so stories of hunting expeditions, raids, and fishing trips were easy
> to elicit. But narratives about the self—particularly what we would call inti-
> mate or revealing narratives—were simply not known. (Linde 1993:47–48)

Rosaldo (1976:122) describes the elicitation of Tukbaw's life history as
"an exploration of a little known cultural domain." This example highlights that while storytelling can be considered a universal activity, what
are considered natural forms of discourse are likely to vary across cultural settings. In addition, it serves to underscore the potential for distortion when "life material is forced into the ethnographer's a priori
(and Western) notion of biography or determined by the ethnographer's
categories of inquiry" (Kendall 1988:12).

As this brief excursion into models of narrative analysis shows, the
terminology surrounding studies of stories follows no single standard.
What does hold across traditions is a need to elaborate a language in
order to analyze that pervasive act—telling a story—and the relation of
that apparently simple act to making decisions, taking future actions,
making sense of experiences, and living a life. The infusion of new vocabulary into narrative studies also points to the contemporary power
of narrative to capture a wide range of concerns, including a search for
more dynamic and agent-centered ways to analyze key aspects of cultural life.

NARRATIVE AS CULTURAL
PROCESS AND SOCIAL DRAMA

As narrative is constructed, narrative constructs. One theme that recurs
throughout these essays is narrative as something that is enacted in
specific contexts and reflects culturally based constructive processes.

These chapters explore stories as ways of thinking through the past, ways of making sense of ongoing situations and guides for future action. They repeatedly stress that narratives shape action just as actions shape stories told about them, and that stories suggest the course of future actions as well as giving form to past experience. The study of narrative becomes a place to explore cultural life as an unfolding personal and social drama.

Geertz (1980) has suggested that there is a broad shift within the human sciences from mechanistic to dramatistic metaphors in the analysis of social life. If anthropologists once primarily saw societies as well-functioning machines or evolving organisms, there has lately been more inclination to think in terms of constructions, performances, enactments, contestations, plots, and counterplots. Narrative easily fits within this family of dramaturgical terms, which emphasize action, motive, event, and process as the key ingredients of social life. Narrative offers an avenue for exploring human temporality, the way we move through time (Ricoeur 1984, 1985, 1987). As the philosopher David Carr (1986:9) argues, "narrative structure pervades our very experience of time and social existence." Telling stories allows anthropologists to attend to temporality in cultural life, enabling them "to deal more directly with change, and thereby to make structural and symbolic studies more dynamic" (E. Bruner 1986a:141). When drama is a root metaphor, life becomes considerably less tidy, its social construction considerably more ambiguous and contested than in traditional structural-functional studies (Turner 1986; Turner and Bruner 1986; Laderman and Roseman 1996; Kapferer 1983; Hinchman and Hinchman 1997). A number of the essays in this volume emphasize illness and healing from the perspective of cultural drama, drawing upon narrative to emphasize how events and experiences are constructed through the complex interactions of agents who occupy different social positions, with differential access to power, and different points of view. The examination of narrative as both social and aesthetic practice connects to growing work in medical anthropology centering on what Laderman and Roseman call "the trope of 'performance'" (1996:3). There are several reasons for the ascendance of narrative, but a considerable one is how useful stories are in helping the anthropologist address life as an unfolding affair, an engagement of actors who very often find themselves in interpretive and practical struggles.

These struggles may concern not only individual contenders (or allies) but also a variety of moral and structural positions. The constructive power of narrative becomes evident when noting its rhetorical force, a theme taken up by many of the essays included here. Because effective stories have perlocutionary power, they can influence the subsequent actions of narrator and audience. Powerful stories can shape future actions in decisive ways, and this only increases the complex and intertwined relation between telling stories and taking actions. The study of narrative has invited investigation of social life as an interplay of differently positioned actors and different moral and persuasive voices. A story, especially a personal story, allows us to see that—from other perspectives and/or through alternative "editing"—other stories might have been told. Even the seductive powers of the compelling story cannot easily disguise its status as a positioned account. Chapters by Riessman, Kirmayer, Wikan, Hunt, and Mattingly especially point toward the complex negotiations and contestations that often surround illness, ones that extend far beyond the illness itself into the very fabric of everyday social life. Chapters by Garro, Good and Good, and by Pollock reveal the way individual narratives become shaped by cultural norms and, in turn, contribute to the development or maintenance of those attitudes and values.

Narrative practices, including who is entitled to tell a story and when it can be told, "reflect and establish power relations in a wide range of domestic and community institutions" (Ochs and Capps 1996:35). Good (1994) writes of an interview situation in Turkey where family members entered into and dominated the telling of the illness story of a young daughter-in-law. Although she was present, the young woman, an outsider who had married into a powerful family, was not allowed to tell her story:

> The image of her sitting quietly while the others told her story reminded us of local power relations in the pragmatics of narrative. Relations of power and gender are expressed not only in the structure of the story, in the point of view it assumes, but in the elementary framing of who is allowed to articulate the illness which belongs not to an individual but to a family. (1994:160)

Entitlement to tell the story of another's illness, however, can also serve as a marker of other types of social relationships. Among the Australian Aborigines of Darwin fringe camps, for example, in cases where persons are "grabbed" by an illness that renders them dependent on others for care, only those who "rescue" the sick are empowered to later recount the story. The ill person is not considered to be of right mind and is not aware of what transpired. But more than this, entitlement to narrate reflects an enduring social relationship, one of indebtedness incurred by the patient: "The debt between patient and caring helper lasts for as long as they both shall live" (Sansom 1982:188).

As many of the essays in this volume point out, the perspective taken in narrative accounts may reflect one's sociocultural memberships, such as professional status (e.g., Hunt 1994; M. Good et al. 1994; Good and Good this volume; Pollock this volume), gender (e.g., Mathews 1992; Hunt this volume; Pollock this volume; Riessman this volume), or an individual's story as drawing on a broader "collective autobiography" (Connerton 1989; see, e.g., Lang 1989; Garro 1995, this volume; White 1991).

Scholars from a variety of backgrounds have turned to narrative to examine questions of special concern to them. Interpretive theorists with a strong phenomenological bent have looked at narrative as a form for representing personal experience as well as at the ways narrative gives expression to and "domesticates" experience by rendering it in cultural form (e.g., Kleinman 1988; Becker 1997). Those concerned with narrative as enactment have examined storytelling as an aesthetic performance that does social work, and looked at the way stories help shape future actions as well as explore past actions (e.g., Kirmayer this volume; Mattingly 1994, 1998a, 1998b, this volume). Cognitive anthropologists have addressed the relationship between personal experience, individual understandings, and cultural models (e.g., Price 1987; Mathews, Lannin, and Mitchell 1994; Garro 1994, this volume). Sociolinguistically inclined studies have examined stories as speech acts, carefully noting the kinds of linguistic rules that govern the generation and suppression of particular narratives and how these communicative acts influence what can be discussed in social encounters (e.g., Brenneis 1996; Haviland 1996; Mishler 1986b).

NARRATIVE AND (ETHNOGRAPHIC) REPRESENTATION

As well as being part of a broad and deep current extending across diverse disciplines, the narrative turn within anthropology has gained momentum from internal critiques of culture theory and practice. Writing about three of the most influential approaches to the study of culture in the 1960s and 1970s—Levi-Straussian structuralism, the Chicago

school of symbolic anthropology, and ethnoscience—Shore notes that
they

> tended to give us disembodied systems, structures, or programs—knowledge
> without any particular knower in mind and structures of thought that lacked
> any flesh-and-blood thinkers. Real people were replaced by hypothetical en-
> tities—"the savage mind," the "typical" or "average" members of a commu-
> nity. People appeared more as the passive sites of cultural programming than
> as purposeful agents, strategists, and meaning makers. . . . We came to know
> more about cultural systems in general than we did about people in particu-
> lar. (Shore 1996:54)

In contrast, during the last two decades, "the agents of culture are no
longer hypothetical or average natives but look like real individuals with
specific histories, particular interests, and concrete strategies. Rather
than as members of homogenous cultures, we now are more likely to
conceive of our natives as enmeshed in complex power relations" (Shore
1996:55) and draw attention to the contested and emergent qualities of
culture. As the preceding section illustrates, narrative meshes easily with
this expansion of the anthropological gaze and has captured the attention of those wishing for an anthropology that allows the individual to
emerge in all her particularity while exploring the relationship between
the personal and the cultural.[5] It has also been taken up by those who
wish to explore how life (both social and individual) unfolds through
time and by those who wish not only to speak of emotion but also to
create it, to write from a place where the reader can also feel something.
When we want to write an anthropology that "breaks your heart," as
Behar (1996) puts it, we tell stories.

Along with a narrative turn, anthropology has also taken a reflexive
turn. Attention to anthropological practices—including the practice of
telling its own and other people's stories—has engendered an intensified
interest in the role of narrative within anthropology. For some, this shifting of attention to narrative is linked to a perceived "crisis" in traditional modes of ethnographic representation (Fischer 1986). Increasingly, anthropologists tell not only the stories of others but personal
stories as well. Ethnographies built around personal stories emphasize
the "de-centered" character of anthropological research and introduce
the anthropologist's voice in no uncertain terms. Viewed in this way,
autobiography may serve as a "handmaiden of ethnography" (Behar
1996:18). Traditional life histories are being reinvented as places in
which personal stories and stories of one's interlocutor co-mingle (Frank
2000). As Behar writes in her eloquent collection of essays, *The Vulner-*

able Observer, "The genres of life history and life story are merging with the *testimonio,* which speaks to the role of witnessing in our time as a key form of approaching and transforming reality" (1996:27).

The telling of personal tales, intersected with observations of one's ethnographic subjects, highlights the place of the anthropologist as personal witness. A powerful example is Renato Rosaldo's (1984) account of his struggle to understand the Ilongot's fierce anger when mourning the death of loved ones. Understanding comes only with the loss of his own wife, as rage overwhelms him. In his essay, he intertwines personal storytelling with a discussion of Ilongot headhunting, recognizing that this personal storytelling is central to his analytic voice. As he states, "The paramount claim made here . . . concerns the ways in which my own mourning and consequent reflection on Ilongot bereavement, rage, and headhunting raise methodological issues of general concern in anthropology" (1984:185). In this volume, Wikan uses narrative to assume a double role, as researcher and as research subject, giving an account of her own illness experience against a backdrop of stories of suffering she has heard and written about. These personal stories are more than seductive ploys that serve to draw the reader in—though they may also be that. They are produced to undermine any pretense to objectivity. They further the reflective stance of anthropology precisely by bringing the researcher out into the open where she, too, may be seen (see also Riessman this volume).

The contemporary interest in investigating lived experience, in "cultural phenomenology" (Csordas 1994b, 1996), embodiment (Csordas 1994a), and a reconsideration of ritual as performance have also abetted the storytelling impulse within anthropology (Mattingly 1998a, this volume). Rather than describing rituals in the language of generic "plot structures" and the "typical event," anthropologists are foregrounding individual performances and the quite specific actions, thoughts, and feelings of particular actors. It should be noted, however, that many anthropologists who write of the "performance of healing" or a "sensuous" anthropology (i.e., one that is able to interpret and examine the nonlinguistic aspects of cultural life), even while telling compelling tales, work to distance themselves from the anthropological focus on narrative and on language or "action as text" metaphors more broadly (Stoller 1989, 1997; Laderman and Roseman 1996; Hughes-Freeland 1998). Narrative, as one genre of discourse, sometimes comes under attack as part of the sweeping critique concerning the role of language as the primary conveyer of cultural knowledge and understanding. Rather than drawing nearer to the body, or the cultural meaning of illness and experience, it is argued that narratives reduce meaning to "mere" text (see Mattingly, this volume and 1998a, for an extended discussion of such objections).

Within anthropology, the growing use of narrative has gone hand in hand with a heightened acknowledgment that the notion of narrative as "representation" is anything but clear. Some would contend that the use of the term "representation" is misleading and others that "representation" entails construction. Whatever one's semantic stance (and consistent with the preceding discussion), a story is never merely a representation if this is taken to be a passive portrait of some prior events or experiences. A story is not neutral. Nor is it a hidden text which the anthropologist somehow unearths like buried treasure. Narratives never simply mirror lived experience or an ideational cosmos, nor is a story a clear window through which the world, or some chunk of it, may be seen. Telling a story, enacting one, or listening to one is a constructive process, grounded in a specific cultural setting, interaction, and history. Text, context, and meaning are intertwined.

The reflexive turn has also resulted in a fundamental critique of ethnographic representation that places narrative at center stage (Fischer and Marcus 1986; Clifford and Marcus 1986; Marcus 1998; Rabinow 1997). Sometimes in this critical and self-conscious movement narrative is treated in grand and abstract terms, inspired in part by Lyotard's (1984) discussion of the postmodern demise of master narratives. But such critiques have also generated quite specific examinations of the narrativizing strategies within ethnographic writing. Reminiscent, but with a different twist, of the potential for life story material to be shaped by the ethnographer's preconceptions both in the field and when transformed into text, Edward Bruner's influential essay "Ethnography as Narrative" asserts that "ethnographies are guided by an implicit narrative structure, by a story we tell about the peoples we study" (1986a: 139). The pivotal claim that Bruner makes is that these underlying narratives precede and give structure to anthropological research. Anthropologists do not build stories out of data, but discover data because of stories that shape their perceptions of the field: "The narrative structures we construct are not secondary narratives about data but primary narratives that establish what is to count as data" (E. Bruner 1986a:142–43).[6] Narratives provide, as Marcus puts it, "fictions of the whole in which to ground [the] facts" (1998:36). Literary theory has offered anthropologists a potent skeptical gaze, which has created a burgeoning interest in the anthropologist as storyteller. The anthropological storyteller who emerges in this portrait is of necessity a storytelling liar, a "trickster," as Crapanzano says. Through narratives, it is argued, cultures and lives are provided a fictional coherence which they lack in actuality (E. Bruner 1984, 1986a; Crapanzano 1984, 1986; Hoskins 1998; Kondo 1990. See Mattingly 1998b and this volume for an extended discussion of this argument). If prior narratives, and often implicit ones, guide the anthropologist's search for data, the narrative aspects of the ethnographic enterprise are not a matter of choosing a particular kind of data to collect or a discursive strategy for presenting the findings. Rather, the task of a reflexive anthropology has been an unmasking of these undergirding narrative structures. From this perspective, explorations of narrative are prompted not only by criticisms of the inadequacy of the traditional ethnographic model but also by a more radical critique concerning the validity, the believability, of any representation at all. While many anthropologists strongly protest the notion that the ethnographic text is necessarily fictive, there is no doubt that debates about the epistemological status of anthropological knowledge have transformed narrative from a specialized interest (especially among linguists and folklorists) to a central construct within the discipline.

It is important to stress that an intensified preoccupation with narrative in the social sciences need not be connected to a postmodern rejection of realist representation nor feature reflexive assessments of the author vis-à-vis the research enterprise. While none of the essays adopts what could be called a postmodern position in any strong sense, several take up questions also posed by postmodernists. These questions, fundamentally philosophical in nature, concern such things as the status of narrative as a model or icon for cultural action or personal experience, and they address the relation between narrative and some external world of events.

TELLING STORIES AND MAKING SENSE: MEDIATING THE PERSONAL AND THE CULTURAL

Whether from the position of observers, listeners, or tellers, the essays in this volume highlight narrative as a mode of thinking, a way of making sense of experience. A number of scholars have pointed to the "vital human capacity" (Shore 1996:319) to confer meaning and create sense out of experience (e.g., Bartlett 1932; J. Bruner 1986, 1990; Goffman 1974; Shore 1996). As noted earlier, Jerome Bruner (1986:11) has portrayed narrative as a fundamental mode of thought that offers a way of "ordering experience, of constructing reality."[7] But, as also highlighted in the introductory section, it is a mode of thinking that marries singular circumstances with shared expectations and understandings acquired through participation in a specific culture. Narrative is linked to human sociality and the human ability to make "cultural sense" of actions. Carrithers (1992) examines narrative thinking from an anthropological point of view, stating that:

> narrative thought consists not merely in telling stories . . . [rather] human beings perceive any current action within a large temporal envelope, and within that envelope they perceive any given action, not as a response to the immediate circumstances or current mental state of an interlocutor or of oneself, but as part of an unfolding story. (82)

In addition, narrative as a mode of thinking can be linked to the growing interest in the situated nature of learning. Lave and Wenger (1991:33–34) explain that "even so-called general knowledge only has power in specific circumstances," being "thoroughly situated, in the lives of persons and in the culture that makes it possible":

> That is why stories can be so powerful in conveying ideas, often more so than the articulation of the idea itself. What is called general knowledge is not privileged with respect to other "kinds" of knowledge. And it too must be brought into play in specific circumstances. The generality of any form of knowledge always lies in the power to renegotiate the meaning of the past and future in constructing the meaning of present circumstances.

Within anthropology (though this is not exclusive to anthropology), what binds together the diversity of analytic approaches to narrative is an appreciation of the intertwining of the personal and the cultural. Thus, concern for narrative reflects an interest in representing those the anthropologist studies, not just as members of a cultural group but as individuals with their own personal histories. Narrative becomes a vehicle for the problematic issue of representing experiences and events as seen from the perspective of particular actors and as elements of a cultural account that can tell us something about a social world, however local that world. In the case of illness, especially long-term illness, treatment settings and health care institutions may form an important part of the social world. The telling of personal experience with a chronic condition may be "deeply embedded within the various institutional structures that influence its production as a story" (Saris 1995:39–40).

Narrative portrayals are also shaped by cultural understandings about appropriate behaviors and feelings. In the naturally occurring accounts of illness recorded in Ecuador by Price (1987), narratives often implicitly, but almost always emphatically, conveyed "I did the right thing." This occurred not only through what was said but also through what was left unsaid. For example, it was expected that mothers, in particular, would make herculean efforts to take care of their ill children without complaint or resentment. These efforts are typically taken for granted and are not highlighted through narrative. In contrast, narratives, told from an observer's viewpoint and put forward as counterexamples, portraying mothers whose response to a child's illness is found wanting, were so emotionally charged "that it can be said that if cultural models of social roles drive the narratives, emotional propositions are the fuel that empower them" (Price 1987:319).

Furthermore, narrative provides a way to approach the relationship between individual and culture by attending to the "role of cultural forms in the creation of meaning" (Shore 1996:316). Learning how to tell a story is a cultural matter, guided by a culture's notions of what constitutes a proper story, who can tell what kinds of stories in what kinds of circumstances, and the like. Creating and conveying meaning through narrative is a constructive process and a learned skill (Bruner and Feldman 1996; cf. Frank 1995:3). Based on a series of developmental studies, Fivush, Haden, and Reese (1996:344) claim that through telling stories with others about the past: "Children are learning the skills of remembering and reminiscing, not the content of particular experiences." Thus, children are not learning *what* to recall, but rather *how* to recall, the culturally appropriate narrative forms for recounting the past. Fieldworkers and other newcomers to cultural settings come to be readers and perhaps tellers of stories consonant with those settings through learning constructive narrative practices. Part of fieldwork in an Anishinaabe community (see Garro in press) involved reaching an understanding of the culturally appropriate narrative form that connects misfortune with culturally defined acts of transgression.

From an anthropological perspective, it is possible to ask how individuals acquire such narrative skills and the ways in which they are culturally embedded. In this volume, the chapter by Good and Good traces how medical students learn to constitute disease through a distinctive set of narrative practices, practices which reflect the fundamental narrativity of clinical reasoning and are learned through practical engagements in clinical settings. To learn to practice, they imply, involves learning how to tell and read a profession's stories. Another example comes from Cain's (1991; see also Steffen 1997) research on how individuals come to reframe their lives as expressed in personal stories told according to the principles of Alcoholics Anonymous (AA). She provides insight into the learning process and its consequences through a compelling analysis of individual narratives at different points in this process. Through participation in AA meetings and assimilating the messages in the stories of established AA members, a culturally specific narrative form or genre is learned, one that provides the schematic basis for the reflexive construction and communication of an individual's past: "The AA member learns the AA story model, and learns to place the events and experiences of his own life into the model, he learns to tell and to understand his own life as an AA life, and himself as an AA alcoholic" (Cain 1991:215). Through this process, an individual's life story comes to more closely resemble the prototypical AA story.[8] The stories of those who fit the AA model of what it means to be an alcoholic come to be resources that may help guide how others come to reconstruct their past. A number of other settings, including therapeutic interactions (as discussed in an earlier section), create opportunities for learning new narrative frameworks for constructing and interpreting experience.

At a pragmatic level, hearing narrative accounts is a principal means through which cultural understandings about illness—including possible causes, appropriate social responses, healing strategies, and characteristics of therapeutic alternatives—are acquired, confirmed, refined, or modified (e.g., Early 1982, 1988; Price 1987). A story about an unusual or novel illness augments the listener's "fund of cultural knowledge" with which to meet the future (Price 1987:315). Stories help to maintain narrative frameworks as a cultural resource for understanding illness experience (Garro in press and this volume). In the Haitian village studied by Farmer (1994), stories told about known individuals with a then unfamiliar illness, AIDS, served as the medium through which broadly shared understandings gradually became established. As these examples illustrate, cultural knowledge informs stories while stories help to link personal experience and cultural meaning, mediating between particularities and generalities.

ILLNESS, HEALING, AND THE
NARRATIVE CONSTRUCTION OF SELF

The concern to mediate between the personal and the social is particularly evident in studies that address the meaning of illness for a person's sense of identity. The search for an experience-near way to explore and represent the lives of others (or occasionally, even one's own life) has drawn anthropologists to stories (e.g., Wikan 1990, 1991, this volume). Within medical anthropology and related writings, narrative provides a means for conveying the biographical disruption caused by illness, especially chronic illness (e.g., Bury 1982; Garro 1992; Kleinman 1988; Williams 1984; Becker 1997). Rather than stories about illness, such accounts are better characterized as being about a life disrupted by illness. Research adopting a life history approach has been particularly valuable in looking at how a chronic or congenital condition shapes a person's sense of identity and selfhood (e.g., Obeyesekare 1981; Frank 1984, 1986, 2000; Kaufman 1988; Monks and Frankenberg 1995; Cain 1991). Life histories offer a processual rather than a static view of cultural life (Peacock and Holland 1993), which has proved useful in tracing illness experience as an ongoing history.

As Arthur Frank stresses, stories of illness are "told *through* a wounded body," for the "body sets in motion the need for new stories when disease disrupts the old stories" (1995:2). In giving voice to illness experiences, narrative is seen as providing a phenomenologically attuned means for enacting bodily experience (e.g., Becker 1997; Murphy 1987; Kleinman 1988; Good 1992; Good and Good 1994). The "body's insistence on meaning" (Kirmayer 1992) gains expression through metaphor and narrative. Narratives, as "extended metaphor" (Ricoeur 1984), draw upon rich connotative images to evoke a world. And while language is not the only means available for communicating and ordering experience, narrative "is an essential resource in the struggle to bring experience to conscious awareness" (Ochs and Capps 1996:23).[9] Based on her extensive research with Americans who have experienced a variety of life disruptions, Becker (1997) suggests that especially in the United States, where "sensation and bodily expression are undervalued" (26) and "verbal self-expression is highly valued" (194), narrative "is our primary means of accessing the world of bodily experience and is essential to our understanding of that experience" (26).[10] Communicating somatic experience through a narrative medium is also a profoundly cultural process:

> The intersection of body and voice is an intimate process that cannot be fully known by others. What *can* be known and is accessible is the way in which culture is manifested in this process. That is, we can understand the permeability of culture through bodily experience as well as through narrative.

> Cultural processes are mediated at their most elemental level through sub-
> jective experience which enables people to take in and reformulate the exter-
> nal world. (Becker 1997:193–94)

In studies of self-making, narrative offers an avenue for linking personal experience to cultural knowledge, norms, and tenets. A number
of studies highlight how culturally based understandings shape or are
reflected in stories about specific, often very personal, experiences with
illness (e.g., Early 1982, 1988; Garro 1988, 1994, 1995; Price 1987;
Mathews, Lannin, and Mitchell 1994; Becker 1994, 1997). Narrative
provides an arena for "coming to terms" (to borrow a phrase from Mathews et al.'s 1994 study) with a problematic experience and making some
sense, at least provisionally, of what is happening. Early, working in
Egypt, found that women use "any of a number of cultural percepts and
a narrative context to negotiate the reality of an episode and of right
curative action" (1982:1491). Ill individuals, particularly when illness
persists, may struggle with multiple, divergent, preexisting culturally
based models with different therapeutic ramifications. Narrative provides a window on the processes involved in aligning an individual's experiences with one or more of these preexisting models and how these
alignments change in light of continuing experiences and new information (Mathews, Lannin, and Mitchell 1994; Hydén 1995). For individuals with a chronic and often difficult to treat illness attributed to the
temporomandibular joint (the condition is commonly referred to simply
as TMJ), narrative provided a vehicle for confronting contradictions between an individual's experience and expectations based on shared cultural models about illness and its care, divergences between what was
expected and what transpired (Garro 1994).

Moreover, individuals diagnosed with TMJ commonly faced significant disruption and alteration in their lives caused by chronic pain and
illness. At a fundamental level, such disruption of the taken-for-granted
world of everyday life can be seen as "nothing less than an ontological
assault" (Pellegrino 1979:44). Through their stories, people conveyed
how the lived experience of chronic pain affected the way they thought
about themselves, their lives, and their futures. Goals, plans, and expectations about life were often radically revised in the face of an illness
with no foreseeable end. At the same time, much of what individuals
said concerned their attempts to maintain a sense of self and purpose in
the face of this profound life disruption (see Brody 1987; Bury 1982;
Kelley 1986:665; Kleinman 1986, 1988; Williams 1984:179). Indeed,
this "dual nature of sickness—the way it can make us different persons

while we remain the same person" (Brody 1987:x) is an integral part of the narratives told by chronic pain sufferers.

Becker (1997) views narratives as enabling the narrator to reestablish a culture-specific sense of order and continuity in life after a disruption. In American culture, such narratives reflect the struggle to come to terms with moral ideologies concerning normalcy in the face of disruptive experiences. Either told to themselves or told to others, narratives are part of the process of healing. When this culture work is successful, "narrative ameliorates disruption: it enables the narrator to mend the disruption by weaving it into the fabric of life, to put experience into perspective" (Becker 1997:166–67; see also Capps and Ochs 1995).

NARRATIVE AS COMMUNICATION

Anthropologists have become increasingly cognizant of the relations between narrative content and the contexts in which narratives are offered, including the position of the ethnographer who has heard the narratives. It is now normative in presentations of narrative material to pay at least "precautionary attention to the role of the ethnographer in the production of ethnographic data" (Herzfeld 1996:74). In addition, anthropologists are more aware of their own role as storytellers—fashioning the stories they "bring back" to effectively communicate messages of their own to a very different audience. As exemplified by the chapters in this volume, anthropologists evince a double concern with narrative. There is a concern to elicit and interpret the stories of informants and a concern to present those stories in a way that draws their readers close—to be, in a sense, a good storyteller of other people's stories.

In presenting the stories of others, anthropologists play a critical role in selecting, juxtaposing, and summarizing material, often from interviews, to represent an individual's "story."[11] While fashioning an account that captures the key points or core aspects is more commonly an undiscussed and rather intuitive analytic process, research devoted to close textual analysis of conversations or interviews serves to highlight the often neglected complexities in identifying and interpreting data as narrative (e.g., Mishler 1986b, Viney and Bousfield 1991). This is exemplified by much of Riessman's work where she focuses on "longer stretches of talk that take the form of narrative—a discourse organized around time and consequential events in a 'world' recreated by the narrator" (Riessman 1990:1195) and explores interpretive possibilities for weaving together these narrative units and how the performance of narrative, and its reading, is a collaborative endeavor (e.g., Riessman 1990, 1993, this volume). Riessman provides a highly reflective account of the multilayered processes and accompanying ambiguities involved in reading and representing interview data to probe what the narrative discourse means (see also Mishler 1986a).

Stories are fashioned to be persuasive accounts. Recounting personal experiences in ways that are vivid, detailed, and/or studded with emotional elaboration contributes to the sense that the narrative is truthful, accurate, or believable (Pillemer 1992; Edwards, Potter, and Middleton 1992). Persuasiveness may derive from re-creating an event in a way that imparts how the event takes on meaning, so that the listener identifies with what is at stake for the teller. Support for one's perspective may also be bolstered by directly or indirectly asserting a correspondence with professional knowledge and culturally authorized discourses. There is a link to social power, as professionals draw upon their claims to knowledge in efforts to construct persuasive narrative scenarios for those who seek their assistance (Hunt 1994; M. Good et al. 1994; Mattingly 1998b; Kirmayer this volume).

Many of the chapters in this volume explore these and other means through which stories gain perlocutionary force. Several draw upon literary theory in their narrative analyses. This concentration on narrative as aesthetic form or aesthetic performance represents a relatively new direction in medical anthropology. In narrative studies of illness and healing influenced by literary traditions, scholars have examined the poetic strategies narrators draw upon to dramatize core cultural beliefs (Bilu and Witzum 1993). They have also attended to the symbolically and metaphorically dense qualities of narratives as these give meaning and coherence to lives (Jackson 1994; Monks and Frankenberg 1995) and "give voice" to the complexities and ambiguities of illness and healing (Sacks 1984, 1995; Frank 1984, 1986, 2000; Coles 1989).

OVERVIEW OF CHAPTERS

While the essays contained in this book have already been mentioned in connection with the themes previously outlined, this closing section discusses each individual chapter with particular attention to the kind of narrative analysis each offers and, when appropriate, the particular analytic tradition drawn upon.

The opening chapter by Byron Good and Mary-Jo DelVecchio Good highlights just how deep narrative runs in the everyday medical world.

Their data can be seen as narrative in (at least) a double sense, for they elicit stories from medical students, which in turn are about medical stories told in the normal course of medical practice. In this phenomenological account, Good and Good consider the path to mature physicianhood as admission into a narrative world and examine how students "enter the world of medical stories" and become transformed through this process. Disturbed by seemingly arbitrary and "fictional" aspects of medical stories early in their clinical training, toward the end they moved to "a deeply embodied sense that truly *medical* stories are mimetic while stories of suffering maintain a fictional quality."

Both this chapter and a later one by Pollock explore the central (and often neglected) moral dimensions of medical practice, noting that narrative seems to provide the place in which difficult and disturbing moral issues can be raised, issues that are neglected within the "scientific" and canonical practices of medical case presentation. Each of these chapters, in different ways, observes how morally central issues are pushed to the margins in canonical discourse. Underscored is another theme that runs through many of the chapters—our human need to tell stories about situations that disturb us, particularly experiences that are either morally ambiguous or morally problematic.

Good and Good introduce the propitious notion of "narrative practices," arguing that narrative infuses all the "closely interlinked *practices* through which the objects of the medical lifeworld are constituted and engaged." They mean more, here, than the simple idea that all case accounts have a narrative structure. Rather, they want to make a more subtle point that the "medicalized object" is "constituted in narrative terms." Their chapter uses narrative to explore the "temporal dimension of disease and the struggle to find coherent plots." While, they grant, temporality does indeed enter the way diseases are understood in medical reasoning (diseases as evolving processes), the narrativity of these constructions of disease is not generally noted. Along with the chapter by Mattingly, this chapter argues for narrative not as a discursive form distinct from social action and practice but as an integral aspect of practice and a structure of temporality.

Linda Garro's chapter examines how the interplay of personal experience and cultural knowledge shapes illness narratives. Her essay, grounded in cognitive theories of both narrative and memory, examines "how cultural knowledge serves as a resource in guiding remembering about the past." She looks at the way cultural knowledge is variably and flexibly drawn upon by members of an Anishinaabe community in of-

fering accounts of their experiences with diabetes: "Through remembering, culturally available knowledge becomes situated knowledge, connected to a particular person, context, and illness history." Many of her
informants recognized limitations in their doctor's explanations of diabetes (e.g., that it was caused by too much sugar or alcohol consumption), especially when these explanations did not accord with their own
experience. In providing alternative explanations, many informants' narratives drew upon a shared narrative of the collective colonial history of
the Anishinaabe, which was interwoven with individual explanations of
illness and personal autobiographies. Garro shows how individual accounts draw strength and verisimilitude as they are nested within accounts of a collective past. Thus individual stories of personal histories
often included accounts of how the Anishinaabe diet had changed over
the years as food supplies became scarce or contaminated by white men's
technology and as the Anishinaabe relied more and more heavily on
white men's foods. Furthermore, these reconstructions of past personal
and collective experience played a powerful role in guiding action, influ-
encing and justifying decisions about how to combat the illness (including decisions to reject the doctor's advice), and shaping expectations
about what the future would hold.

Linda Hunt's chapter also highlights illness narratives as guides to
present and future actions, in her case, through the refashioning of social roles in local cultural worlds. Drawing on fieldwork with cancer patients in Oaxaca, Mexico, she examines the illness narratives of two
Mexican patients stricken with cancer who have had surgery in which
part of their reproductive systems were removed. She explores the ways
the stories they construct of their illness intersect with their evolving life
stories, particularly how they are able to use their illness to reconstruct
problematic gender identities. She focuses on the creation of an illness
narrative as a reflective process, noting that the chronically ill individual
"may enter into a period of self-reflection and reorientation: a moment
where conventional structure is realigned with personal endeavor as
well as social constraint." She argues, "In examining the strategic implications of illness narratives, we open a window onto understanding the
rhetorical processes (Brodwin 1994) by which chronic illness and its associated role disruptions are woven into ongoing negotiations over questions of power and powerlessness within patients' lives." Hunt's essay
thus connects the strategic construction of illness narratives with the
reconstruction of gender roles which "effectively turned suffering into

a social asset, and role destruction into an opportunity for personal empowerment."

Donald Pollock's chapter returns us to stories told by physicians, but these are quite different from the ones considered by Good and Good. Pollock looks at published autobiographical accounts written by physicians and examines what such accounts can tell us when viewed from the perspective of the reader rather than that of the writer or teller of the tale. Pollock explores the connection between the narrative form and the messages these accounts convey not only about the personal lives of their narrators but also about the social world of medicine. As he puts it, he is attempting to read physician narrative through the history of medicine, that is, to see how these accounts as narrative genres have been shaped by the shifting social scene within medicine itself. He singles out two genres of physician tales for analysis. One is the "female physician" story, which he uses to explore the emergence of feminist issues in medicine. Another genre is the "training tale"—autobiographies that concern the novice physician and his apprenticeship. He examines these as morality tales that comment on changes in medicine that their authors (and quite likely the reading public) find disturbing or problematic. Most particularly, he asks, how does a genre of narrative, such as the training tale, gain authenticity? Why is it that such tales written by novices are so popular? He concludes that they offer a "counterpoint" to "the extravagant, almost science-fiction-like promises of the medical essayist," who promotes medicine as a practical advance of technology and science.

The chapter by Catherine Riessman, drawing on a sociolinguistic tradition of narrative analysis, takes a close look at the emergence of meaning in an interview setting through the interactions of a woman telling a series of interlinked stories and her audience. The narrative text examined here is not a finished product as in Pollock's chapter but is far more fragile and emergent. Riessman situates her analysis in relation to the problem of infertility in India and the tremendous stigma attached to those who cannot conceive. Her essay moves between broad cultural and feminist concerns and in-depth analysis of a set of narrative performances as she examines "the interactional production and performance of narrative" in her encounters with one informant. Through her presentation of these narrative performances, Riessman offers both a subtle portrayal of childlessness for one young woman and a discussion about the cultural meaning of childlessness in a South Indian context as she considers how women combat a subordinated status. This essay also offers an account of Riessman's own shifting interpretations of the stories she is told and how she revises her understanding of them. She notes the way narrative meanings are problematic and ambiguous because these are shaped by the particular interactional context in which the stories are told and the role of the interviewer in shaping the narrative performance.

Laurence Kirmayer also emphasizes interactional context in his chapter, but this time through an analysis of a clinical encounter between a psychiatrist and a patient in which the different perspectives each brings to the encounter prevent the construction of any coherent story. Kirmayer introduces a framework for the analysis of clinical narratives drawn from rhetoric or "the verbal art of persuading others." While approaching narrative through an exploration of the poetics of discourse, Kirmayer challenges reliance on literary models that treat narratives as texts to be read because, he argues, these presume more coherence than one finds in everyday storytelling—at least in clinical sessions. He insists on considering narrative as a social process, as an enactment, and as a place in which the issues of power and legitimacy (Whose story gets to be the authoritative version?) are of central concern.

Kirmayer reflects on the relationship between narrative and personal identity, touching upon some of the questions about narrative memory and narrative reconstruction raised by Garro. His concerns about narrative coherence also enter into this discussion. Kirmayer notes that "in acute illness, narratives are often fragmentary or undeveloped" and that metaphors, rather than narratives, may play a more significant role in shaping the ill person's experience of illness and sense of self. His chapter contemplates the connection between self-identity and narrative coherence. He contends that if it is true that "through narrative we construct a morally valued and conceptually coherent identity and sense of self," as many argue, "a corollary of this synthetic function of narrative is that identity can become fragmented through ruptures in narrative."

Cheryl Mattingly's chapter concerns what she calls "emergent narratives," stories that are created largely through actions rather than through words. She, too, explores the interaction between health professionals and clients, focusing on a single clinical encounter between an occupational therapist and a patient. Like Kirmayer, she also draws upon literary notions of narrative to consider the poetics of the clinical interaction. Unlike Kirmayer, she relies on philosophical hermeneutics rather than rhetoric in considering the place of narrative in clinical work, and she explores the narrative structure of action rather than narrative discourse. She engages debates within literary theory and anthropology concerning the relationship between life as narrated and life as lived. She asks: "Might it be possible to avoid both naive realism *and* 'action-as-text' semiotic treatment of social life while preserving the idea that stories and action have a special correspondence?" The problem, she notes, "is how to bring these two terms—narrative and action—into a close interpretive relationship without reducing either to a pale copy, a 'mere' representation or enactment of the other. How do we see narrative in terms of life and life in terms of narrative without loss of richness and complexity, without neglecting the phenomenological complexities of lived experience and the creative artifice of narrative?"

Her chapter differs in other ways from both Kirmayer's and the final chapter in this collection by Dreier. They emphasize the conflicts and contestations within therapy as the various agents with their own perspectives and their own stakes try to shape therapeutic time to further their particular concerns, tending to get in each other's way in the process of doing so. Kirmayer takes a medical encounter and examines how, throughout the conversation, different story lines or narrative possibilities are tendered and contested by the two participants. In his example there is a failure to construct a shared narrative to guide future joint action. By contrast, Mattingly explores how collaborative therapeutic interactions lead to the creation of narrative within clinical time. Based on videotape analysis of a therapeutic interaction between a therapist and a nine-year-old patient with sensory and motor difficulties, an encounter that involves exercises and play rather than a conversation, she argues that narratives may be created in action even if never explicitly told. Such emergent narratives question the presumption that lived experience lacks narrative form.

The chapter by Unni Wikan is unique in telling a personal story about illness. She interweaves autobiography with material from her ethnographic research to explore the complex relationship between illness narratives, illness experience, and personal identity. She begins with a story of her own about an illness experience and then relates a story from her ethnographic work, told by a poor woman living in Cairo whom she has known for many years. She uses these stories both to say some things about the surprises of illness and how it speaks to a person's sense of self and to raise a series of critical questions about narrative theory. Wikan wonders about the usefulness of recent terminology surrounding studies of narrative (including the very use of the term "narrative"). She critiques the predominance of the "I" in many life story and autobiographical accounts of illness, which may pay insufficient attention to the web of social relations into which the illness falls. She also questions the notion that stories provide a coherence that is missing in lived experience, contending that stories that are told are not so coherent as theorists sometimes lead us to believe.

Wikan also raises a concern about illness narratives themselves. Perhaps we make too much of them, or misread what we hear, when we elicit illness narratives as researchers. She asks, "How can we know that the illness narratives we elicit as researchers tap the experience of suffering? People's compelling concerns could be different; they need not be the illness, even when illness looms large in a person's life." Her question has particular salience for those who study illness among the very poor, as Wikan has. Poverty itself can create such an array of difficulties that physical illness, even significant illness, may not figure as tremendously important in and of itself. Her call to interweave the study of illness with concerns that may run much deeper, such as intimate social relationships or economic struggles, echoes themes also developed in Hunt's chapter.

One of Wikan's most cogent points is that the stories she can tell about her illness experience are, like her life itself, without a clear sense of beginning, middle, and end. Or, rather, while she can locate a clear beginning, the rest is still unfolding. She reflects on the story she tells about her illness, saying, "I certainly did *not* know where to stop, as I began telling you my story. . . . Nor did I know, as I began telling you my story, where it would take me. For it (my life, my illness) branches off in all kinds of directions." Her words resonate with Kirmayer's when he claims that coherent narratives are less likely to be experience-near than those that are more fragmented. But even stories whose end is unclear can be told. "Stories," she writes, "can just as well be made out of beginnings, a good beginning."

Ole Dreier's chapter provides the most sustained challenge to narrative analysis in this group of essays. He raises themes that concern conflict, power, and legitimacy as he examines a series of interactions between a family psychotherapist and family members. Like Kirmayer, he too highlights the fragile and contested character of clinical interactions, but his chapter provides an intriguing contrast to Kirmayer's because he brings a very different analytic frame to bear. Drawing from his background in critical psychology and practice theory, he uses the constructs of "social practices" and "social contexts" to argue that practices and contexts provide the key structuring devices of everyday life, and that in these everyday contexts (unlike the therapeutic one), talk is not necessarily the primary medium through which family members create and maintain their relationships. He disputes the centrality of narrative as a model for social life in general and points out that through emphasizing the temporal dimension of human experience, narrative models downplay the complex spatial embeddedness of everyday social life. In addition to a temporal dimension, we simultaneously inhabit and move across many diverse contexts and structures of social practice, which have their own distinct social rules, expectations, and the like.

Dreier examines psychotherapy as one context (and a temporary one) in the many contexts of family members' everyday lives. He focuses on "how clients reflect on the meaning of sessions as part of their ongoing everyday life," drawing upon interviews with family members about therapy, family problems, and family life. He challenges certain widely held assumptions about why therapy effects change. From his data, he concludes that therapy does not teach family members to talk or solve problems together in a particular way so much as to provide a peculiar setting distinctly different from any pattern of interaction that occurs ordinarily among family members. It is this enduring difference, and the strategic use family members make of it, that creates possibilities for change in family relationships. However, the uses and meanings individual members make of sessions are neither obvious nor congruent. He argues that research on therapy is misleading because "the dominant tradition of research analyzes therapy viewed within the context of sessions," but to really understand the effects of therapy it is important to regard clients as "experiencing agents . . . in and across the various contexts of their everyday lives."

We continue our discussion of this collection in the final chapter through some extended reflections on how illness and healing are constructed through narrative. We examine points of both convergence and divergence across this group of essays. Stories may be good things to think with, but it is important to be self-conscious about what sort of things they are, what they help us think about, and when they limit our view. In the epilogue, we propose to do some of that.

NOTES

1. This quote comes from Young's description of the psychiatric unit. His analyses of PTSD and what transpires in diagnosis and treatment are complex. Some of his ideas linking narrative and clinical practices will be examined in a later section.

2. Another innovative approach examines how narrative models offer alternative ways to understand clinical problems. In his book *Achilles in Vietnam: Combat Trauma and the Undoing of Character,* Shay (1994) draws parallels between the story recounting the downfall of the hero Achilles in Homer's *Iliad* and the accounts of combat trauma and postwar experiences told by Vietnam veterans. Mishler (1995:98), in his précis of Shay's book, states:

> His analysis is an imaginative and instructive example of the contribution of a narrative approach to a complex psychological and social problem. It allowed him to enlarge the scope of our understanding of trauma and its consequences beyond the narrow medical model of posttraumatic stress disorder. Shay taught us that the effects of combat trauma—and perhaps other traumas as well—depend on whether or not it occurs against a background of betrayal by a moral authority. If it does, it sets off a process that leads to the "undoing of character"— not simply bad dreams or psychosomatic symptoms. And he teaches us as well that we can arrive at this understanding by listening to and analyzing stories, because narrative is the form through which the process is represented.

3. Of course, narratives are often included in traditional cultural acts, ritual acts (courtroom dramas, for example) that carry illocutionary force as well.

4. Although beyond the scope of this chapter to discuss in detail, the surge of interest in narrative in cognitive psychology combined with the prevailing schema-based constructive view of human cognition leads into questions about the relationship between language, memory, and experience—between using culturally appropriate narrative forms and the organization of experience and how the act of narration affects memory for that experience and thus future reconstructions of the experience (see, e.g., Schank 1990; Fivush, Haden, and Reese 1996).

5. It should be noted that Shore, among others, does not view these developments as "wholly salutary," for they have come at a serious cost: "As the concrete person has been given new life in anthropology, the very concept of culture that has been at the heart of the discipline has receded from view and is all but lost to us" (1996:55; cf. Strauss and Quinn 1997). Rather than expansion of the anthropological gaze, the situation is but a shift in focus with one blind spot replaced with another. Shore entreats anthropologists to strike a balance between a focus on particular persons within a culture and attention to the development of culture theory. Encompassing narrative as a type of cultural model, Shore writes: "I am very sympathetic with the anthropologist's shift of attention to human agency and contingency in cultural life. Yet properly conceived, this focus should lead us further *into* issues of the relations among culture, mind and models, rather than signal a retreat from the cognitivist paradigm" (1996:55). The chapter in this volume by Garro (see also Garro in press) is oriented around such an exploration.

6. To provide support for his social constructionist position, Edward Bruner takes the dominant story told by anthropologists about American Indians in the 1930s and contrasts it with the quite different story told in the 1970s. Intriguingly, though, he argues that "both American anthropologists and American In-

dians share the same narratives as they are both part of the same larger society during the same time frame. If this is so, the subject-object distinction is dissolved and it becomes difficult to differentiate the outside view and the inside view. Anthropologists and Indians are co-conspirators who construct their ethnography together, in part because they share the same plot structures" (1986b:19).

7. With reference to Jerome Bruner, Donald (1991) points to the emergence of narrative thinking as a key transition in his evolutionary account based on the interdependence of culture and cognition. From a different perspective, Sperber (1985) suggests that narrative may provide a useful entrée to learning about human cognitive abilities. Starting with the observation that stories tend to be easily remembered, Sperber asks what are the formal properties of such representations that relate to their psychological properties and thus make them more susceptible to becoming cultural representations (i.e., widely distributed).

8. J. Bruner maintains "we *become* the autobiographical narratives by which we 'tell' about our lives" (1987:15) so that "a life is not 'how it was' but how it is interpreted and reinterpreted, told and retold" (31). Without presuming any universality for life stories, Bruner's position holds that the process of narrating past events shapes future remembering of these events.

9. Ochs and Capps (1996:19) define narratives of personal experience quite broadly to include "verbalized, visualized, and/or embodied framings of a sequence of actual or possible life events."

10. Giving narrative voice to bodily experiences, however, can pose its own challenges, as the following quote from a woman who suffers from panic attacks and agoraphobia illustrates: "It's sort of strange talking about these things, you know? I mean it took me quite a while to even begin to put it into words for other people, you know people who hadn't experienced panic themselves, because these *attacks* or whatever you want to call them were so strange" (Capps and Ochs 1995:175).

11. Mishler (1995:95) describes "the typical problem of a narrative researcher: namely, how to extract a narrative from a stretch of discourse." Calling for a more reflective stance among researchers he aptly notes: "we do not *find* stories; we *make* stories" (117).

REFERENCES

Agar, M. 1980. Stories, background knowledge and themes: Problems in the analysis of life history narratives. *American Ethnologist* 7:223–39.

Aristotle. 1970. *Poetics*. Translated by G. Else. Ann Arbor: University of Michigan Press.

Austin, John. 1962. *How to do things with words*. Cambridge, Mass.: Harvard University Press.

Bal, Mieke. 1985. *Narratology: Introduction to the theory of narrative*. Toronto: University of Toronto Press.

Barclay, Craig R., and Peggy A. DeCooke. 1988. Ordinary everyday memories: Some of the things of which selves are made. In *Remembering reconsidered:*

Ecological and traditional approaches to the study of memory, edited by
U. Neisser and E. Winograd, 91–125. Cambridge: Cambridge University
Press.

Barthes, Roland. 1974. *S/Z: An essay*. New York: Hill and Wang.

Bartlett, Frederic C. 1932. *Remembering: A study in experimental and social
psychology*. Cambridge: Cambridge University Press.

Bauman, Richard. 1986. *Story, performance and event: Contextual studies of
oral narrative*. Cambridge: Cambridge University Press.

Becker, Gay. 1994. Metaphors in disrupted lives: Infertility and cultural constructions of continuity. *Medical Anthropology Quarterly* 8:383–410.

———. 1997. *Disrupted lives: How people create meaning in a chaotic world*.
Berkeley and Los Angeles: University of California Press.

Behar, Ruth. 1996. *The vulnerable observer: Anthropology that breaks your
heart*. Boston: Beacon Press.

Bilu, Y., and E. Witzum. 1993. Working with Jewish ultra-Orthodox patients:
Guidelines for a culturally sensitive therapy. *Culture, Medicine, and Psychiatry* 17:197–233.

Bohannon, Laura. 1966. Shakespeare in the bush. *Natural History* 75 (August–
September): 28–33.

Brenneis, Donald Lawrence. 1984. Grog and gossip in Bhatgaon: Style and substance in Fiji Indian conversation. *American Ethnologist* 11:487–507.

———. 1996. Telling troubles: Narrative, conflict, and experience. In *Disorderly
discourse: Narrative, conflict, and inequality*, edited by C. L. Briggs, 41–52.
New York: Oxford University Press.

Brenneis, Donald L., and Laura Lein. 1977. "You fruithead": A sociolinguistic
approach to children's disputes. In *Child discourse*, edited by S. E. Tripp and
C. M. Kernan, 49–66. New York: Academic Press.

Briggs, Charles, ed. 1996. *Disorderly discourse: Narrative, conflict and inequality*. New York: Oxford University Press.

Brody, Howard. 1987. *Stories of sickness*. New Haven, Conn.: Yale University
Press.

Broyard, Anatole. 1992. *Intoxicated by my illness*. New York: Potter.

Bruner, Edward M. 1984. Introduction: The opening up of anthropology. In
Text, play and story, edited by E. Bruner, 1–16. Prospect Heights, Ill.: Waveland Press.

———. 1986a. Ethnography as narrative. In *The anthropology of experience*,
edited by V. M. Turner and E. M. Bruner, 139–55. Urbana: University of Illinois Press.

———. 1986b. Introduction: Experience and its expressions. In *The anthropology of experience*, edited by V. M. Turner and E. M. Bruner, 3–30. Urbana:
University of Illinois Press.

Bruner, Jerome. 1986. *Actual minds, possible worlds*. Cambridge, Mass.: Harvard University Press.

———. 1987. Life as narrative. *Social Research* 54:11–32.

———. 1990. *Acts of meaning*. Cambridge, Mass.: Harvard University Press.

———. 1996. *The culture of education*. Cambridge, Mass.: Harvard University
Press.

Bruner, Jerome, and Carol Fleisher Feldman. 1996. Group narrative as a cultural context of autobiography. In *Remembering our past: Studies in autobiographical memory,* edited by D. C. Rubin, 291–317. Cambridge: Cambridge University Press.

Burke, Kenneth. 1945. *A grammar of motives.* Berkeley and Los Angeles: University of California Press.

Bury, M. 1982. Chronic illness as biographical disruption. *Sociology of Health and Illness* 4:167–82.

Cain, Carole. 1991. Personal stories: Identity acquisition and self-understanding in Alcoholics Anonymous. *Ethos* 19:210–53.

Capps, Lisa, and Elinor Ochs. 1995. *Constructing panic: The discourse of agoraphobia.* Cambridge, Mass.: Harvard University Press.

Carr, David. 1986. *Time, narrative and history.* Bloomington: Indiana University Press.

Carrithers, Michael. 1992. *Why humans have cultures: Explaining anthropology and social diversity.* Oxford: Oxford University Press.

Chamberlain, Mary, and Paul Thompson, eds. 1998. *Narrative and genre.* London: Routledge.

Clifford, James, and George Marcus, eds. 1986. *Writing culture: The poetics and politics of ethnography.* Berkeley and Los Angeles: University of California Press.

Cole, Michael. 1996. *Cultural psychology: A once and future discipline.* Cambridge, Mass.: Harvard University Press.

Coles, R. 1989. *Stories and theories: The call of stories.* Boston: Houghton Mifflin.

Connerton, Paul. 1989. *How societies remember.* Cambridge: Cambridge University Press.

Crapanzano, Vincent. 1977. The life history in anthropological fieldwork. *Anthropology and Humanism Quarterly* 2:3–7.

———. 1980. *Tuhami: Portrait of a Moroccan.* Chicago: University of Chicago Press.

———. 1984. Life histories. *American Anthropologist* 86:953–60.

———. 1986. Hermes' dilemma: The masking of subversion in ethnographic description. In *Writing culture,* edited by J. Clifford and G. Marcus, 51–76. Berkeley and Los Angeles: University of California Press.

Csordas, Thomas, ed. 1994a. *Embodiment and experience: The existential grounding of culture and self.* Cambridge: Cambridge University Press.

———. 1994b. *The sacred self: A cultural phenomenology of charismatic healing.* Berkeley and Los Angeles: University of California Press.

———. 1996. Imaginal performances and memory of ritual healing. In *The performance of healing,* edited by C. Laderman and M. Roseman, 91–113. New York: Routledge.

Culler, Jonathon. 1981. *The pursuit of signs: Semiotics, literature, deconstruction.* Ithaca, N.Y.: Cornell University Press.

D'Andrade, Roy G. 1992. Schemas and motivation. In *Human motives and cultural models,* edited by R. G. D'Andrade and C. Strauss, 23–44. Cambridge: Cambridge University Press.

Donald, Merlin. 1991. *Origins of the human mind: Three stages in the evolution of culture and cognition.* Cambridge, Mass.: Harvard University Press.

Early, E. A. 1982. The logic of well-being: Therapeutic narratives in Cairo, Egypt. *Social Science and Medicine* 16:1491–97.

———. 1988. The Baladi curative system of Cairo, Egypt. *Culture, Medicine, and Psychiatry* 12:65–83.

Edwards, Derek, Jonathan Potter, and David Middleton. 1992. Toward a discursive psychology of remembering. *The Psychologist* 5:441–46.

Eisenberg, Leon. 1981. The physician as interpreter: Ascribing meaning to the illness experience. *Comprehensive Psychiatry* 22:239–48.

Farmer, Paul. 1994. AIDS: Talk and the constitution of cultural models. *Social Science and Medicine* 38:801–10.

Fischer, Michael. 1986. Ethnicity and the post-modern arts of memory. In *Writing culture: The poetics and politics of ethnography,* edited by J. Clifford and G. Marcus, 194–233. Berkeley and Los Angeles: University of California Press.

Fischer, Michael, and George Marcus, eds. 1986. *Anthropology as cultural critique: An experimental moment in the human sciences.* Chicago: University of Chicago Press.

Fisher, Walter R. 1997. Narration, reason and community. In *Memory, identity, community: The idea of narrative in the human sciences,* edited by L. P. Hinchman and S. K. Hinchman, 307–27. Albany: State University of New York Press.

Fitzgerald, Joseph M. 1996. Intersecting meanings of reminiscence in adult development and aging. In *Remembering our past: Studies in autobiographical memory,* edited by D. C. Rubin, 360–83. Cambridge: Cambridge University Press.

Fivush, Robyn, Catherine Haden, and Elaine Reese. 1996. Remembering, recounting, and reminiscing: The development of autobiographical memory in social context. In *Remembering our past: Studies in autobiographical memory,* edited by D. C. Rubin, 341–59. Cambridge: Cambridge University Press.

Forster, E. M. 1927. *Aspects of the novel.* New York: Harcourt Brace Jovanovich.

Frank, Arthur. 1995. *The wounded storyteller: Body, illness, and ethics.* Chicago: University of Chicago Press.

Frank, Gelya. 1984. Life history model of adaptation to disability: The case of a "congenital amputee." *Social Science and Medicine* 19:639–45.

———. 1986. On embodiment: A case study of congenital limb deficiency in American culture. *Culture, Medicine, and Psychiatry* 10:189–219.

———. 1996. Life history. In *Encyclopedia of Cultural Anthropology,* edited by D. Levinson and C. Ember. Vol. 2: 705–8. New York: Henry Holt.

———. 2000. *Venus on wheels: Two decades of dialogue on disability, biography, and being female in America.* Berkeley and Los Angeles: University of California Press.

Freud, Sigmund. 1920. *A general introduction to psychoanalysis.* New York: Boni and Liveright.

Garro, Linda. 1988. Explaining high blood pressure: Variation in knowledge about illness. *American Ethnologist* 15:98–119.

———. 1992. Chronic illness and the construction of narratives. In *Pain as human experience,* edited by M. J. DelVecchio Good, P. Brodwin, B. Good, and A. Kleinman, 100–137. Berkeley and Los Angeles: University of California Press.

———. 1994. Narrative representations of chronic illness experience: Cultural models of illness, mind, and body in stories concerning the temporomandibular joint (TMJ). *Social Science and Medicine* 38:775–88.

———. 1995. Individual or societal responsibility? Explanations of diabetes in an Anishinaabe (Ojibway) community. *Social Science and Medicine* 40: 37–46.

———. In press. The remembered past in a culturally meaningful life: Remembering as cultural, social and cognitive process. In *The psychology of cultural experience,* edited by H. Mathews and C. Moore. Cambridge: Cambridge University Press.

Garro, Linda, and Cheryl Mattingly, guest editors. 1994. Narrative representations of illness and healing. *Social Science and Medicine* 38 (6).

Geertz, Clifford. 1980. Blurred genres: The refiguration of social thought. *American Scholar* 80:165–79.

Gennette, Gerard. 1982. *Figures of literary discourse.* New York: Columbia Uniersity Press.

Gergen, K., and M. M. Gergen. 1997. Narratives of the self. In *Memory, identity, community: The idea of narrative in the human sciences,* edited by L. P. Hinchman and S. K. Hinchman, 161–84. Albany: State University of New York Press.

Goffman, Erving. 1974. *Frame analysis.* Cambridge, Mass.: Harvard University Press.

Good, Byron J. 1992. A body in pain: The making of a world of chronic pain. In *Pain as human experience,* edited by M. J. DelVecchio Good, P. Brodwin, B. Good, and A. Kleinman, 29–48. Berkeley and Los Angeles: University of California Press.

———. 1994. *Medicine, rationality, and experience: An anthropological perspective.* Cambridge: Cambridge University Press.

Good, Byron J., and Mary-Jo DelVecchio Good. 1994. In the subjunctive mode: Epilepsy narratives in Turkey. *Social Science and Medicine* 38:835–42.

Good, Mary-Jo DelVecchio. 1995. *American medicine: The quest for competence.* Berkeley and Los Angeles: University of California Press.

Good, M. J. DelVecchio, P. Brodwin, B. Good, and A. Kleinman, eds. 1992. *Pain as human experience: An anthropological perspective.* Berkeley and Los Angeles: University of California Press.

Good, M. J. DelVecchio, B. J. Good, T. Munakato, Y. Kobayashi, and C. Mattingly. 1994. Oncology and narrative time. *Social Science and Medicine* 38:855–62.

Goodwin, Charles. 1984. Notes on story structure and the organization of participation. In *Structures of social action,* edited by M. Atkinson and J. Heritage, 225–46. Cambridge: Cambridge University Press.

Goodwin, Majorie Harkness. 1990. *He-said-she-said: Talk as social organization among Black children.* Bloomington: Indiana University Press.

Hahn, R. H. 1995. *Sickness and healing.* New Haven, Conn.: Yale University Press.

Haviland, John Beard. 1977. *Gossip, knowledge, and reputation in Zinacantan.* Chicago: University of Chicago Press.

———. 1996. "We want to borrow your mouth": Tzotzil marital squabbles. In *Disorderly discourse: Narrative, conflict, and inequality,* edited by C. L. Briggs, 158–203. New York: Oxford University Press.

Herzfeld, Michael. 1996. Embarrassment as pride: Narrative resourcefulness and strategies of normativity among Cretan animal-thieves. In *Disorderly discourse: Narrative, conflict, and inequality,* edited by C. L. Briggs, 72–94. New York: Oxford University Press.

Hinchman, L. P., and S. K. Hinchman. 1997. *Memory, identity, community: The idea of narrative in the human sciences.* Albany: State University of New York Press.

Holland, Dorothy, and A. Kipnis.1994. Metaphors for embarrassment and stories of exposure: The not-so-egocentric self in American culture. *Ethos* 22: 316–42.

Hoskins, Janet. 1998. *Biographical objects: How things tell the stories of people's lives.* New York: Routledge.

Hughes-Freeland, Felicia. 1998. Introduction. In *Ritual, performance, media,* edited by F. Hughes-Freeland, 1–28. London: Routledge.

Hunt, Linda M. 1994. Practicing oncology in provincial Mexico: A narrative analysis. *Social Science and Medicine* 38:843–53.

Hunter, Kathryn. 1991. *Doctors' stories: The narrative structure of medical knowledge.* Princeton, N.J.: Princeton University Press.

Hydén, Lars-Christer. 1995. The rhetoric of recovery and change. *Culture, Medicine and Psychiatry* 19:73–90.

Hymes, Dell H. 1981. *"In vain I tried to tell you": Essays in Native American ethnopoetics.* Philadelphia: University of Pennsylvania Press.

Iser, W. 1978. *The act of reading: A theory of aesthetic response.* Baltimore: Johns Hopkins University Press.

Jackson, Jean. 1994. The Rashomon approach to dealing with chronic pain. *Social Science and Medicine* 38:823–33.

Jakobson, Roman. 1960. Closing statement: Linguistics and poetics. In *Style in language,* edited by T. Sebeok, 350–77. Cambridge, Mass.: MIT Press.

———. 1971. Shifters, verbal categories and the Russian verb. In *Roman Jakobson: Selected writings,* 2:130–47. The Hague: Mouton.

Johnson, N. S., and J. M. Mandler. 1980. A tale of two structures: Underlying and surface forms in stories. *Poetics* 9:51–86.

Kapferer, B. 1983. *A celebration of demons: Exorcism and the aesthetics of healing in Sri Lanka.* Bloomington: Indiana University Press.

Kaufman, Sharon. 1988. Illness, biography and the interpretation of self following a stroke. *Journal of Aging Studies* 2:217–27.

Kelley, M. P. 1986. The subjective experience of chronic disease: Some implications for the management of ulcerative colitis. *Journal of Chronic Diseases* 39:653–66.

Kendall, Laurel. 1988. *The life and hard times of a Korean shaman.* Honolulu: University of Hawaii Press.

Kirmayer, L. 1992. The body's insistence on meaning: Metaphor as presentation and representation in illness experience. *Medical Anthropology Quarterly* 6:323–46.

———. 1994. Improvisation and authority in illness meaning. *Culture, Medicine and Psychiatry* 18:183–214.

Kleinman, Arthur. 1986. Illness meanings and illness behavior. In *Illness behavior: A multidisciplinary model,* edited by S. McHugh and M. Vallis, 149–60. New York: Plenum Press.

———. 1988. *The illness narratives: Suffering, healing, and the human condition.* New York: Basic Books.

———. 1995. *Writing at the margin: Discourse between anthropology and medicine.* Berkeley and Los Angeles: University of California Press.

Kondo, Dorinne. 1990. *Crafting selves: Power, gender and discourses of identity in a Japanese workplace.* Chicago: University of Chicago Press.

Labov, W. 1972. The transformation of experience in narrative syntax. In *Language in the inner city,* edited by W. Labov, 354–96. Philadelphia: University of Pennsylvania Press.

———. 1981. Speech actions and reactions in personal narrative. In *Analyzing discourse: Text and talk,* edited by D. Tannen, 219–47. Washington, D.C.: Georgetown University Press.

Labov, W., and J. Waletzky. 1967. Narrative analysis: Oral versions of personal experience. In *Essays in the verbal and visual arts,* edited by J. Helm, 12–44. Seattle: University of Washington Press for the American Ethnological Society.

Laderman, C., and M. Roseman, eds. 1996. *The performance of healing.* New York: Routledge.

Landau, Misia. 1997. Human evolution as a narrative. In *Memory, identity, community: The idea of narrative in the human sciences,* edited by L. P. Hinchman and S. K. Hinchman, 104–18. Albany: State University of New York Press.

Lang, Gretchen Chesley. 1989. "Making sense" about diabetes: Dakota narratives of illness. *Medical Anthropology* 11:305–27.

Langer, Susanne. 1953. *Feeling and form: A theory of art.* New York: Scribner.

Langness, L., and G. Frank. 1981. *Lives.* Novato, Calif.: Chandler and Sharp.

Lave, Jean, and Etienne Wenger. 1991. *Situated learning: Legitimate peripheral participation.* Cambridge: Cambridge University Press.

Linde, Charlotte. 1993. *Life stories: The creation of coherence.* Oxford: Oxford University Press.

Luria, A. R. 1968. *The mind of a mnemonist.* New York: Basic Books.

———. 1972. *The man with a shattered world: The history of a brain wound.* Cambridge, Mass.: Harvard University Press.

Lyotard, J. 1984. *The postmodern condition: A report on knowledge.* Minneapolis: University of Minnesota Press.

MacIntyre, Alisdair. 1980. Epistemological crises, dramatic narrative, and the philosophy of science. In *Paradigms and revolutions,* edited by G. Gutting. South Bend, Ind.: University of Notre Dame Press.

———. 1981. *After virtue: A study in moral theory.* South Bend, Ind.: University of Notre Dame Press.

Mancuso, J. C. 1986. The acquisition and use of narrative grammar structure. In *Narrative psychology: The storied nature of human conduct,* edited by T. R. Sarbin, 91–110. New York: Praeger.

Mandler, Jean M. 1984. *Stories, scripts and scenes: Aspects of schema theory.* Hillsdale, N.J.: Lawrence Erlbaum.

Marcus, George. 1998. *Ethnography through thick and thin.* Princeton, N.J.: Princeton University Press.

Mathews, Holly. 1992. The directive force of morality tales in a Mexican community. In *Human motives and cultural models,* edited by R. D'Andrade and C. Strauss, 127–62. Cambridge: Cambridge University Press.

Mathews, Holly, D. R. Lannin, and J. P. Mitchell. 1994. Coming to terms with advanced breast cancer: Black women's narratives from eastern North Carolina. *Social Science and Medicine* 38:789–800.

Mattingly, Cheryl. 1991a. The narrative nature of clinical reasoning. *American Journal of Occupational Therapy* 45:998–1005.

———. 1991b. Narrative reflections on practical actions. In *The reflective turn,* edited by D. Schon, 235–57. New York: Teachers College Press.

———. 1994. The concept of therapeutic emplotment. *Social Science and Medicine* 38:811–22.

———. 1998a. *Healing dramas and clinical plots: The narrative structure of experience.* Cambridge: Cambridge University Press.

———. 1998b. In search of the good: Narrative reasoning in clinical practice. *Medical Anthropology Quarterly* 12:273–97.

Mattingly, C., and L. C. Garro. 1994. Introduction: Narrative representations of illness and healing. *Social Science and Medicine* 38:771–74.

Mishler, Elliot. 1986a. The analysis of interview narratives. In *Narrative psychology: The storied nature of human conduct,* edited by T. R. Sarbin. New York: Praeger.

———. 1986b. *Research interviewing: Concept and narrative.* Cambridge, Mass.: Harvard University Press.

———. 1995. Models of narrative analysis: A typology. *Journal of Narrative and Life History* 5:87–123.

Monks, J., and R. Frankenberg. 1995. Being ill and being me: Self, body, and time in multiple sclerosis narratives. In *Disability and culture,* edited by B. Ingstad and S. R. Whyte, 107–34. Berkeley and Los Angeles: University of California Press.

Murphy, Robert. 1987. *The body silent.* New York: Henry Holt.

Neisser, Ulric. 1994. Self-narratives: True and false. In *The remembered self,* edited by U. Neisser and R. Fivush, 1–18. Cambridge: Cambridge University Press.

Obeyesekare, G. 1981. *Medusa's hair: An essay on personal symbols and religious experience.* Chicago: University of Chicago Press.

Ochs, Elinor, and Lisa Capps. 1996. Narrating the self. *Annual Review of Anthropology* 25:19–43.

———. In press. *Living narrative.* Cambridge, Mass.: Harvard University Press.

Ochs, Elinor, R. C. Smith, and C. E. Taylor. 1996. Detective stories at dinnertime: Problem solving through co-narration. In *Disorderly discourse: Narrative, conflict and inequality,* edited by C. L. Briggs, 95–113. New York: Oxford University Press.

Peacock, J., and D. C. Holland. 1993. The narrative self: Life stories in process. *Ethos* 21:367–83.

Pellegrino, E. D. 1979. Toward a reconstruction of medical morality: The primacy of the act of profession and the fact of illness. *Journal of Medicine and Philosophy* 4:32–56.

Pillemer, David B. 1992. Remembering personal circumstances: A functional analysis. In *Affect and accuracy in recall: Studies of "flashbulb" memories,* edited by E. Winograd and U. Neisser, 236–64. Cambridge: Cambridge University Press.

Polkinghorne, Donald E. 1991. Narrative and self-concept. *Journal of Narrative and Life History* 1:135–53.

Price, Laurie. 1987. Ecuadorian illness stories: Cultural knowledge in natural discourse. In *Cultural models in language and thought,* edited by D. Holland and N. Quinn, 313–42. Cambridge: Cambridge University Press.

———. 1995. Life stories of the terminally ill: Therapeutic and anthropological paradigms. *Human Organization* 54:462–69.

Propp, Vladimir. 1968. *Morphology of the folk tale.* Translated by L. Scott. Austin: University of Texas Press.

Rabinow, Paul. 1997. *Essays on the anthropology of reason.* Princeton, N.J.: Princeton University Press.

Radin, P. [1926] 1983. *Crashing thunder: The autobiography of an American Indian.* Lincoln: University of Nebraska Press.

Ricoeur, Paul. 1984. *Time and narrative.* Vol. 1. Translated by K. Blamey and D. Pellauer. Chicago: University of Chicago Press.

———. 1985. *Time and narrative.* Vol. 2. Translated by K. Blamey and D. Pellauer. Chicago: University of Chicago Press.

———. 1987. *Time and narrative.* Vol. 3. Translated by K. Blamey and D. Pellauer. Chicago: University of Chicago Press.

Riessman, Catherine K. 1990. Strategic uses of narrative in the presentation of self and illness: A research note. *Social Science and Medicine* 30:1195–200.

———. 1993. *Narrative analysis.* Qualitative Research Methods, vol. 30. Newbury Park, Calif.: Sage.

Rosaldo, Renato. 1976. The story of Tukbaw: "They listen as he orates." In *The biographical process: Studies in the history and psychology of religion,* edited by F. E. Reynolds and D. Capps, 121–51. The Hague: Mouton.

———. 1984. Grief and a headhunter's rage: On the cultural force of emotions. In *Text, play and story: The construction and reconstruction of self and society,* edited by E. M. Bruner, 178–95. Prospect Heights, Ill.: Waveland Press.

———. 1986. Ilongot hunting as story and experience. In *The anthropology of experience,* edited by V. M. Turner and E. N. Bruner, 97–138. Urbana: University of Illinois Press.

Sacks, Oliver. 1984. *A leg to stand on.* New York: Summit Books.

———. 1987a. Foreword. In A. R. Luria, *The man with a shattered world: The history of a brain wound.* Cambridge, Mass.: Harvard University Press.

———. 1987b. *The man who mistook his wife for a hat and other clinical tales.* New York: Perennial Library.

———. 1995. *An anthropologist on Mars.* New York: Knopf.

Sansom, Basil. 1982. The sick who do not speak. In *Semantic anthropology,* edited by D. Parkin, 183–95. London: Academic Press.

Saris, A. Jamie. 1995. Telling stories: Life histories, illness narratives, and institutional landscapes. *Culture, Medicine and Psychiatry* 19:39–72.

Schafer, R. 1981. *Narrative actions in psychoanalysis.* Worcester, Mass.: Clark University Press.

———. 1992. *Retelling a life: Narration and dialogue in psychoanalysis.* New York: Basic Books.

Schank, Roger C. 1990. *Tell me a story: A new look at real and artificial memory.* New York: Scribner.

Shay, J. 1994. *Achilles in Vietnam: Combat trauma and the undoing of character.* New York: Atheneum.

Shore, Bradd. 1996. *Culture in mind: Cognition, culture, and the problem of meaning.* New York: Oxford University Press.

Spence, Donald. 1982. *Narrative truth as historical truth.* New York: Norton.

Sperber, Dan. 1985. Anthropology and psychology: Towards an epidemiology of representations. *Man* 20:73–89.

Steffen, Vibeke. 1997. Life stories and shared experience. *Social Science and Medicine* 45:99–111.

Stoller, Paul. 1989. *The taste of ethnographic things: The senses of anthropology.* Philadelphia: University of Pennsylvania Press.

———. 1997. *Sensuous scholarship.* Philadelphia: University of Pennsylvania Press.

Strauss, Claudia, and Naomi Quinn. 1997. *A cognitive theory of cultural meaning.* Cambridge: Cambridge University Press.

Turner, Victor. 1986. *The anthropology of performance.* New York: PAJ Publications.

Turner, Victor, and Edward M. Bruner, eds. 1986. *The anthropology of experience.* Urbana: University of Illinois Press.

Viney, Linda L., and Lynne Bousfield. 1991. Narrative analysis: A method of psychosocial research for AIDS-affected people. *Social Science and Medicine* 32:757–65.

Waitzkin, Howard, and Theron Britt. 1993. Processing narratives of self-destructive behavior in routine medical encounters: Health promotion, disease prevention, and the discourse of health care. *Social Science and Medicine* 36:1121–36.

Waitzkin, Howard, and Holly Magaña. 1997. The black box in somatization: Unexplained physical symptoms, culture and narratives of abuse. *Social Science and Medicine* 45:811–25.

White, Geoffrey M. 1991. *Identity through history: Living stories in a Solomon Islands society.* Cambridge: Cambridge University Press.

White, Hayden. 1980. The value of narrativity in the representation of reality. In *On narrative,* edited by W. J. T. Mitchell, 1–23. Chicago: University of Chicago Press.

Wikan, Unni. 1990. *Managing turbulent hearts: A Balinese formula for living.* Chicago: University of Chicago Press.

———. 1991. Toward an experience-near anthropology. *Cultural Anthropology* 6:285–305.

Williams, Gareth. 1984. The genesis of chronic illness: Narrative reconstruction. *Sociology of Health and Illness* 6:175–200.

Young, Allan. 1995. *The harmony of illness.* Princeton, N.J.: Princeton University Press.

Zimmerman J., and V. Dickerson. 1994. Using a narrative metaphor: Implications for theory and clinical practice. *Family Process* 33:233–45.

TWO

"Fiction" and "Historicity" in Doctors' Stories

Social and Narrative Dimensions of Learning Medicine

BYRON J. GOOD and
MARY-JO DELVECCHIO GOOD

In recent years, social scientists, medical ethicists, and scholars from the medical humanities have begun to investigate narrative dimensions of medical practice (Mishler 1986a, 1986b; Brody 1987; Kaufman 1993; Kleinman 1988; Hunter 1991; Mattingly 1991, 1994; B. Good 1994; M. Good 1995). Little surprise. The moment one attends to narrative, it becomes clear that stories and storytelling—narratives and narrative practices—have a central role in medical practice. Physicians talk in stories, whether discussing patients anecdotally or analyzing "cases" in formal settings such as morbidity and mortality conferences or grand rounds. They teach through stories. Clinical pedagogy has traditionally focused on making rounds to patients' bedsides, presenting individual cases, and reviewing relevant medical science in the context of clinical narratives and problem solving. More recently, this approach has been extended to preclinical teaching of the basic biological sciences—as part of "problem-based learning" curricula—on the assumption that clinical cases or clinical stories should serve as the fundamental units for learning and organizing medical knowledge. And behind the formal use of clinical cases in medical education lies a whole genre of wisdom literature, in which physicians recount stories of patients they have treated and reflect on what they have to teach all of us not only about pathophysiology but also about human suffering and the human condition.[1]

Narrative extends beyond pedagogy, however. Physicians practice in stories. They carry out their work by developing narrative accounts of

patients and formulating therapeutic activities in relation to these accounts. They reason and make decisions in narrative terms. And they
fight with each other through narrative, telling stories about each other
and contesting the veracity of the stories that other physicians tell or
have told about their patients (M. Good 1995).

And how do we know this? How do we, as social scientists, understand the nature of medical practice and its relation to the inner life of
physicians? We know, of course, largely through the stories they tell us.
We ask medical students or physicians to tell us about patients they have
seen, about difficult moments in their training or ethical conflicts they
face, about mistakes they have made and had to live with, about their
conflicts with other physicians, and they tell us stories. Little wonder
there is new attention to narrative theory in the analysis of medical
practice.

In spite of the ubiquity of storytelling in medical settings or in research with health care practitioners, one prominent form of critique of
medical care has been based on physicians' failure to recognize the narrative dimensions of the illness experience, to attend to the stories patients tell. Physicians constitute "disease" as disordered physiological
structure and function, set within abstract, medicalized time (Frankenberg 1988), or as "dehistoricized objects-in-themselves" (Young 1982:
275). Thus, while patients experience "sickness" in the context of life
narratives, the lived body, and diverse forms of social relations and
power structures, medicine constructs the objects of therapeutic attention as ahistorical, atemporal, and nonsocial dimensions of the medicalized body.[2]

In this chapter we reflect on narrative practices in medicine and the
apparent contradiction between the ubiquity of stories in clinical practice and the critique of medicine for its willful neglect of the narrative dimension of illness. We do so by examining how a group of medical students enter the world of medical stories, learning to read and tell stories,
coming to experience the power that follows from a story told accurately and reflecting—through stories—on the moral dimensions of
medicine at its limits. In particular, drawing on a distinction made by
Ricoeur (1981:287–96), we are interested in exploring how students
move from an early sense of disease as viewed through the lens of the basic sciences to an acute awareness of the "fictional" quality of medical
stories, to a sense of their absolute "historicity," a deeply embodied
sense that truly *medical* stories are mimetic while stories of suffering
maintain a fictional quality.

SOURCES: A STUDY OF PHYSICIANS
IN TRAINING AT HARVARD MEDICAL SCHOOL

The research on which this chapter is based was a study of how young men and women enter the world of medicine, undertaken in the context of a major and much heralded curricular reform at Harvard Medical School, which produced the "New Pathway in General Medical Education." For more than four years, along with two of our graduate students,[3] we interviewed a cohort of more than sixty medical students, selected primarily from the graduating class of 1990. One of us (BG) also participated in three of the major basic science blocks in the new curriculum, attending tutorials, lectures, and laboratories as an anthropologist researcher.

The primary aim of the research was to develop a phenomenological account of how students enter the highly specialized lifeworld of medicine—how they find their way imaginatively and practically into that world and its objects, crafting selves and developing the knowledge and skills appropriate to their work as physicians. We focused specifically on the evolution of "competence" as students moved from raw beginners to apprentices to practicing physicians. We discussed the terror and joy they felt in gaining competence to work with desperately sick patients, their experiences of total absorption in the world of medicine, and their fears of loss of self as they became more and more deeply engaged. We followed students over time, observing the emergence of a sense of professional selfhood in a context in which "competence" is a symbol of extraordinary potency, in which making mistakes is a necessary part of learning, and in which errors and poor judgment can have devastating consequences for patients as well as those who are learning to be physicians.[4]

Among the findings that emerged from our analysis of the interview data and observations, two have special relevance for investigating the narrative structure of medical knowledge. First, we came to understand the importance of a number of distinctly medical "practices" that serve as basic building blocks, or "formative principles," of medical practice and knowledge.[5] Students enter the phenomenal world of medicine not merely by mastering a body of basic medical sciences, by learning an enormous technical vocabulary, and by developing clinical experience, although these are essential to becoming physicians. Students enter the lifeworld of medicine by learning to engage in a set of distinctly medical practices. In the first two years of medical training—the "basic science" years—anatomy and histology laboratories are designed to teach medical students a set of visual practices, ways of seeing and interacting with the world consonant with a distinctively medical ontology. From anatomy laboratory, with its systematic exploration of the "natural" structures of the physical body, to the exploration of diverse cellular structures seen through increasingly powerful levels of the microscope, disease comes to be *seen* in all its materiality, and a hierarchy proceeding downward from gross anatomy to cellular structure to molecular and genetic levels is interpreted as movement from surface manifestation to deeper levels of causality (cf. B. Good 1994:ch.3). These fundamentally visual practices serve as the building blocks for medical knowledge throughout the physician's lifetime.

In their third and fourth years, during their clinical training, students enter medical discourse by learning to engage in more specifically narrative practices. They learn basic writing practices, narrative representations of patients in medical charts. They learn speaking practices—how to present patients to other physicians, how to interview patients to gather appropriate information, how to discuss an illness and its likely course with patients and family members, and how to gain consent from patients to participate in procedures and treatment. And they learn clinical reasoning, grounded in a sense of the temporal emergence of disease, and develop a repertoire of procedures which they are competent to undertake. One primary conclusion from this research is thus that any study of medical knowledge requires sustained analytic attention to these elementary and closely interlinked *practices* through which the objects of the medical lifeworld are constituted and engaged.

A second conclusion from this research is that these practices all have a narrative dimension. This is neither obvious nor trivial. It *is* obvious that case accounts presented during rounds or written in charts have a narrative structure. They tell more or less detailed stories of a patient and his or her disease. They describe the onset of symptoms, the crisis that brought the patient to the medical system, the course of the illness as it is known, and what is being done. What is less obvious, however, is the extent to which the medicalized object—the disease, the body, pathophysiological processes, the patient—is constituted in narrative terms, and the extent to which forms of reasoning, the interpretation of empirical findings, and treatment processes are all narrative in structure. The temporal dimension of disease and the struggle to find coherent plots become more obvious after medical students enter the clinics, but from the earliest years diseases are interpreted as evolving processes, whether studied through longitudinal paper cases or as disease processes (metastasis, inflammatory responses) with distinctive stages. What is seldom recognized, however, is the play between fictional and realist dimensions of medical narratives as students enter the world of medicine.

In the following pages, we draw on our interviews with Harvard medical students to explore the evolving meaning of medical narratives, as well as how students' stories provide access to an inner world of experience.

ENTERING A WORLD OF STORIES: EMBODYING THE MEDICAL HABITUS

We asked a third-year student whom we were interviewing to tell us about his recent pediatrics rotation and what experiences made him feel like he was gaining competency. "Not a lot," he said, laughing. "Write-ups. I got better at doing write-ups. They got less painful to do. Progress notes." "A very important part of medicine?" we asked. "Very important part. Learning to talk in the right way, another part. Like learning to communicate."

Learning to write and talk the right way implies not only learning the vocabulary of medicine and the technical knowledge it conveys but also learning to tell a medical story, tailored to a particular context and audience, particularly during medical rounds: "I think the main thing . . . you learn [is] kind of the daily rhythm, which is rounds in the morning, work rounds, . . . attending rounds, . . . visit rounds. . . . A big part of rounds is presenting cases, and in some ways that's probably the biggest thing medical students learn."

At the heart of rounds are case presentations, a genre of stories that are stereotyped in format but vary in length depending on the context. "Morning rounds, you give short stories, bullets. Attending rounds, you give longer stories. Presenting admissions, you give even longer stories. . . . And in teaching experiences there are illustrative stories. That's a whole other kind of story." And what is the structure of these case presentations?

> Telling a story is definitely one of the things, I mean that's often what you're kind of told. . . . You have to organize things into some kind of a story, whether you choose to do it chronologically or whether you choose to do it from the basis of one particular disease process or something, even though it might not be exactly a chronological progression or something, but definitely you're often told to, encouraged to tell a story in some way.

One of the classic ways of presenting a case is as a diagnostic story.

> I've been told a number of times by house officers . . . that you should be sort
> of leading up to something which is your differential diagnosis, and that you
> should tell the story of this patient such that you'll persuade your audience
> of your final, most likely diagnosis, or of your differential, and why you've
> included certain diseases and excluded others. Then if you tell your story such
> that it points in some direction, then you give some totally different differen-
> tial, then . . . you've just confused everyone.

The nature of the story must be "edited" for a particular context.
One student told of an early experience on surgery:

> It was probably my first patient, and I started to go into this whole thing
> about why the person's here, what we found on the physical exam, and of
> course none of this was what [the chief resident] wanted to hear. It was like
> he wanted a two-second blurb on this person on how they were doing. . . .
> He just jumped down my throat. He said, "All right, what are you doing?
> Why are you wasting my time? Just get to the important stuff." When I didn't
> know what the important stuff was, he got even more mad.

Learning what "the important stuff" is and how to present it in a persuasive way is central to becoming a physician. It requires that one know
enough about the patient's condition, the disease processes, the diagnostic possibilities, and the appropriate treatments to sort through a chart
and present the critical issues in a minute or two. It requires the ability
to tell a good story, organized chronologically, tracing origins and consequences of the disease process, or outlining a diagnostic puzzle. It requires skills in performance and articulation (M. Good 1995:chs. 6,7).
And it requires learning to interact with patients in a way that reveals
"the important stuff," sorting through patients' stories to find the data
necessary to tell an appropriate medical story to more senior physicians.
"They don't want to hear the story of the person. They want to hear the
edited version," a student said of rounds.

This general description of how students learn the basic narrative
practices essential to being competent physicians is broadly accurate.
However, it is a rather stereotyped account, silencing the deep anxieties
students experience as they begin encountering patients, learning how to
read their stories, and learning to take actions that have enormous consequences. Listening to students going through the process provides a
more complex sense of the emergence of the medical world and an evolving sense of the relation between medical narratives and the physical body.

THE MEDICAL STORY AS "FICTIONAL"
AND THE EMERGENCE OF MEDICAL "REALISM"

A number of the passages quoted previously were drawn from an interview with a third-year medical student who was in one of his early clinical rotations. We began interviewing this student two years earlier, when he was a first-year medical student just beginning his basic science courses and learning to interview patients as part of his "patient-doctor" class. In our very first interview, he told of an experience examining a patient. His description contrasts with his later discussions of interviewing and presenting patients and sheds light on the evolution of the medical perspective. "I never anticipated what a terrifying experience it was emotionally to see patients," he told us.

> I couldn't believe it! I'd even seen patients before [when he was a research interviewer]. But I was frightened. It was as if a woman came in a room you were in and started taking her clothes off! This time I was going to have to do the exam. I was the only one who was going to do it, and it happened too fast. I didn't get anything that I needed. I couldn't believe how anxiety-producing it was. I felt like the patient was acting in a way that made presumptions about my competence, that I should explain myself, excuse myself.

He went on to tell the story of this early clinical encounter when he was asked to interview and do a physical exam on a young woman suffering from asthma. The woman made it clear that because he was a medical student she did not want him to examine her, and she only agreed to lift her shirt so he could listen to her lungs when he insisted. Since he was obviously not yet a physician, he felt extremely uncomfortable trying to take control of the interaction. Yet he knew his preceptor expected him to act as though he were in control.

> Clearly I'm being told my job is to control that interaction. There's a message, very strong, that if you let the patient take over, you don't have that kind of time, you don't get anywhere, you ask an open-ended question, but you guide. You give the illusion of the patient controlling the situation when in fact you're controlling the situation.

He described feeling that he was being taught a series of "tricks of the trade," ways of making the patient feel in control of the situation when in reality the doctor is. And he reflected rather bitterly on his memories of years of being a patient himself—he had had cancer before entering medical school—feeling that he had been tricked or "fleeced" by his doctors.

He went on to tell how he felt he had to live up to the expectations to act like a physician, and that these included learning how to "present" the patient properly and describe her in writing in the chart. "You don't talk about your patient," he said, "you 'present' your patient." Learning how to present to his preceptor was critical. "And they told you how they wanted a presentation done?" we asked.

> We're supposed to get more sophisticated—or more indoctrinated—about presenting our patients each time we see them. And learning that as a systematic way of organizing what you want to say. The problem of course is that the organization often dictates what you say and what you don't say. There's no category for miscellaneous perception or for how I felt about this experience, or, gee, you might want to think about why this person said what they did.

Thus, although he described the characteristics of a case presentation in a manner similar to his description two years later, his experiential perspective on participating in those narrative practices changed quite dramatically. In his initial years, he did not feel "authorized" to "cross the boundary" with a patient, to engage the patient from a position of power and tell her story from that position. Such authorization would come later, when he described with growing excitement the importance of presenting information so it could be used efficiently by the medical team. Only then could he participate in constituting the case as a project, a temporal ordering of illness processes that projected technical interventions as the work of the physicians.

In the early years of clinical work, this lack of authority gives students a tremendous sense of the conventionality or arbitrariness of medical practice, of the story that is told of a patient and the actions that result. For a time, the sense of realism of medical claims engendered in the basic science years is called into question. Another student told of a pediatrics case his team was seeing at the time we were speaking. "We have a kid on our team right now who has a very unusual constellation of symptoms, and no one really knows what the heck is going on . . . ," he said. "What is the case?" we asked.

> Well, it's a kid with a strange rash and failure to thrive. People just aren't really sure how to tie it all together. But I guess what I'm trying to convey is . . . it doesn't seem very scientific. . . . I mean the first two years of medical school, you get the feeling that everything is very scientific, you're learning science. Then this kid comes in with this funny set of symptoms, and a medical student . . . does the most in-depth write-up because the interns don't have the

time . . . then you do reading for it that night, and that's why it takes from three in the afternoon until nine at night. Then he comes up with his differential, which is what he got from the textbook that happened to be in the conference room or whatever and that he remembers from his pathophysiology course, and maybe the intern has a couple of other ideas, but that's only what two people remember, and there are obviously a zillion other syndromes and diseases and weird things that they may not have seen or don't remember, that they never even learned about, and one of those things may be what this patient has.

He went on to describe the apparent hit-or-miss quality of particular diagnoses being put on or omitted from the differential diagnosis in cases such as this, noting research that indicates how unlikely it is that a diagnosis will ultimately be made that is not on the first differential. The seemingly random process of thinking up potential diagnoses—"if they remembered it that particular minute at three in the morning or whatever"—thus disturbed him. "So that's kind of where it seems to me the arbitrariness comes in," he concluded. This conventionality is particularly troubling when cases go awry, or when the student does a rotation on a service such as neurology, where many of the patients have had strokes associated with other treatments they have received, such as those on a coronary care unit.

At the same time that students have experiences indicating that clinical stories have a relatively arbitrary relation to reality, challenging the naturalistic or representational character assumed basic to the narrative practices they observe, they also begin to have experiences of the efficacy of a well-told story. This same student described a rotation on a pediatrics emergency service as a clerkship "that sort of changed me more than others as far as bringing me along the road to being a doctor." In this setting, medical students are allowed to see patients with non-life-threatening conditions before they have been seen by other physicians.

> You're the first one to walk in the room. You say, "Hi, I'm you know, a medical student working in the emergency room and [I want to] ask you a few questions and examine you, and then one of the other doctors will be in to see you with me." I was seeing maybe five patients a day or six, or even more, and just one right after the other. After a while you just become totally at home because you have to, walking into a room, introducing yourself to a complete stranger, doing a history and physical, and trying to make sense of the situation and come up with a diagnosis, and come up with a treatment plan and write it up very concisely on one sheet of paper because that's the way the ER works, deciding whether they need to be admitted or not, what tests to order.

He went on to describe how the routine of seeing patients with similar conditions led to a new confidence that he could work in a clinical setting. We asked what problems he saw most frequently.

> Probably the most common thing was asthma attacks. Childhood's a big asthma age, and when kids have real bad asthma attacks and the parents can't take care of it at home, . . . then they come to the emergency department. You really get good at dealing with asthma. The first time I saw asthma I had to ask every step of the way what you do. By the end I sort of had learned the algorithm and the protocol. There's a set kind of protocol of graduation in level of treatment. First you start with inhalers, and if two or three don't work, then you go to IV. Put an IV in and give IV meds and see if those work after a few hours, and if they don't, then the kid usually gets admitted. So there's kind of a gradually escalating level of treatment that gets done. Eventually the picture clicks for you, and you realize that that's what you do, and then you go off and do it on your own.

The student begins to recognize prototypical patterns, learns to place a patient along a typical continuum of illness, and discovers the efficacy of formulating disease in this fashion and responding accordingly. Clinical stories thus come to be seen less and less as arbitrary or "fictional," and more as having a "realist" quality: they represent reality in a fashion that allows routine but powerful interventions.

ABSORBED BY MEDICAL POWERS

The student we have been quoting went on to describe other far more complex experiences that represented the power of medical interventions in a quite dramatic way:

> The other day, my very first day in the emergency ward at the Mass. General on surgery—we do two weeks in the emergency in the minor surgery department, but as a student you get called in to help on codes to do things like draw bloods every now and then, or more often than not, run them up to the lab—they brought this guy in who jumped off the Tobin Bridge, I think. On arrival he wasn't breathing, his heart wasn't beating, and all his bones were broken. They wheeled him in, he's moribund, and the EMTs are giving their rapid-fire history, which is what they do when they bring a real emergency in like this. . . . They're giving all the pertinent data, everything's moving really fast [he snapped his fingers rapidly], and within five minutes they had opened this guy's chest and were doing open-chest heart massage. The senior resident had this guy's heart in her hand. I was in the room, twenty-five people were in the room, but here they bring this guy in, and the senior resident cuts, makes an incision between his fourth and fifth rib, or something below the

armpit. Then they put the rib spreader in and pulled out the guy's heart. They incised the pericardia, I guess they clamped the aorta. They clamp the descending aorta so that all the blood squeezed out of the heart will go to the brain and the coronary arteries so that you save the brain and the heart, which are the most important, obviously. At least you're able to survive ischemia. So here the senior resident has the guy's heart under his right armpit and she's squeezing on his heart. There's only so far you can pull it, but there it is hanging, dangling outside the guy's chest. Meanwhile, I was helping the junior resident put a chest tube on the other side. I didn't even know which end of the chest tube is the right end to go in. I handed it to him the wrong way. Blood is gushing out and splashing all over my shoes. Someone says, "Where did this guy come from?" And someone jokes, "Probably San Francisco." Meanwhile, blood is gushing out all over the floor. I'm thinking, "Christ, how [much blood is] getting all over my shoes?" Anyway, they only did the code for about five minutes because it was obvious the guy was dead when he hit the door, and he wasn't going to be anything but dead. Like you said, no one even knew what the man's name was. Five minutes after the code had started, the attending said, "This man's dead. Stop the code." Almost everyone leaves the room except a nurse or two to help clean up. They said, "Which medical student wants to practice suturing and sew this guy's chest back together?"

"What does it feel like?" we asked him. "Is it kind of shocking?"

I don't know, I guess it's a complicated set of feelings for me. . . . I think the things that I experience most poignantly about it are I have a lot of trouble dealing with the fact that it's exciting to be in that situation. There's all this action and sense of urgency, and everything feels vital. You feel important in some way, or like you could be important. Then they're doing these things. I mean, how many people in the world have the experience of seeing a man's chest opened and his heart being open-chest heart massaged before your very eyes? It's like *Star Trek* or something. It's not anything you can put in any context of the rest of your life or anything that anyone can describe to you. The level of violation of everything you consider human, and yet you know it's in the cause of saving someone's life. They wouldn't do it, I'm sure, unless there were cases where that did save the person's life.

As if to illustrate this, to indicate the rather bizarre legitimacy of behaving in ways that apparently "violate everything you consider human," he went on immediately to tell of a twenty-year-old woman who had been in a car accident and suffered a small tear between the vena cava and right atrium of her heart, who had been brought to the same surgery unit. She was in intensive care, apparently stable, when suddenly this portion of her heart ruptured and she went into cardiac arrest.

One of the cardiac surgeons happened to be there, and they opened her chest there, and half a liter of blood came out of her pericardium. They immediately rushed her to the OR. Her hematocrit was 8 when they got her there, normal is about 38 or something. She should be dead, but they saved her life. They must have given her twenty-five units of blood, I don't know, tons of blood, and basically sewed her heart back together. The next day she was talking and asking for, I don't know, lipstick or her mother to bring in her makeup kit or something, and that girl should be dead. She was dead, and they brought her back to life, just a miracle what happened to that woman.

He again reflected on the power of the drama, the power only par-tially conveyed by the story as he could tell it to us, that drew him into medicine and revealed the power of medicine.

> I guess I got sidetracked, but . . . it's such an . . . amazing thing that I guess the voyeuristic side of me gets excited by being privileged to be an observer in these situations, of these scenes that so few people are privileged to be a part of. . . . I just haven't come to terms with it yet, but I feel very guilty about being excited about being able to see that kind of stuff. For me, that's a lot of my personal experience of what it feels like.

This engagement in the drama of medicine increases as students come to be more and more full participants in the drama. Ironically, it is of-ten on the most demanding rotations, on rotations when the student is in the hospital constantly, working every third night—rotations about which students most complain—that a real sense of being able to con-trol the course of events begins to overtake the young physician.

> You're totally absorbed, and you're there in the hospital so often that you don't miss . . . a beat on your patients. You know everything that happens to them.
>   And, you know, inevitably when you have a lighter call schedule, you're coming in and asking people to tell you, you know, nurses or whoever was covering, . . . what happened with Mrs. Jones, you know, in the past 24 hours that I was off. This kind of feeling like, if, if, if, you know, I should have been there. I should have been the one that did it. I should have seen everything. I shouldn't have to ask anyone to cover my ass. And if I do it's because, you know, I wimped out. I fell short. I wasn't really doing my job. I should be liv-ing in the hospital [chuckles] all the time. You know. I should get rid of my apartment. And, um, I think, I think there's a lot of truth to that.

In periods of such complete absorption, young physicians begin to have a real sense of power, a sense that patients are truly depending on them, and that because they are following the patients so closely, they can actually affect their disease processes, ensure that things will go well. Along with this goes a sense of camaraderie with other physicians—"it's kind of like entering the priesthood or something. I mean, you sort of feel like you're in the, you know, . . . the cathedral of surgery of the Western world or something."

> I mean, there were moments when I thought, hey, . . . I'm kind of getting drawn into this a little bit. I mean I've been in this hospital more hours than most of, you know, 99.9 percent of the people I'm walking by in the hallways. And, you know, it kind of gives you a little bit of a, puts a little bit of a swagger in your walk or something. . . . I mean . . . there's kind of a real brotherhood that develops with people that you're working with. . . . And there's a real sense that anyone who does any less is a wimp . . . not only a wimp, but a bad doctor. . . . it's immoral to do any less. Or unethical. You're neglecting your patients. You can't be as good a surgeon 'cause you aren't doing it enough. And no one complains about it. And these people work just ungodly hours. I mean it's, it's ungodly. It really is.

At these times, the world of the hospital truly becomes paramount. It is the central reality, what really matters most in the world. All else begins to be largely irrelevant. A young woman we were interviewing told of a time when she was working intensely in a neurology service with patients who had suddenly been struck down—by a stroke or a car accident that caused a brain injury—and crossed that "slim line" from consciousness and health to entering a vegetative state. One afternoon the student left the hospital and went to Harvard Square, "just to get my watch fixed, you know, a mundane detail."

> I happened to walk by this Urban Outfitters or whatever, and I saw this woman, you know, [picking out] a miniskirt, intently selecting a color matching her outfit. The irony was just like . . . so incredible! I was just dumbf . . . [laughs] dumbfounded watching this . . . creature doing this thing. And thinking back . . . in this hospital . . . not so far down the road, . . . people are lying there, you know, didn't know right from left. And if I take a crowbar and struck this girl in the head, she'll be . . . like that. Strip off all her, you know . . . aaii! it's just amazing. And this fiction, you know, even you and I are sitting here talking about this, . . . It boils down to . . . mm, oh, just such a slim . . . [her voice trailed off].

The hospital thus emerges as the site of what is most important in the world, a setting where physicians deal in the most elemental terms with biological reality and where ultimate issues are revealed and engaged, in both material and moral terms.

MEDICINE AS MORAL DRAMA—AND MORAL FAILURE

The young man whose interview we have been quoting, a student planning to become a psychiatrist who was surprised to have been so drawn into the drama of surgery, returned twice during the interview to a long reflection on a case where medicine seemed far less benign than in the other cases he reported, far less a source of power and efficacy. The case provided a counterpoint to his discussions of being absorbed into the world of medicine.

> The first month of my very first rotation, I had a patient who was, um, a forty-year-old, fortyish-year-old Japanese woman with, um, with end-stage liver disease from hepatitis, chronic hepatitis. You know, otherwise perfectly healthy person, um, who was being evaluated for a liver transplant . . . And, who, ah, was just a really sweet woman and who I really got to be quite fond of, and, um, who was . . . was kind of like an innocent in the lion's den.

He described how, perhaps because she was Japanese, this woman was not a "cynical consumer" like many of his other patients. In fact, he wished she were more so, more "streetwise," "a little more cynical or skeptical for her own protection."

> Nonetheless, I . . . got to be pretty fond of her, and she was very sick. And, um, she was being evaluated for this transplant and proceeding so far, you know, successfully through the evaluation process. . . . Which involved making sure she, you know, had a good enough heart function and all the other things. And no other terrible diseases so that she'd have a good chance of, you know, surviving the transplant and having good life expectancy afterward, or whatever. And, um, one of the procedures she had to go through was a biopsy of some abnormality that they had seen on her adrenal gland or on her kidney, or something. And, ah, and, ah, in doing the biopsy they had to stick a needle in to take a sample, and because of her liver disease she had a coagulation disorder.
>
> But apparently, and the numbers indicating that were in her chart, but apparently they do these biopsies all the time on patients with those kind of numbers and don't give any supplementary platelets or coagulation factors, that patients with her kind of numbers survive the procedure or whatever. And, [clears throat] um, so she had the biopsy, seemed to be fine, and that night went to sleep and I guess was found sometime in the middle of the night to be, um, delirious or something like that like.
>
> As it turned out, she was bleeding internally and, you know, very quickly decompensated and couldn't be revived and died. Basically she bled to death . . . into her abdomen. And, um, I hadn't been on call that night, so I, you know, missed the whole thing. And I came in early the next morning, you know, to pre-round, you know, find out how she was doing, and I came into her room to find an empty bed and lots of blood on the floor. And, I think, you know, someone was mopping up the blood, or something. And, um, you know, instantly knew something was wrong and I talked to her nurse. And she said, you know, informed me, oh, didn't you know, she died a couple of hours ago.

He described how he particularly remembered that no one on the team really talked about the event. He had a good, caring, down-to-earth junior resident, who was very humane with his patients. But he barely mentioned the case.

> And I remember just being really shocked and kind of feeling kind of bereft that there was kind of no processing. No, no sort of time or anything, no words spent on trying to deal with, you know, the loss. And, . . . he sort of described what had happened in a very medical kind of way. Um, when we were on our morning rounds, and then it was briefly talked about in a very similar medical kind of way in, um, our attending rounds that week.
>
> You know, maybe a couple of days later or something, where the attending, who was . . . a very senior white-bearded gentleman, physician, internist talked about, you know, what had happened. And expressed some some, you know, sadness at the loss. And talked about whether platelets should have been given or not. And the repercussions in the department of radiology and all that kind of stuff. And then the patient was later presented, I think at the end of the week, at grand rounds.
>
> And, um, it just sort of became, from the minute of her death it seemed like, you know, from the moment I arrived, it seemed like it became progressively more medicalized, the whole experience, and no one ever looked back. And, um, I mean, more medicalized in the sense that, you know, we talked about it a little on our team rounds, and then at attending rounds it was a little more formal medical-type discussion.
>
> And then grand rounds, you know, [there were] slides of the biopsy specimen and this and that and rapid-fire clinical summary and then, you know, just totally medical and impersonal. And, um, I remembered, you know, just kind of feeling like, . . . hold the bus, you know, I'm not there yet. I can't, I'm not ready . . . to just talk about the medical stuff. You know, aren't we going to kind of, you know, feel sad for a few minutes here. . . . I just really felt blindsided. And like I needed to sort of grieve about it in some way. But, you know, it just never happened.

He described how he simply had to process the experience himself— "walking down the hallway between this or that task."

> And I guess eventually it became the past. But that was, I don't know, that was a pretty upsetting experience, . . . just to have some, a patient that you really were, ah, felt a fondness for. Who you felt like you had established some kind of relationship of trust with and to have really what felt like a complete betrayal of trust occur. You know, where she didn't die because of her disease, really. She died because of a procedure. And, um, to feel like you were, that I had been a part of that betrayal of trust in some way. Like, you know, I mean I, ah, . . . I thought about what if I had, maybe I should have, you know, circled the platelet deficiency with a red magic marker or something. I mean should I have called someone? Or what could I have done dif-

ferently? Even though I was, you know, a total peon in the whole group of people taking care of her.

In this experience, another dimension of the medical story was revealed. It was a dimension that Habermas (1987:318ff.) calls the "colonization of the life world," "an elitist splitting-off of expert cultures from contexts of communicative action in daily life," in this case a splitting off of the technical dimensions of care from the humane experiences of care and its failures, even for the practitioners involved. The failure of medical care was progressively told as a medical story, a story of a procedure that failed, a story told in work rounds, in attending rounds, and ultimately in grand rounds. It was a story in which the dimensions of ultimacy were clearly edited out, never made a part of the medical story. And the telling of the story, or not telling the story, made very clear to the student the nature of the lifeworld of medicine into which he was entering.

This "colonized" dimension of the medical lifeworld is seldom fully embodied or incorporated by the physician. Indeed, recounting stories such as that told by this student serves as a clear counterpoint to the telling of stories on rounds. It is a story told to the ethnographers in the "reflective mode" (M. Good 1985, 1995), an alternative accounting that brings the soteriological, as well as affective, dimensions back to the fore. Stories such as these complement the formalized medical stories of the wards, revealing aspects of the inner life of medicine and serving in a modest way to protest against dehumanizing aspects of ward culture. Seldom, however, do they lead to serious efforts to change the structure of clinical life. Even more seldom do they lead to any serious questioning of the basic structure of the narrative practices through which disease is constituted as the object of medical attention.

FINAL REFLECTIONS

Students enter the world of medicine by learning how to constitute disease through a set of distinctive narrative practices. They gain competence as they learn to tell stories that accurately represent physiological reality and provide a basis for effective interventions. Maturing as physicians involves early experiences of naive realism, periods of disillusionment and a sense of the arbitrariness of the claims of medicine, periods of a sense of the absolute power of medicine, and, for many, an increasingly complex understanding about the relations among medical narratives, the human body, and the experiences of their patients.

The stories students tell about their experiences indicate a complex set of reflections on this process. The "inner life" of physicians is hardly a simple reflection of the "medical model" or medical ontology so widely analyzed by social scientists. On the one hand, students are drawn by the power of the medicalized representation of the body, "voyeurs" to remarkable and "inhuman" interventions, fascinated by their own growing power to treat complex medical conditions in an effective manner. On the other hand, students *experience* the conventionality of medical practice. They see procedures done in a ritual-like fashion. They observe practices that are effective in the short term but have few long-term benefits, perceiving outcomes from a commonsense rather than medical perspective. And they observe the fundamental failure of medical practitioners to attend to the affective and moral dimensions of their work, noting the impact of this failure for both the practitioners and their patients.

We have attempted to trace the maturing of medical students through time in part by noting an interplay between what Ricoeur calls "fictional" and "historical" dimensions of medical narratives. In his essay "The Narrative Function," Ricoeur addresses the relation between fiction and history as forms of narrative. He acknowledges the obvious— that the two make quite different claims to represent reality. However, by focusing on the "unity of reference which might correspond to the unity of sense in the narrative genre" (1981:288), Ricoeur develops three arguments: that there is more fiction in history than the positivist conception of history admits, that fictional narratives are more mimetic than positivism allows, and that "the references of empirical narrative and fictional narrative *cross upon* what I provisionally called historicity or the historical condition of man" (1981:289).

Issues of fact and reference are somewhat different for medicine than for history, but an interplay between fictional and historical or realist experiences is a part of the developing experience of physicians. On the one hand, although students and physicians are quick to recognize narrative dimensions of their practice, the term *story* seems to imply a fictional quality lacking the urgency to be accurate in representing disease and responding. Good histories are crucial; accurate representation is essential to good medicine. On the other hand, "fictional" qualities of medicine are also part of the experience of maturing physicians. Medical accounts seem more conventional than realist, at times, decisions arbitrary. Physicians learn to distrust patients' stories as inaccurate by purpose or by accident. They learn to "edit" patients' accounts. And at times, medical history is juxtaposed to patients' fictions as the real to the unreal.

At their best, however, physicians come to a deeper sense of how fiction and history coexist as forms of understanding disease and human suffering (cf. Kleinman 1988). *Poiesis* and *mythos* are present alongside *mimesis* in illness narratives and the medical imaginary. Clinical narratives (M. Good 1995) serve not only to represent the "history of the potentialities of the present" but also "to open up the real to the possible" (Ricoeur 1981:295). And physicians' narratives, told in the "reflective mode," represent a form of critical consciousness in relation to the incessant instrumentalism of medical practice.

Physicians—and medicine—are seldom "at their best," of course. There is a constant threat that medical practice will be fully penetrated by economic and administrative rationality, by medical forms of instrumental rationality that subsume "the voice of the lifeworld" of both patients and practitioners, leading to further "colonization" of medical practice and critical consciousness. At no time in recent history has this threat been greater, as the language of profit and managed care, commoditization, and competition comes more and more to dominate medical discourse. Critical analysis and political responses are fully appropriate. At the same time, we remain convinced that attention to the narrative dimensions of medicine has the potential not only to engender and sustain a humane dimension of medical care but also to incorporate critical elements of the medical consciousness into those policy and political debates that too often reproduce the instrumental rationality we seek to criticize.

NOTES

1. Oliver Sacks's writing (e.g., 1973, 1985) is only a recent example of a genre that has a long history in Europe and North America (cf. Hunter 1991). See B. Good (1994:ch. 6) for a review.

2. For a fuller analysis of "how medicine constructs its objects," see B. Good (1994). A similar critique of medicine as constituting disease is presented there: "Disease occurs not only in the body—in the sense of an ontological order in the great chain of being—but in time, in place, in history, and in the context of lived experience and the social world. Its effect is on the body in the world! And for this reason, I have argued, narratives are central to the understanding of the experience of illness" (1994:133). For a creative examination of how social and

historical memories are appropriated into bodily experience, see Kleinman and Kleinman (1994).

3. Eric Jacobson and Karen Stephenson participated in the research as interviewers and collaborators.

4. All these issues are dealt with at length in M. Good, *American Medicine: The Quest for Competence* (1995), which serves as backdrop for this paper. See also M. Good (1985), M. Good and B. Good (1989), and B. Good (1994:ch. 3).

5. The term *formative principles* is taken from Cassirer's *Philosophy of Symbolic Forms* (1955) and is a key analytic category in B. Good, *Medicine, Rationality and Experience: An Anthropological Perspective* (1994) used for investigating the relationships among the interpretive practices of medical care, the medical lifeworld, and forms of knowledge of that world that serve as the basis for routine clinical work.

REFERENCES

Brody, Howard. 1987. *Stories of sickness.* New Haven, Conn.: Yale University Press.

Cassirer, Ernst. 1955. *The philosophy of symbolic forms.* Vol. 1, *Language.* New Haven, Conn.: Yale University Press.

Frankenberg, Ronald. 1988. "Your time or mine?" An anthropological view of the tragic temporal contradictions of biomedical practice. *International Journal of Health Services* 18:11–34.

Good, Byron J. 1994. *Medicine, rationality and experience: An anthropological perspective.* Cambridge: Cambridge University Press.

Good, Mary-Jo DelVecchio. 1985. Discourse on physician competence. In *Physicians of Western medicine,* edited by R. Hahn and A. Gaines, 247–68. Dordrecht: D. Reidel.

———. 1995. *American medicine: The quest for competence.* Berkeley and Los Angeles: University of California Press.

Good, Mary-Jo DelVecchio, and Byron J. Good. 1989. "Disabling practitioners": Hazards of learning to be a doctor in American medical education. *Journal of Orthopsychiatry* 59:303–9.

Habermas, Jürgen. 1987. *The theory of communicative action.* Vol. 2, *Lifeworld and system: A critique of functionalist reason.* Translated by Thomas McCarthy. Boston: Beacon Press.

Hunter, Kathryn Montgomery. 1991. *Doctors' stories: The narrative structure of medical knowledge.* Princeton, N.J.: Princeton University Press.

Kaufman, Sharon. 1993. Toward a phenomenology of boundaries in medicine: Chronic illness experience in the case of stroke. *Medical Anthropology Quarterly* 2:338–54.

Kleinman, Arthur. 1988. *The illness narratives: Suffering, healing and the human condition.* New York: Basic Books.

Kleinman, Arthur, and Joan Kleinman. 1994. How bodies remember: Social memory and bodily experience of criticism, resistance, and delegitimation following China's Cultural Revolution. *New Literary History* 25:707–23.

Mattingly, Cheryl. 1991. The narrative nature of clinical reasoning. *Journal of American Occupational Therapy* 45:998–1005.

———. 1994. The concept of therapeutic "emplotment." *Social Science and Medicine* 6:811–22.

Mishler, Elliot. 1986a. *The discourse of medicine: Dialectics of medical interviews.* Norwood, N.J.: Ablex.

———. 1986b. *Research interviewing: Context and narrative.* Cambridge, Mass.: Harvard University Press.

Ricoeur, Paul. 1981. *Hermeneutics and the human sciences.* Edited and translated by John B. Thompson. Cambridge: Cambridge University Press.

Sacks, Oliver. 1973. *Awakenings.* New York: Dutton.

———. 1985. *The man who mistook his wife for a hat and other clinical tales.* New York: Summit Books.

Young, Allan. 1982. The anthropologies of illness and sickness. *Annual Review of Anthropology* 11:257–85.

THREE

Cultural Knowledge as Resource in Illness Narratives

Remembering through Accounts of Illness

LINDA C. GARRO

The narrative accounts examined in this chapter situate the occurrence of illness within the context of a person's life, relating how the past is remembered in accounting for a present condition. While not all illness conditions lead to retrospective assessments, remembering the past often accompanies the search for meaning, explanation, and treatment occasioned by illness. In talking about illness, whether one's own or another's, individuals remember, drawing on their experiences and knowledge to link the past with present concerns and future possibilities. The approach taken here relates cognitive perspectives on memory to how cultural knowledge serves as a resource in guiding remembering about the past (see also Garro in press).

Consistent with cognitively oriented psychological theories about memory, remembering is best understood as typically reconstructive rather than simply reproductive (Bartlett 1932). Poised between past and future, remembering is an active, constructive process; "what we recall depends on what we now believe as well as on what we once stored" (Neisser 1988a:49). As persons talk about their experiences, past events are reconstructed in a manner congruent with current understandings; the present is explained with reference to the reconstructed past; and both are used to generate expectations about the future. In response to a disruptive life event like illness, the reconstruction of the past in accounting for an illness, and dealing with the illness in the present and future, are often closely connected.

A relatively new area of psychological inquiry with potential relevance to understanding how illness accounts are remembered and told is autobiographical memory (two edited collections, Rubin 1986 and 1996, provide a good introduction to this rapidly growing and diverse literature). Although more restricted operational definitions are often used in research, *autobiographical memory* can be broadly defined as "the capacity of individuals to recollect their lives" (Baddeley 1992:26). Some of the interest in autobiographical memory research reflects a trend within cognitive psychology to study the everyday uses of memory—"how people use their own past experiences in meeting the past and future . . . under natural conditions" (Neisser 1978:13). As memories are often recalled as stories, researchers from very diverse perspectives (contrast the introduction from Rubin 1996 with Singer and Salovey 1993) highlight the role of narrative in communicating the remembered past. Narrative accounts convey the effort to make sense of the past from the perspective of the present. In going beyond a recitation of what merely happened, these accounts point to meaningful connections among events and states of affairs.

While there are some notable exceptions, autobiographical memory research has tended to be oriented around issues involving the recall of discrete events in an individual's past and is often concerned with the question of accuracy (i.e., how well memories reflect past events). Accuracy of memory is an important and complex issue, of special relevance to legal testimony and survey research, but it may be of limited applicability to understanding remembering in many other real-world situations. Bartlett, who first talked of remembering in terms of reconstruction, claimed that in "a world of constantly changing environment, literal recall is extraordinarily unimportant" (1932:204). By treating autobiographical memory as primarily a record of the past, researchers have paid much less attention to how memory can serve as a resource in everyday life (cf. Robinson 1986:23). Consideration of remembering within the context of daily life leads to questions such as how remembering the past relates to what is done in the present or planning for the future (Neisser 1988b), how an understanding of the past helps individuals give meaning to their lives and the world (Bruner 1990), or how hearing the remembered accounts of others augments the listener's "fund of cultural knowledge with which to meet future illnesses" (Price 1987:315). And it is issues like these that are of interest here.

Culturally available knowledge about illness and its causation can also be seen as a resource that may guide the interpretation and reconstruction of past experience.[1] The relationship between what is "known" and what is "remembered" is explored in this chapter using accounts of diabetes obtained during the course of fieldwork in an Anishinaabe community. While the accounts presented in later sections of this paper are more complex, a very simple example can be provided here. The understanding that diabetes can develop from eating too much sugar is widely shared and thus can be considered part of what is "known" about the condition (although, as will be discussed later, this is not the only "known" shared explanatory framework for diabetes). In contrast to this general knowing, an example of "remembering" comes from a woman who talked about eating a lot of candy bars during her first pregnancy and connects this with a subsequent diagnosis of diabetes. As this example shows, remembering conveyed through a narrative account is not separate from what is known. Rather, through remembering, culturally available knowledge becomes situated knowledge, connected to a particular person, context, and illness history. Narrative provides a window on the processes involved in relating individual experience to preexisting explanatory frameworks available within a cultural setting (cf. Cain 1991; Mathews, Lannin, and Mitchell 1994).

This comparison of what is known with what is remembered brings to mind the well-known theoretical distinction in cognitive psychology between semantic and episodic memory. At a general level, episodic memory is defined as "the recording and subsequent retrieval of memories of personal happenings and doings," while semantic memory can be characterized as "knowledge of the world that is independent of a person's identity and past" (Tulving 1983:9). Despite significant controversy within psychology about different "kinds" of memory and distinct memory systems, the episodic/semantic distinction is seen as having heuristic value, providing a useful way of classifying different types of knowledge (Mandler 1985; see also Neisser 1988c). Although there has been considerable discussion concerned with whether the constructs of autobiographical memory and episodic memory should be considered equivalent or if episodic memory encompasses more than autobiographical memory (a particularly cogent discussion can be found in Brewer 1996), my purpose in introducing these constructs is to show that the distinction made here between what is known and what is remembered is compatible with current cognitive theories. With reference to the semantic/episodic distinction, D'Andrade has stated that culture seems to have its greatest effect on semantic memory (1995:217). Much work in cognitive anthropology, from differing theoretical perspectives, has focused on shared cultural knowledge, on representing aspects of the way the world is understood to be within particular cultural settings.

Although coming at somewhat similar issues from a different angle, Borofsky (1994) recently proposed a continuum between "knowledge" and "knowing." At the "knowledge" end of the continuum is "understanding that is definite and delineated" and that may be treated as specific "facts" (335). Within a cultural setting, Borofsky describes knowledge as relatively constant—across time, across informants, and across context. In contrast, "knowing" is understanding that is "more fluid and flexible in character"; "affirmations that tend to vary with varying contexts" (335). While Borofsky's complex essay warrants more discussion than space here permits, this knowledge/knowing continuum parallels the semantic/episodic distinction in pointing to general knowledge versus understandings as observed in specific contexts. In addition, the fluidity of "knowing" is consistent with the observation that the same individual may give different narrative accounts in different contexts (Lang 1990).

Remembering is reflexive and generative. It may be long after the occurrence of a past experience that it becomes meaningfully connected to a current illness through a reflexive assessment. Relating preexisting explanatory frameworks to personal experience is also a generative process, involving the linking of the remembered past to plausible interpretations within the framework of possibilities afforded by culture. While the cultural understandings often can be said to be shared, there may be considerable variability and flexibility in how they are instantiated in acts of remembering.

Reference to the framework of possibilities afforded by culture or to culturally available knowledge is intended to recognize that remembering may be shaped by sources of information that are not widely shared in a cultural setting. This may include what is acquired through culturally provided tools such as books and television. Understandings about illness and treatment, like other aspects of cultural knowledge, are socially distributed within a cultural setting (D'Andrade 1995). Interactions with others, perhaps particularly those who claim knowledge of illness and its treatment, may be cited as a source of validation for one's perspective, contributing to the credibility and persuasiveness of the account presented. In addition, such interactions may come to guide how an individual reconstructs the past. Kleinman's (1980) formulation of clinical interactions as transactions between explanatory models is clearly pertinent. Through such interactions, a person seeking care may come into contact with an essentially new framework or a new application of an existing framework, with this new knowledge playing a constitutive role in the reorganization and interpretation of past experiences. A similar reframing process occurred in a number of the narrative accounts obtained from members of a support group for individuals with problems associated with the temporomandibular joint (the condition is commonly referred to simply as TMJ). As a consequence of patients' being given a diagnosis of TMJ and through their interactions with others, including treatment providers and support group members, narrative accounts came to be structured around a shared model for TMJ (Garro 1994). Because knowledge about TMJ is not generally shared in North American culture, the shared model expressed by members of this group cannot be considered shared cultural knowledge, but it is culturally available knowledge.

While cultural knowledge may guide remembering along certain lines, relating culturally available knowledge to a particular life context does not happen in a straightforward, deterministic manner (cf. Price 1987: 330). A number of studies point to multiple, even conflicting, explanatory frameworks that can potentially be applied to individual illness cases. Farmer's (1994) portrayal of the emerging cultural model of AIDS within a Haitian village encompassed two disparate explanatory frameworks, either "naturally" (e.g., sexual contact with someone who "carries the germ") or "unnaturally" (with AIDS being willfully and maliciously "sent" by another person).[2] In an essay on understandings about illness in the same Anishinaabe community referred to earlier, I noted (Garro 1990:443) that some illnesses, especially those that do not respond to treatment or that are deemed "unusual" (suspicion may be sparked for a variety of reasons), raise etiological questions that may lead to "a constant entertaining of alternative explanations" with divergent, and at times highly significant, implications for appropriate treatment. Good and Good (1994) discuss "subjunctivizing tactics" in Turkish epilepsy narratives. Drawing on the available body of cultural knowledge, these narratives contained multiple perspectives suggesting alternative plots about the source and outcome of the illness, which justified continued care-seeking and sustained hope for the possibility of cure.

Within the Anishinaabe community, however, a diagnosis of diabetes does not raise critical etiological concerns of the kind described in the preceding paragraph. Indeed, many of those interviewed expressed similar understandings about diabetes and, as will be seen in the specific case examples, would note connections between specific life circumstances and a given explanatory framework. Rather than embedding alternative, contradictory plots or explanations in their accounts, individuals would often demonstrate the compatibility of possible explanatory frameworks. This can be seen in the previously mentioned account from the woman who linked diabetes with eating too many candy bars during pregnancy. In addition to indicating that diabetes results from individual dietary choices like consuming too much sugar, she also pointed to broader societal changes, contrasting the healthy "wild" foodstuffs eaten in the old days with the unhealthy, contemporary, store-bought foods that had resulted in a dramatic increase in sickness, including diabetes, throughout the community.

While the approach taken here does not preclude the potential for "multiple readings" within the narratives, to adopt Good and Good's phrase (1994:835), attention is directed to remembering and how the personal past is conveyed through narrative. In the three accounts that follow, cultural understandings or what is "known" about illness and diabetes can be said to be generally shared and serve as resources in reconstructing the past, but resources that are variably drawn upon and linked to personal experience and history through "remembering."

DIABETES IN AN ANISHINAABE COMMUNITY

In this section I present a rather abbreviated synopsis of the research project (additional details, including more information about the community, are available in Garro 1995, 1996). The research site is an Anishinaabe reserve community located in Manitoba, Canada. Anishinaabe, and its plural, Anishinaabeg, are how people refer to themselves within the community, although Ojibway or Saulteaux may also be used when communicating in English with individuals from outside the community. While some children speak only English, it is a community where most adults still speak their own language, Anishinaabemowin, and prefer it in most social settings.

As in many other First Nations' communities across North America, there has been a relatively rapid increase in cases of maturity-onset diabetes occurring since World War II, an increase that was documented for the general area of my fieldwork site in publications that started to emerge around the mid-1980s (e.g., Young et al. 1985). When I first started fieldwork in 1984, I had no plans to do specific interviews on understandings for particular illnesses. But as I spoke with community members, a recurring topic concerned diabetes and high blood pressure, and how these were "new" illnesses that had not been present in the community in the "old days" but now were so common that some said it seemed as if "everybody is diabetic." The emergence of diabetes and high blood pressure as important health problems has occurred over the same time period as the move toward an economy based on purchased foods.

In Anishinaabemowin, *diabetes* translates as "sweet sickness" or "sugar sickness." As the name suggests, diabetes is seen as linked to sugar, and consuming a lot of sugar (through foods or alcohol) often came up in informal discussions of how someone could develop this illness. Diabetes was also often described as a "white man's sickness." An illness labeled as a white man's sickness is seen as occurring for the first time after Europeans came to North America (other illnesses commonly referred to with this label include measles, tuberculosis, chicken pox, cancer, and high blood pressure). Talk about diabetes may bring up strongly articulated contrasts between the healthy and fortifying foods obtained through Anishinaabe subsistence activities in the past and the comparatively unhealthy reliance on the store-bought foods of the Anishinaabe present. As mentioned previously, these two broad explanatory frameworks are not necessarily seen as contradictory and were often proffered by the same person.

To further explore how community members made sense of these "new" illnesses, I carried out interviews with individuals who had been diagnosed with either diabetes or high blood pressure. In both studies, two interview formats were used. The first consisted of a series of open-ended questions based on Kleinman's explanatory model interview format (Kleinman 1980). In the second, individuals were presented with a series of statements and asked whether each was true. These statements were based on comments made in earlier informal interviews with community members—many came out of discussions about diabetes or high blood pressure, others came out of discussions of other illnesses. Although this analysis will not be presented here, the responses to these statements were examined using cultural consensus analysis (Romney, Weller, and Batchelder 1986; for an analysis of the diabetes data, see Garro 1996). Overall, however, the interviews provided support for shared cultural understandings about diabetes and the two broad explanatory frameworks described earlier.

How an individual understands an illness reflects both personal experience with this and other illnesses and information obtained through other sources, such as interaction with others. Diabetes, as well as individual experiences with this illness, are topics of conversation. Scattered throughout the interviews are observations attributed to other individuals, especially other persons who have been diagnosed with diabetes.

Information from the biomedically oriented health professionals who provide treatment and health education services is also important. Unlike in juvenile diabetes, where heredity is considered to be a significant contributor, concerns about weight are often implicated in maturity-onset diabetes. While there is some variability among health professionals (see Garro 1996), in the majority of cases the emphasis is on weight (and not specifically on sugar consumption) and on efforts to convince patients to make comprehensive lifestyle changes in diet and exercise in order to lose weight. Anishinaabe healers, when consulted, are typically asked for herb-based medicines, said to be effective in controlling diabetes. Anishinaabe healers are rarely contacted about possible alternative diagnoses after a physician's diagnosis of diabetes.

Given the interview context, a difficult issue to assess concerns the extent to which individuals feel obliged to provide certain kinds of narrative accounts, such as those judged to be compatible with the counsel of health care workers. An earlier essay (Garro 1995) discussed how individuals talked about diabetes both as a result of individual dietary choices, often attributing these ideas to physicians and other health professionals, and as a "white man's sickness" linked to environmental and societal changes (both were expressed in the woman's account described in the introductory section). The focus here, however, is not on representing typical accounts, nor on describing consensus and variation within the community, but rather on narrative as a reflexive, generative, and flexible mode of thinking.

"That's how someone used to eat in the past"

When I spoke with the fifty-eight-year-old woman I'll call Ellie Spence, she described herself as no longer having diabetes. But, as became clear while we talked, her experience with diabetes led to significant and ongoing changes in the way she and her family ate. Like the other individuals interviewed, Mrs. Spence had been contacted by a staff person from the local health center, who asked permission for me to speak with her about diabetes. The visit to her home was somewhat unusual because before introductions and explanations about the research were made, she launched into her account:

I'll say where somebody gets sugar diabetes is the food we eat. Nobody ate
canned food before [pause]. It's the white man's fault. White people put too
much chemicals in the food. Anishinaabeg never had sugar diabetes. Nobody
ate canned meat before. What someone used to eat was salt pork, dried beans,
and eggs. Other things were also eaten. People would plant their own gardens
for the winter. Corn was planted, for they would eat it during the winter
along with other foods. For example, soup was made. In the past, Anishinaabeg used to eat cow hocks, like the pork hocks they have today. That's
how someone used to eat in the past.

Mrs. Spence continued by enumerating more of the foods people used to
eat when she was a child, a time before diabetes was known in the community. She talked about foods that were gathered, about fishing and
hunting, and described the different ways the foods were prepared by her
mother. She concluded her introductory statement with the following:

This is why I think someone has sugar today because of the foods someone
eats now. I also did quit eating the foods I used to eat before. I quit food or
meat from the can. Another thing, canned milk was never used before—no
canned milk in earlier days. Now I never use that milk. That canned milk.

Mrs. Spence became even more explicit later when commenting on her
situation when she was diagnosed with diabetes:

What I think is because of the foods. I was working at [name of business located off the reserve] at the time. I never ate right. We always ate "Klik" or
"Spork" [these refer to canned meat products], anything at all, so that is
where I think it came from. I was always busy and I had no time to cook a
proper meal.

In constructing this account, Mrs. Spence taps into the broader discourse about "white man's sickness." When talking about illness conditions as "white man's sicknesses," individuals often mentioned the chemicals sprayed on crops or used in processing foods, such as canned foods.
Typically, such statements are not tied to an individual's personal history but are comments about the community history, which help to
explain the relatively recent emergence of white man's sicknesses, like diabetes, and the substantial number of persons diagnosed with these illnesses. Most remarks about "white man's sickness" can be understood
as "a making sense of the past as a kind of collective autobiography"
(Connerton 1989:70). Connerton (1989:21) identifies two types of narrative contexts used to understand others, but which may also be ap-
plicable to understanding oneself:

We situate the agents' behaviour with reference to its place in their life history; and we situate that behaviour also with reference to its place in the his-

tory of the social settings to which they belong. The narrative of one life is part of an interconnecting set of narratives; it is embedded in the story of those groups from which individuals derive their identity.

Remarks about "white man's sickness," whether integrated into a personal story or not, are often affectively laden, linked as they are to the disruption and destruction of the Anishinaabe way of life, which has been ongoing since first contact with Europeans. Such comments clearly take a moral stand and implicitly condemn prevailing practices in contemporary society. They can also be viewed as expressions of resistance to the tendency of biomedically oriented practitioners to highlight individual responsibility for diabetes through making recommendations that patients lose weight, change their diet, and get more exercise (Garro 1995).

Mrs. Spence's account stands out as distinctive because this collective memory has become personal knowledge, grounded in the particulars of her own life history. But the link between eating canned foods and developing diabetes was only reflexively established a number of years after her initial diagnosis and only after other explanatory frameworks had been found wanting. Mrs. Spence originally ascribed her diabetes to eating sugar and then to drinking alcohol. But when eliminating these items from her diet led to no change in her diabetes, Mrs. Spence revisited other possible explanations for diabetes within the context of her own past.

The last time Mrs. Spence went for a checkup at the local health center, she was told she no longer has diabetes. She credits this improvement to her return to the foods she remembers eating while growing up. Mrs. Spence's diet is based on foods her mother used to prepare, she has replanted her vegetable garden, and she obtains wild meat and fish whenever possible. With few exceptions, she does not eat canned foods but justifies her family's consumption of some particular types of canned foods, such as tomatoes, by pointing out: "Tomatoes have been in cans for a long time. I remember my mother buying them in cans a long time ago." Mrs. Spence also justifies her continued use of sugar, a food item many people with diabetes say should be avoided, by using only the brown and maple sugars with which her mother cooked.

What is remembered in this narrative relates her past to present understandings and future plans. Mrs. Spence's actions are consistent with generally shared cultural understandings concerning diabetes, and they also fit her own personal experience. But it should also be noted that this is a relatively unique response, although there were others who talked about the health benefits associated with eating wild meat or having gardens.

"My kids don't let me do anything"

Although Mrs. Green was the person I came to interview, her husband joined in on our conversation. After I explained why I had come, Mr. and Mrs. Green started to list the individuals they knew, including family members, who had been diagnosed with diabetes. At the end, they commented that everybody seemed to be getting diabetes and that the "new food" was causing "a lot of sicknesses."

Like Mrs. Spence, Mr. and Mrs. Green also attribute diabetes to changes in diet occurring within the relatively recent past. But, unlike Mrs. Spence, and like most others in the community, this collective explanation for diabetes is not central to Mrs. Green's personal narrative. She explained: "Nobody knows which one, because you eat everything. You don't know which one causes it." While this attribution presages a bleak future for the whole community, it appears to have little motivational force in their lives (see Strauss 1992:3, D'Andrade 1992). Mrs. Spence is atypical; most of those who talked about changes in diet did not see truly feasible alternatives to what they were currently eating. Even though wild meat is widely perceived as more salubrious than meat bought in stores, agricultural spraying and other modern practices are often seen as contaminating all foods, including wild foods. The uncontaminated foods of the Anishinaabe past are simply not to be found in present-day circumstances.

Mrs. Green talked about other people who either did or did not have diabetes. She told of a friend who "doesn't eat sweets but yet she got it." Mr. Green pointed out that he was the one who put lots of sugar in his tea. So, Mrs. Green, who is not fond of sweet foods or drinks, dismisses sugar consumption as an explanation for her diabetes. Mrs. Green also commented that her husband drinks a lot but that he didn't have sugar diabetes. In initiating the discussion of these possible causes, sugar and drinking, Mrs. Green reveals her knowledge of the common explanatory frameworks. That others commonly explain diabetes by reference to histories of eating too many sweets or drinking is what Mrs. Green "knows" about diabetes, but in addition she "remembers" specific instances that do not fit these generally shared understandings.

It became clear as our discussion continued that while the positioning of Mrs. Green's history within the context of broader dietary changes represents a plausible account of her diabetes, in other words a possible version, it did not capture the meaning of diabetes for Mrs. Green or her response to this illness.

Mrs. Green told how "all of sudden she had sugar diabetes," an occurrence she linked with preexisting high blood pressure, citing the doctor as the one who pointed to this connection. Mr. Green explained how her high blood pressure resulted from working too hard, and the subsequent failure to stop working so hard after developing high blood pressure resulted in diabetes. According to Mrs. Green, the symptoms she attributes to high blood pressure are now accompanied by other symptoms seen as resulting from high blood pressure. The emergence of diabetes is taken by the whole family as an indicator of her deteriorating condition.

This reconstructed narrative, which connects diabetes and high blood pressure, is a powerful one for the Green family and derives its motivational force primarily from cultural knowledge about high blood pressure (Garro 1988). But it was only after Mrs. Green was diagnosed with diabetes that changes occurred at the family level. Mrs. Green states that since the diabetes diagnosis "my kids don't let me do anything" by assuming all of the household chores and thus making it possible for her to take things easier and get more rest. This construction also strengthens Mrs. Green's claim that her teenage children shouldn't stay out late giving her a "hard time" because the "doctor told me not to worry so much." While there were other individuals with high blood pressure who later developed diabetes, the linking of the two conditions did not figure prominently in other narrative accounts, nor did it provide an arena for constructing a response to illness. Working too hard and worrying too much are explanatory frameworks closely tied to high blood pressure, but such issues do not typically arise in accounting for diabetes. Frequent references to the physician's comments provide validation for embedding diabetes within a preexisting explanatory framework associated with high blood pressure.

"That's because of those bombs they're testing"

Mrs. Brenda Stevenson provides a distinct, yet similar, narrative reconstruction, again based on shared cultural understandings about diabetes. Forty-nine years old at the time of the interview, Mrs. Stevenson had been taking diabetic medications for nine years. A few years before the interview, one of her legs had been amputated because of diabetic complications. Like Mrs. Green, Mrs. Stevenson raises some of the explanatory frameworks closely associated with diabetes only to reject them. Simply eating too many sweet foods cannot be the cause, because she knows someone who has diabetes but who never touched sweets or sugar. She also knows many people who are overweight but who don't have diabetes. It couldn't come from drinking, because she never drank, and anyway, if that were true, then there should be more diabetes "because everybody drinks." Mrs. Stevenson went on to buttress this argument with personal testimony, claiming: "Whatever the doctor told me, I tried it, but it didn't help me. I went worse. Now I just eat normal the way I eat." For example, the doctor told her not to eat too many sweets, but when she did this, it had no effect on her illness. On the contrary, she says she often feels better when she eats sweets. Mrs. Stevenson feels that there is little she can do in response to this illness, except to maintain her strength by eating well and normally and taking her prescribed medication, which she likens to vitamins because they "build you up" and help the body deal with poorer quality contemporary foodstuffs.

Although Mrs. Stevenson is dismissive of the advice she attributes to her own doctor, she referred back to a newsreel she watched years previously:

> A long time ago there was a doctor . . . about thirty years ago, when we used to have those picture shows here. And that doctor told everything about how you are going to be, you're going to have sore bones, you're going to have headaches. That's because of those bombs they're testing, he said. That's going to settle down. You'll even get it from the milk, you'll get it from the crop. He told us everything in that news. That's why people are going to get weaker and weaker, he said. I believe that now.

Mrs. Stevenson remembers this newsreel as a portent of what later came to pass. Diabetes is but one of the consequences of the ongoing contamination of the environment and food supply by white men. Other events, like the Chernobyl nuclear disaster, were cited, and Mrs. Stevenson pointed to the ubiquity of chemicals throughout the food chain. Unlike those of Mrs. Spence and Mrs. Green, Mrs. Stevenson's personal history is irrelevant to understanding why she developed diabetes. It makes no sense to her to single out any particular foods because "you can get it from anyplace." For Mrs. Stevenson there is no escape.

On a visit to Mrs. Stevenson's home several months after the interview, I spoke with her and her daughter, Barbara, about a recent health problem of Mrs. Stevenson's. This conversation is detailed here because it illustrates how switching between interpretive frameworks helps to provide a rationale for responding to illness. Mrs. Stevenson told of how an infection had developed in her remaining foot and the physician warned that another amputation might be necessary. Barbara, in hopes of averting a second amputation, consulted an Anishinaabe healer to see if the problem was a result of diabetes or something else. For a presumed complication of diabetes, this was a quite unusual step. It was also an action taken completely on Barbara's personal initiative and without informing her mother. Typically, if Anishinaabe healers are consulted about cases of diabetes, it is only to request herbal preparations seen as effective against diabetes. But, with the threat of a second amputation, Mrs. Stevenson's case was also highly unusual, and this raised etiological concerns, at least for Barbara.

The healer explained that while Mrs. Stevenson did indeed have diabetes (a "white man's sickness"), there was another cause for the infected foot (an "Anishinaabe sickness"), broadly indicating that it was attributable to an inappropriate past action by Mrs. Stevenson (see Garro 1990 for further discussion of these issues). He asked Barbara to bring Mrs. Stevenson to see him and suggested that she would know why the infection had developed. For an illness of this type, remembering an appropriate past incident is an integral part of treatment. Being told what the healer said, Mrs. Stevenson did indeed remember a failure to keep a sacred promise she made when much younger, a pledge to dance in the annual Sun Dance for a three-year period. The pledge was broken when she did not participate during the third year. When visiting the healer, Mrs. Stevenson was advised how to make amends and was also provided with an herbal preparation for soaking her foot. Mrs. Stevenson and her daughter both acknowledged the healer's role in averting the amputation by providing a way of redressing the underlying problem. In this instance, the healer guided Mrs. Stevenson to consider a different illness condition with an alternative explanatory framework, but it was Mrs. Stevenson who reflexively evaluated the applicability of his advice within the context of her own life.

CONCLUDING COMMENTS

While "white man's sicknesses" and the contamination of contemporary foods came up in many of the interviews, in only a relatively few instances, including two of the narratives recounted here, is this collective reconstruction used to elucidate personal history (cf. Brodwin 1995; Lang 1990). This may be a reflection of the interview context. Still, narratives of this type serve to reinforce the connection between collective history and illness, helping to maintain this explanatory framework as a cultural resource for understanding individual illness experience as well as an explanation of why diabetes and other "white man's sicknesses" have emerged as significant health concerns in recent years.

These narratives also point to the wide range of possible explanatory frameworks in memory that can serve as additional resources when those more closely associated with an illness condition do not seem to fit a personal reconstructive context. One example of this can be seen in the situating of Mrs. Green's experience with diabetes within the shared cultural model for high blood pressure. Mrs. Green's report of the co-occurrence of symptoms ascribed to high blood pressure and those attributed to diabetes helps justify this connection. An instance of a more radical shift to an entirely distinct explanatory framework can be seen in the redefinition of Mrs. Stevenson's foot infection as an "Anishinaabe sickness" rather than as a complication resulting from diabetes. Further evidence that this is a significant departure from more conventional ways of talking about diabetes is that unlike, say, sugar or drinking, which were often advanced only to be dismissed as not relevant to an individual's story, "Anishinaabe sickness" was never put forward simply to reject it. Indeed, asking specifically about a connection between diabetes and Anishinaabe sickness was typically considered a quite humorous question.

Both Mrs. Green's and Mrs. Stevenson's accounts show how remembering can be guided by others, albeit in a selective fashion, and especially by those in healing roles. The physician and the Anishinaabe healer are both used to validate a particular narrative reconstruction. Mrs. Stevenson also couches her discussion of "white man's sickness" with reference to a physician on a newsreel and predictions of increased illness as a result of environmental contamination. In all three of these instances, these allusions to specialists can be seen as contributing to the credibility and hence the persuasiveness of the story. Still, it is only the broad narrative contour that is framed with reference to the specialist; the story is filled in and reconstructed within the context of individual lives, and it is this elaboration that contributes even more to the compelling quality of these accounts (see Pillemer 1992:244–45).

These three case examples illustrate how through "remembering" their experiences with diabetes, individuals variably draw upon culturally shared knowledge in constructing a narrative account. With reference to understandings about diabetes, the culturally available explanatory frameworks do not shape the construction of illness experience in a deterministic fashion but are flexible and provide relatively wide latitude for constructing a narrative that is both plausible and consistent with individual experience. Attending to the "known" and the "remembered" illuminates how culturally available knowledge serves as a resource in assigning meaning and in responding to illness.

NOTES

1. One form of representation widely accepted in cognitive science is the schema. Schemas are the underlying cognitive construct for the explanatory frameworks presented in this chapter. More formally, cognitive schemas can be defined as "learned internalized patterns of thought-feeling that mediate both the interpretation of on-going experience and the reconstruction of memories" (Strauss 1992:3; the phrase "thought-feeling" comes from Wikan 1989). Accordingly, cultural schemas or cultural models can be seen as those cognitive schemas that are generally shared in a particular setting. Cognitively oriented anthropologists have long been interested in how generally shared cultural schemas come to be constitutive of individual-level schemas.

2. Farmer's processual ethnography is also of interest because he claims that in the development of a cultural model for AIDS, illness stories of known individuals "provide the matrix within which nascent representations were anchored" (1994:801). Consensus in the meanings associated with AIDS emerged and became established through the generation and discussion of illness stories.

REFERENCES

Baddeley, Alan D. 1992. What is autobiographical memory? In *Theoretical perspectives on autobiographical memory,* edited by M. A. Conway, D. C. Rubin, H. Spinnler, and W. A. Wagenaar, 13–29. Dordrecht: Kluwer.

Bartlett, Frederic C. 1932. *Remembering: A study in experimental and social psychology.* Cambridge: Cambridge University Press.

Borofsky, Robert. 1994. On the knowledge and knowing of cultural activities. In *Assessing cultural anthropology,* edited by R. Borofsky, 331–47. New York: McGraw-Hill.

Brewer, William F. 1996. What is recollective memory? In *Remembering our past: Studies in autobiographical memory,* edited by D. C. Rubin, 19–66. Cambridge: Cambridge University Press.

Brodwin, Paul E. 1995. Discussants' comments at a session entitled "Narrative as construct and as construction: Stories in a world of illness" (part 1). Ninety-third Annual Meeting of the American Anthropological Association, Washington, D.C., November.

Bruner, Jerome. 1990. *Acts of meaning.* Cambridge, Mass.: Harvard University Press.

Cain, Carole. 1991. Personal stories: Identity acquisition and self-understanding in Alcoholics Anonymous. *Ethos* 19:210–53.

Connerton, Paul. 1989. *How societies remember.* Cambridge: Cambridge University Press.

D'Andrade, Roy G. 1992. Schemas and motivation. In *Human motives and cultural models,* edited by R. G. D'Andrade and C. Strauss, 23–44. Cambridge: Cambridge University Press.

———. 1995. *The development of cognitive anthropology.* Cambridge: Cambridge University Press.

Farmer, Paul. 1994. AIDS-talk and the constitution of cultural models. *Social Science and Medicine* 38:801–9.

Garro, Linda C. 1988. Explaining high blood pressure: Variation in knowledge about illness. *American Ethnologist* 15:98–119.

———. 1990. Continuity and change: The interpretation of illness in an Anishinaabe (Ojibway) community. *Culture, Medicine and Psychiatry* 14:417–54.

———. 1994. Narrative representations of chronic illness experience: Cultural models of illness, mind and body in stories concerning the temporomandibular joint (TMJ). *Social Science and Medicine* 38:775–88.

———. 1995. Individual or societal responsibility? Explanations of diabetes in an Anishinaabe (Ojibway) community. *Social Science and Medicine* 40: 37–46.

———. 1996. Intracultural variation in causal accounts of diabetes: A comparison of three Canadian Anishinaabe communities. *Culture, Medicine and Psychiatry* 20:381–420.

———. In press. The remembered past in a culturally meaningful life: Remembering as cultural, social and cognitive process. In *The psychology of cultural experience,* edited by H. Mathews and C. Moore. Cambridge: Cambridge University Press.

Good, Byron, and Mary-Jo DelVecchio Good. 1994. In the subjunctive mode: Epilepsy narratives in Turkey. *Social Science and Medicine* 38:835–42.

Kleinman, Arthur. 1980. *Patients and healers in the context of culture.* Berkeley and Los Angeles: University of California Press.

Lang, Gretchen Chesley. 1990. "In their tellings": Ethnographic contexts and illness narratives. Paper presented at the Eighty-ninth Annual Meeting of the American Anthropological Association, New Orleans, November.

Mandler, George. 1985. *Cognitive psychology: An essay in cognitive science.* Hillsdale, N.J.: Lawrence Erlbaum.

Mathews, Holly F., Donald R. Lannin, and James C. Mitchell. 1994. Coming to terms with advanced breast cancer: Black women's narratives from eastern North Carolina. *Social Science and Medicine* 38:789–800.

Neisser, Ulric. 1978. Memory: What are the important questions? In *Practical aspects of memory,* edited by M. M. Gruneberg, P. E. Morris, and R. N. Sykes, 3–24. London: Academic Press.

———. 1988a. Five kinds of self-knowledge. *Philosophical Psychology* 1:35–59.

———. 1988b. Time present and time past. In *Practical aspects of memory: Current research and issues.* Vol. 2, *Clinical and educational implications,* edited by M. M. Gruneberg, P. E. Morris, and R. N. Sykes, 545–60. Chichester, England: Wiley.

——. 1988c. What is ordinary memory the memory of? In *Remembering reconsidered: Ecological and traditional approaches to the study of memory,* edited by U. Neisser and E. Winograd, 356–73. Cambridge: Cambridge University Press.

Pillemer, David B. 1992. Remembering personal circumstances: A functional analysis. In *Affect and accuracy in recall: Studies of "flashbulb" memories,* edited by E. Winograd and U. Neisser, 236–64. Cambridge: Cambridge University Press.

Price, Laurie. 1987. Ecuadorian illness stories: Cultural knowledge in natural discourse. In *Cultural models in language and thought,* edited by D. Holland and N. Quinn, 313–42. Cambridge: Cambridge University Press.

Robinson, John A. 1986. Autobiographical memory: A historical prologue. In *Autobiographical memory,* edited by D. Rubin, 19–24. Cambridge: Cambridge University Press.

Romney, A. Kimball, Susan C. Weller, and William H. Batchelder. 1986. Culture as consensus: A theory of culture and informant accuracy. *American Anthropologist* 88:313–38.

Rubin, David C., ed. 1986. *Autobiographical memory.* Cambridge: Cambridge University Press.

——, ed. 1996. *Remembering our past: Studies in autobiographical memory.* Cambridge: Cambridge University Press.

Singer, Jefferson A., and Peter Salovey. 1993. *The remembered self: Emotion and memory in personality.* New York: Free Press.

Strauss, Claudia. 1992. Models and motives. In *Human motives and cultural models,* edited by R. G. D'Andrade and C. Strauss, 1–20. Cambridge: Cambridge University Press.

Tulving, Endel. 1983. *Elements of episodic memory.* Oxford: Oxford University Press.

Wikan, Unni. 1989. Managing the heart to brighten face and soul: Emotions in Balinese morality and health care. *American Ethnologist* 16:294–312.

Young, T. Kue, L. L. McIntyre, Joseph Dooley, and J. Rodriguez. 1985. Epidemiological features of diabetes mellitus among Indians in northwestern Ontario and northeastern Manitoba. *Canadian Medical Association Journal* 132:793–97.

FOUR

Strategic Suffering

Illness Narratives as Social Empowerment among Mexican Cancer Patients

LINDA M. HUNT

The disruption experienced by people living with chronic illnesses such as cancer is at once that of the "disease" itself (the physical disruptions it produces as an objective, biological entity) and that of the "illness" [1] (the experience of disruption of the expected, the taken-for-granted). Chronic illness thus may present the afflicted with permanent challenges to their identity: it does not permit one to go on living in an undisputed, familiar world (Good 1994; Garro 1994; Good and Good 1982). The core experience of serious chronic illness has often been characterized as an existential loss, a break in the usual rhythm of life (Cassell 1982; Erwin 1984; Kaufman 1988; Williams 1984; Williams and Wood 1986). Bury (1982) describes chronic illness as introducing "biographical disruption," a time in which the normal social structures and roles of reciprocity and support are disrupted. A critical dilemma that people encounter when struggling to face such permanent loss of normal roles is how to reconstruct a sense of continuity of self and role responsibilities, since in many ways performance of roles is what defines one's personhood (Bury 1982; Cassell 1982).

When viewed in these terms, the disruption introduced by chronic illness may appear in purely negative terms: something has been lost, and the loss is something to be coped with and endured. However, examination of people's long-term adaptations to chronic illness reveals that the initial phase of disruption is often followed by a period of reorganization and reconstruction of the self and one's place in the world. Becker

(1997) has shown that people confronted by major disruptions to their lives, such as chronic illness, use narratives to restructure their sense of self and social location, telling stories that both articulate and mediate disruption. She argues that narrative thus holds a potent constructive capacity, through which people find the power to resist and restructure ideas of normalcy that do not fit with their experience, as they reconfigure their disrupted identity.

Because chronic illness can produce major disruptions to core components of identity, such as social roles and relationships, narratives concerning such illnesses hold the potential not only of articulating the disruptions experienced but also of reconfiguring one's very social identity. This is so because the narrative portrayal of events is in essence performative, and as such is capable of both expressing and enacting visions of reality. Brodwin (1994), in examining the rhetorical aspect of chronic pain representations, notes that illness can provide an idiom for communication that is capable of at once expressing a lack of sense of control and of generating a sense of mastery. This performative nature of narrative is especially compelling when considered in terms of the permanent disruptions to identity that chronic illness implies. The restructuring of self and social identity that occurs in response to chronic illness requires a long-lasting performance, a kind of pilgrimage into a sustainable construction of a changed self and roles (Frankenberg 1986).

Within the process of narrative reconstruction of the chronically ill self, the individual may enter into a period of self-reflection and reorientation: a moment where conventional structure is realigned with personal endeavor as well as social constraint (Monks and Frankenberg 1988). As patients move from the liminality of illness crisis back into a complex lifeworld, their illness narratives have a potential for affecting strategic changes in terms of the broad context of their lives. Some take this opportunity to redefine the self and social roles in ways that address broader personal and social conflicts and contradictions than those encountered in the illness itself. In naming the heroes and villains, dramatic conflicts and resolutions that compose the illness narrative, the teller may influence the ways the illness and, indeed, the self are conceived and understood.

An important function of illness narratives is to integrate illness into the larger context of life (Jackson 1989; Mattingly 1994, 1998; Mattingly and Garro 1994). Illness narratives are produced intersubjectively. In dialogue with those around them, patients produce stories about the causes and effects of their illness that connect it in direct ways with their evolving life story (Hunt 1994, 1998). Illness representations are thus constituted as a sum of patient presentations and audience interactions (Strauss and Corbin 1984). The narrative reconstruction of the chronically ill self is thus necessarily positioned within power relationships.

Becker (1997), in examining the process of narrative reorganization of the self and social life following disruptive events, found that such reconstructions often serve to create a sense of biographical continuity. However, in cases where the preexisting power relationships were dysfunctional, continuity may not be a desirable end. I wish to propose that in such cases, the telling of illness narratives may be taken up as an opportunity to reorder contentious elements of the social field, creating new meanings and relationships. Illness narratives may thus respond to the disruption of identity introduced by chronic illness by generating a strategically revised identity, creating a new place in the social world that resolves conflicts and difficulties rooted in the broad context of the teller's life. In examining the strategic implications of illness narratives, we open a window onto understanding the rhetorical processes (Brodwin 1994) by which chronic illness and its associated role disruptions are woven into ongoing negotiations over questions of power and powerlessness within patients' lives.

To explore these dynamics, this chapter presents an analysis of the illness narratives of two Mexican patients who have undergone surgical removal of part of their reproductive systems as a treatment for cancer. It will examine how their illness narratives transform the gender liminality resulting from the illness and surgery into revised social identities that address their long-standing difficulties with the ideal gender roles of their culture. An important aspect of these narratives is that while they legitimize nonconformity to prescribed gender roles, they do so without challenging the authority of the larger cultural concept of appropriate behavior for men and women in their society. It will be argued that, in these cases, use of illness narratives is neither manipulative nor revolutionary but instead reflects the practical outcome of people creatively constructing a revised identity when confronted with the permanent disruptions presented by living with chronic illness.

CHANGES IN SOCIAL IDENTITY
AND ILLNESS NARRATIVES

In Mexico, as in much of the world, cancer has a powerful metaphoric dimension; it conjures images of an insidious invasion of the victim by a ruthless aggressor that slowly, but inevitably, destroys the person from within (Adonis 1978; American Cancer Society 1980; Antonovsky 1972; Balshem 1991, 1993; Brody 1988; Chavez et al. 1995; Dreifuss-Kattan 1990; Finkler 1991; Garro 1990; M. J. Good et al. 1990, 1992, 1994; Gordon 1990; Hunt 1992, 1993, 1994; Kagawa-Singer 1993; Mathews, Lannin, and Mitchell 1994; Panourgia 1990; Patterson 1987; Saillant 1990; Sontag 1977). Coming to terms with having such an illness necessarily presents a myriad of challenges to the everyday sense of self in the world.

Previous studies of cancer patients' changing identities have primarily considered the cognitive or psychological adjustments that individuals make to cope with their disease (Aaronson 1990; Bolund 1990; Dreifuss-Kattan 1990; Haes 1988; Lowitz and Casciato 1988; Weisman 1979). These studies commonly focus on the intrapsychic dimension of responding to the challenges of cancer. They examine the psychological "coping mechanisms" that patients may draw upon in learning to live with their illness. However, when considered within their larger social and cultural context, such "coping mechanisms," in addition to their psychological functions, are necessarily constrained by and responsive to the pressing problems of negotiating mutual rights and responsibilities between individuals, in terms appropriate to the local moral and cultural world (cf. Kleinman and Kleinman 1991). "Having cancer" requires mobilizing resources for treatment, eliciting assistance for caring for the patient, and renegotiating the privileges and obligations of the patient within familial and other social hierarchies. Shifts in personal identity in having cancer therefore emerge in the context of a larger social framework, subsuming questions of domination and subordination.

The disruptions in social identity introduced by cancer and its treatment not only present a challenge to existing social relations but also, in thrusting patients into a state of indeterminacy and ambiguity, provide an opportunity to negotiate new identities in what Rosaldo has called "the social space within which creativity can flourish" (Rosaldo 1993: 112; see also Gutmann 1996). Chronic patienthood, in its very liminality and marginality, implies a level of role flexibility that may contain a moment of potential empowerment (cf. Frankenberg 1986; Turner 1969; Van Gennep 1960). At these moments, illness narratives have the potential to constructively redefine one's place within the social world (cf. Mattingly 1994, 1998; Mattingly and Garro 1994), simultaneously articulating and configuring the disaster of having cancer in innovative and strategic ways. Individuals, in the process of producing illness narratives, thus move between multiple ways that the sick role could be constructed, achieving altered identities not passively but through selective action (Uzell 1974). The orientations to the illness and its treatment they thereby generate have relevance in the specific terms of their broader sets of interests, needs, and circumstances (cf. Bourdieu 1977; Sahlins 1976).

In analyzing the illness stories that Mexican cancer patients shared with me, I have found that often, in the course of rebuilding a workable image of themselves, the world, and their place in it, patients generate narratives that forge an identity around patienthood in ways that negotiate issues of social empowerment. Such illness narratives may result in a revised version of old roles that constitute a new and enhanced place for the patient within the social world.

THE RESEARCH PROJECT

The case material presented here is drawn from an ethnographic study of hospital-based cancer care in Santo Domingo,[2] a provincial capital in southern Mexico of about five hundred thousand people. The study included extensive interviews with forty-three cancer patients and their families, as well as observations in the oncology clinics of the three major hospitals in town.[3]

Two case examples will be presented in order to explore how illness narratives may be used to reconstruct the altered self in response to the serious existential challenges presented by cancer and its treatment, and how that reconstruction is related to the broader social field. It will be shown that, in generating a revised identity in the face of chronic illness, illness narratives embed ongoing negotiations over contentious elements in patients' social world such as struggles over legitimacy or victimization.

This argument is built on interpreting the stories that patients and their families told me in interviews, but it is extended to contexts beyond the interview situation. In so doing, it is presumed that these stories reflect the intersubjective nature of narrative, having been developed within the more generalized social dialogue of everyday life, wherein the disruptive aspects of chronic illness and its treatment are integrated into ongoing social life. This presumption is based on two sets of observations. First, the narratives themselves cite negotiations and resolutions that have taken place with others in the social lives of the patients. It therefore seems reasonable to assume that similar narrative constructions have been used in interactions with the people to whom they refer.

Second, in many cases family members participated in the interview and often jointly produced the illness narrative related to me, indicating that such illness narratives both are publicly generated within the social sphere and represent a habitual rhetorical style.

The variety of conflicts and strategies expressed and configured in the narratives of the group studied were nearly as numerous as the patients. This discussion will therefore be limited to the circumstances of two specific cases. Still, it should be noted that almost all those interviewed had, over the course of many months and often years, constructed the chronic aspect of cancer patienthood in a way that had important implications for resolving contentious aspects of their lifeworld. It will be argued here that this reflects the embeddedness of the process of generating an illness story. In integrating chronic illness and its treatment into everyday life, the pressing issues encountered in everyday social interactions, and the conflicts and goals of those interactions are the material out of which the illness narratives are constructed. The narratives therefore necessarily have salience for addressing the issues most at stake for the person telling the story.

GENDER ROLES AND REPRODUCTIVE CANCERS

The two cases chosen for detailed examination here present an interesting set of contrasts. Both patients suffered from cancer of their reproductive systems, and both had been successfully treated sometime earlier by surgical removal of the affected organs. The specific nature of these cancers and their obvious close relationship to disruptions of gender identity have opened parallel opportunities for these patients to reflect on and reformulate their respective gender roles. Preexisting conflicts which each experienced around the ideal roles of dutiful wife and devoted son, respectively, have become the focus of their narrative reconstructions of a larger, culturally normative narrative of appropriate gender roles. They each exhibit a strategic use of their illness stories in which they have found legitimacy for nonconformity to prescribed gender roles through narrative representations in ongoing negotiations over the impact of their illness and treatment.

Sexual Politics and Cervical Cancer

First, let us consider the case of Isabela Martinez, a sixty-eight-year-old indigenous woman, the mother of thirteen children. She, like most women in this study, employed a rhetoric consistent with the cultural norm that the greatest achievements women can strive for lie in their devout fulfillment of their role as mother and wife. In Latin American culture, the ideal wife is often characterized as selfless, morally pure, and dedicated to children and husband.[4] This image includes an expectation that she be unfailingly receptive to her husband's sexual advances (Bartra 1987; Foster 1967; Lewis 1963; Rubel 1966; Shedlin and Hollerbach 1981). In her discussion of her illness with me, Isabela made it clear that she did indeed view sexual submission to her husband as a marital duty, but one that had been abused by him. In examining her illness narrative, we can see that she has reconstructed her postsurgical self in ways that both express and reformulate the difficulties she has suffered in this domain.

Isabela and her husband were both from poor campesino families, but they had established a successful business of buying and selling shoes. They lived in considerable comfort in a nice brick house near the center of town in a large indigenous village outside of Santo Domingo. What Isabela at first thought were symptoms related to the miscarriage of her fourteenth child she later discovered were caused by advanced cervical cancer. I spoke with her in her home, three years after she had a hysterectomy as treatment for the cancer. Her prognosis was very good, and she continued to go to the oncology clinic every six months for follow-up visits.

In the course of discussing her illness with me, Isabela made frequent references to the number and frequency of her pregnancies. Her reproductive history was central in her story of the etiology of her illness. The timing and number of her children were things over which she clearly felt she had had no control. Interestingly, she began her illness narrative with reference to her husband's sexual expectations of her. When asked how she had become ill, she said:

> I married when I was seventeen years old, and when I was eighteen I had my first child. And right away, in one year I turned around and had another. And right away again, the next year, and again, another child. . . . That was because when each child was just eight days old my husband wanted to have relations with me. On the eighth day after the birth, my husband would want to have relations with me. Like that, like that, like that. That is how it was. That's why every year, every year, every year, I had a child, that's why there are thirteen.

Isabela went on to describe her current experience of her illness, indicating that she had constructed her illness in a way that had turned the suffering associated with the illness into a resource for dealing with the long-term conflicts she had experienced regarding her wifely role obligations. She told me:

> [Since the hysterectomy] I have had burning pain [*ardores*], burning pains. That's why not anymore, I haven't been able to—I still haven't had relations with him. I don't have any relations with my husband, because I'm afraid. "I don't know if it's going to hurt me," I say. . . . "No, no, no, no I can't." Because this pain burned me, and that was because I had relations with my husband. So no, I don't have relations with him. Because I had been ill. So no more, he's touched me only two times. But I don't want to anymore because I imagine that I'm going to feel more pain.

In Isabela's narrative of the etiology and effect of her illness, we see that she has seized the opportunity to reconstruct her identity such that her rejection of her husband's advances is normalized and legitimized. She has turned her suffering into a form of social empowerment. The destructive force of the cancer and the defeminizing nature of the surgery allowed her the flexible moment of liminality wherein it was possible to reformulate her gendered identity. Her illness narrative shows her employing a previously unavailable power to refuse her husband's sexual demands. She has thus managed to preserve her social identity as dutiful wife, while resisting the culturally mandated marital requirement for sexual submission. Her narrative emphasizes and elaborates the suffering she experienced related to her cancer and surgery, such that she is able to effectively resist what she views as exploitative behavior on the part of her husband. She accomplishes this while avoiding any necessity to question or revise the normative moral code of wifely compliance.

Her unusual openness in confiding this rather intimate story allows us some understanding of a phenomenon that was hinted at by four other women in the study. They each mentioned that they had ceased sexual activity following hysterectomies or mastectomies, but only Isabela's narrative offered detailed insight into the sexual politics underlying such behavior. Additionally, the illness narratives of several other women were constructed around a history of physical and emotional abuses suffered at the hands of their husbands or other male relatives. Their illness narratives display and challenge issues of abuse of social power, articulating a previously suppressed voice—a voice made available to them by virtue of the liminality found in being a cancer patient.

In a similar vein, the following case shows how a young man's illness narrative reconstructs a male identity disrupted by cancer and its treatment, in a way that effectively legitimizes nonconformity to culturally defined male role responsibility.

Family Obligation and Testicular Cancer

Latin American male identity, often glossed as "machismo," has been the subject of a great deal of speculation among literary critics and social scientists (see, e.g., Goldwert 1982; Bartra 1987; Paz 1961; Limón 1994). The Latin American male identity is often characterized, in simple terms, as a dominating assertive figure, ruling his wife and family. However, as Gutmann (1996) has argued, gender identity is never simple but instead is profoundly complex. His analysis of male gender identity in Mexico City examines this complexity. He points out that the obligation of taking responsibility for the well-being and support of one's family is also a central aspect of what it means to be a "good man" in Latin America. The dilemma faced by the man in the next case stemmed from conflicts surrounding this caretaking identity. Even prior to becoming ill, he had struggled to be a "good son" but found himself in a nearly impossible situation. In collaboration with his family, he produces an illness narrative that reconstructs a post-illness identity which provides a more tenable social role for himself. As in the case of Isabela, this is accomplished without having to revise the central cultural norm of appropriate male behavior.

Although at twenty-five Roberto Juarez had no children and had never married, he was single-handedly supporting a large family, including his parents, five younger siblings, an alcoholic brother-in-law, and assorted nephews and nieces. The family lived in a small, crowded adobe hut in a farming village twenty miles to the south of Santo Domingo. They owned two small plots of rocky, unproductive land on which they grew corn and beans for the family to eat. In recent years, Roberto's three older brothers had left to start their own families, and his father had become incapacitated with a back injury, leaving Roberto to work the land alone. In addition to the hard labor of tilling, planting, and harvesting, he also worked a few days a week for a bricklayer, working long hours carrying cement and bricks for very low wages.[5] Between the farm and his job, Roberto worked constantly, but still the family was desperately poor. His mother kept a few goats and pigs, and she made tortillas to sell, but that was the extent of the family's resources.

Roberto was in follow-up care for testicular cancer when I met him. A year and half earlier he had been diagnosed with early-stage cancer (seminoma in situ), and one testicle had been surgically removed at that time as treatment. This type of cancer is considered extremely treatable, and Roberto's postsurgical prognosis was excellent.[6]

When I went to their house to talk to Roberto, his whole family sat with us on the ground in front of their hut, and both parents joined him in answering my questions about his illness. They said that when Roberto had first become ill, his testicle had become extremely swollen, he was unable to walk, and his skin had turned dark green, as though he were being poisoned. Frightened, they took him to see a doctor, who told them that he needed an operation. He said it would cost a lot of money, which they didn't have. They took Roberto to another doctor and were told the same thing. The family faced a real dilemma: the cost of the surgery was prohibitive, but Roberto couldn't work to support the family in the condition he was in. Roberto explained: "At first I was thinking of making the sacrifice, and not having the operation. Well, that it might be better if I would die. . . . But then I thought: 'If this is taken away, I'll be better and I will work more and harder.' That's what I thought . . ."

Thus Roberto's narrative is structured in a way that foregrounds his desire to fulfill his obligation as caretaker. However, as the plot unfolds, we see this desire quickly thwarted. He explained that the family finally sold some of their few belongings and one of their plots of land and he had the surgery. He said:

> So we all pitched in and put together the money. It was everything we had. It came to three million pesos.[7] We paid cash. . . . And because of this, for my fault, I've left them poorer than they were before. The doctor told me that with just the operation I would get better, but here it is a year and a half later, and I still can't work hard. . . . Now I don't have the tumor, but I still can't work. It made it harder because now I can't lift heavy things, I can't. I can't work like I worked before . . . I had the surgery, and it came out well. After a year I wanted to work, but I still can't. I'm only half working now, which is all I can do. . . . What I think is that since they cut the testicle from me, I can't anymore. . . . I try to be like everyone else, but . . . I'm not the same as I was when I was born.

His mother interrupted: "That's why now he can't work like before, like he used to work. . . . He always worked hard, he didn't want to give in, but it's beat him. His illness has beat him. . . . He's suffered a lot."

Roberto, as the only able-bodied adult male in his family, was faced with the impossible obligation of single-handedly sustaining a large family with very limited resources. His illness narrative elaborates the emasculating aspect of his cancer treatment, the loss of his testicle, into a loss of his strength and stamina, and thus redefines his role in the household. His mother's reiteration of this construct illustrates how this configuration has become an effective and accepted part of his reconstructed social identity.

It is interesting to consider the joint nature of how Roberto's illness narrative has been constructed. It is not a simple matter of his convincing others to grant him release from role obligations. It is a mutual construction by him and his mother, which has a rather sophisticated strategic payoff. It at once achieves the desired role release, while salvaging Roberto's reputation as a "good son" without requiring a challenge or revision of the authoritative cultural model of male identity.

DISCUSSION

It is perhaps counterintuitive to think of becoming a cancer patient as a means of empowerment, but this was a striking feature of these case examples. Both Isabela and Roberto had been thrust into a liminal state with regard to their gender identity by the nature of their particular types of cancer and the surgical removal of part of their gendered organs. They have thus found themselves in a somewhat ambiguous moment, wherein the applicability of the cultural gender norms is subject to renegotiation. In dialogue with those about them, they produce illness narratives that reconstruct their gendered social roles such that they are exempt from participation in certain prescribed behaviors which prior to their illness had proved untenable for them.

In the process of narratively reconstructing an identity in the face of the disruption posed by their chronic condition, these patients addressed pressing gender role issues that had long plagued them in the course of their everyday lives. The nature of their particular cancers and the disruptive effect of their symbolically emasculating and defeminizing treatments had created a moment of indeterminate gender role identity for each of them. Through their illness narratives they had at once found a voice for their role frustrations and created legitimated new roles for themselves, both expressing and resolving some of the difficult social issues with which they had long been grappling. Through her narrative, Isabela both underscored the burden she felt in the sexual demands of her husband and found the power to resist the situation. Roberto's narrative focused on the loss of his manhood and effectively produced a social accord about the limits of his abilities to fulfill excessive familial obligations.

These cases were not unique. The illness narratives of many patients in this study had similar strategic effects, configuring the illness and its impact on their identities in ways that were socially empowering. For example, there was the illiterate wife who had sustained thirty years of beatings from an abusive husband. Her illness narrative cited his abuse as the cause of her brain cancer, and she thereby publicly challenged her husband and for the first time was able to be recognized as his victim. Another was the aging patriarch whose struggle with his sons to maintain control over the family farm was manifest and negotiated in the competing narratives both he and they told of the father's illness (Hunt 1992).

The clinical literature might construct the phenomenon to which I refer as "secondary gain": the interpersonal advantages that result when one has the symptom of a physical disease, including such things as increased attention from family members, financial gain, and release from work or other social obligations (Barsky and Klerman 1983). This literature is concerned with the impact of these factors on individual patients' motivations to stay ill or become well, and on the tendency toward somatization. This implies that patients may consciously or unconsciously hold ulterior motives that may underlie their failure to get well (see, e.g., Fishbain et al. 1995; Schoen 1993).

The central concern in identifying secondary gain is to determine the validity of subjective reports of pain and disability. It is a judgmental and simplistic model, devised to evaluate the authenticity, in medical terms, of patient complaints. By focusing the present analysis on the embeddedness of illness narratives in broader contexts of personhood and social life, we move toward a fuller understanding of narrative's performative nature. The complex process of reorganization of identity and social relations cannot be credibly reduced to the rudimentary terms of the specific advantages that may accrue to the patient. Characterizing the strategic suffering accomplished by the illness narratives described here as expressions of patients' manipulative or duplicitous motives would fail utterly to comprehend the highly intricate relationship between the expressive and instrumental aspects of the narrative reconstruction of the chronically ill self (Becker 1997; Frankenberg 1986). Instead, the strategic success of these narratives should be seen as an expression of the resilience and adaptability of the human spirit. These patients are neither exploitative nor inauthentic, but rather are involved in a process wherein adversity is incorporated into their ongoing biographies in creative and useful ways. They have effectively reconstructed a place for themselves in the world that is in some ways better for them than the place they occupied prior to the illness's disruptive effects.

Social researchers examining issues of political and economic domination have often argued that the disempowered find and use whatever resources are available to them to gain some ability to deal with oppressive conditions (see, e.g., Ong 1987; Scott 1985). This is in some ways what we have seen in the cases of Isabela and Roberto. As they narratively connect the cause and effects of their illness and treatments to their ongoing lives, they effectively convert the liminality of cancer patienthood into a social resource. In a fascinating process of inversion carried out through narrative, weakness becomes power, and disability becomes a tool.

Should the strategic impact of these illness narratives then be understood in political terms, as a form of resistance to class- and gender-based oppression? Previous researchers working from the feminist and critical anthropology traditions have explained the power relationships expressed in patients' constructions of cancer and other health problems as manifestations of class and gender conflict (see, e.g., Balshem 1993; Martin 1987). In drawing such a conclusion, two important assumptions are necessary: first, that disempowered people perceive their situation as oppressive, and second, that they act out of a motivation to resist that oppressive structure.

Neither of these assumptions is supported by the present analysis. In the two case examples, it is noteworthy that the role reconstructions the narratives produce do not challenge core local cultural concepts of gender roles, but instead are consistent with them. The narratives act to resolve the disjuncture each has encountered between personal experiences and normative expectations about how life should be (Becker 1997), without contesting the cultural constructs of ideal gender roles. Rather than undertake a major revision of standard conventions and mores, these transformations instead draw on normative cultural roles to construct and articulate the new model itself. In these examples we see that cultural ideals give the images and motives that are simultaneously the basis of disruption and of reorganization. Through intersubjective narrative representations of the causes and consequences of their illnesses, these patients produce a revised notion of order that restructures their disrupted identities in ways that transcends victimhood (Ortner 1995; cf. Bruner 1990; MacIntyre 1981). In the process of reconstructing their disrupted identities, they manage to resolve long-standing social conflicts, without needing to take the more radical epistemological step of defining the existing structure as oppressive, and resisting it.

Through their strategic use of illness narratives, these patients responded to the permanent identity loss produced by the chronic illness and its treatment in socially empowering ways. They accomplish this without the need to question the authority of the dominant cultural ideologies about power and obligation. In the very identity loss and liminality that chronic illness introduces, they have found an opportunity for socially empowering reflection and reorientation (Monks and Frankenberg 1988). As these cases have illustrated, illness narratives may be used to restructure one's social roles in strategically advantageous ways, both without losing legitimacy and without having to challenge the dominant model.

By examining the constructive nature of illness narratives, we have seen that patients' narrative performance is capable of enacting (Brodwin 1994) a new, more empowered position for themselves. In the process of defining a changed self, a self with a chronic illness, these patients have effectively enacted social change. In the process of weaving alternative forms of coherence, they simultaneously reflect cultural norms, address contradiction, and realign power relations (cf. Ortner 1995).

CONCLUSION

Illness narratives are generated in an intersubjective dialogue, articulating the illness and its effects with the broader context of life's issues and goals. Through strategically constructed illness narratives, many patients in this study effectively turned suffering into a social asset, and role destruction into an opportunity for personal empowerment. In the long-term frame of the process of adjustment to chronic illness and its treatment, the illness became a central element in the plot of an altered life story with new themes, tensions, and antagonists, a revised system of power, and a transformed protagonist. In the process of forging revised identities in place of those disrupted by the cancer and its treatment, these patients rebuilt workable versions of the world and their place in it.

The examination of the strategic implications of illness narratives does not require making judgments about the manipulative or political intentions of the actors. The purposes and tactics of the patients in this study, while perhaps encompassing some of these motives, are more completely understood as expressive and instrumental narratives that are highly complex, individual and socially located efforts to generate a new, viable place in the social world.

This analysis has allowed us to consider the highly integrated nature of the physical and social disruptions produced by chronic illness and the embeddedness of the process of reorganization people undertake in reconstructing an identity in the context of such an illness. We have seen how illness narratives can result in a reorientation to the self that is shaped not simply as a reconstructive effort to create a sense of continuity in the face of disruption, but also can be a means of affecting change in contentious social roles and relationships. As part of the ongoing interpersonal interactions of patients and those around them, illness narratives may perform important work in ongoing negotiations about mutual rights and responsibilities in the social world. They can become potent micropolitical tools, reforging the disrupted identities of patients. Strategic use of illness narratives can act to legitimize nonconformity to prescribed roles while averting the necessity to call for revision of the moral principles underlying those roles.

ACKNOWLEDGMENTS

An earlier version of this paper was presented at the annual meeting of the American Anthropological Association, Washington, D.C., November 1995. This chapter is based on research supported in part by the National Science Foundation under grant no. BNS8916157 and by Wenner-Gren grant no. Gr.5183. Any opinions, findings, conclusions, or recommendations expressed in this paper are mine and do not necessarily reflect the views of these foundations. I wish to express my gratitude for the cooperation and support of the patients and physicians who participated in this study, who generously shared their stories with me. I also wish to thank Paul Brodwin, Cheryl Mattingly, Linda Garro, Carole Browner, and two anonymous reviewers for many useful comments on an earlier draft of this paper.

NOTES

1. The word *disease* is used here to refer to physiological dysfunction itself, as understood according to physicians' theories of disorder, and is contrasted with *illness,* which is the experiential aspect of disorder (Kleinman 1988).

2. All proper names are pseudonyms.

3. A full description of the methodology and sample used in this study appears in Hunt 1992.

4. For a critique of this characterization, see Browner and Lewin (1982).

5. About $3.50 U.S. per day.

6. In the United States the five-year survival rate for surgically treated early stage seminoma is 99 percent (Einhorn et al. 1988).

7. About $1,070 U.S.

REFERENCES

Aaronson, Neil. 1990. Quality of life assessment in cancer clinical trials. In *Psychosocial aspects of oncology,* edited by J. Holland and R. Zittoun. Berlin: Springer-Verlag.

Adonis, Catherine. 1978. French cultural attitudes toward cancer. *Cancer Nursing* 1:111–13.

American Cancer Society. 1980. *A study of black America's attitude toward cancer and cancer tests.* New York: American Cancer Society.

Antonovsky, A. 1972. The image of four diseases held by the urban Jewish population of Israel. *Journal of Chronic Diseases* 25:375–84.

Balshem, Martha. 1991. Cancer, control and causality: Talking about cancer in a working-class community. *American Ethnologist* 18:152–72.

———. 1993. *Cancer in the community: Class and medical authority.* Washington, D.C.: Smithsonian Books.

Barsky, A. J., and G. L. Klerman. 1983. Overview: Hypochondriasis, bodily complaints and somatic styles. *American Journal of Psychiatry* 140:273–82.

Bartra, Roger. 1987. *La jaula de la melancolía: Identidad y metamorfosis del Mexicano.* Mexico City: Grijalbo.

Becker, Gay. 1997. *Disrupted lives: How people create meaning in a chaotic world.* Berkeley and Los Angeles: University of California Press.

Bolund, Christina. 1990. Crisis and coping: Learning to live with cancer. In *Psychosocial aspects of oncology,* edited by J. C. Holland and R. Zittoun. Berlin: Springer-Verlag.

Bourdieu, Pierre. 1977. *Outline of a theory of practice.* Cambridge: Cambridge University Press.

Brodwin, Paul. 1994. Symptoms and social performance: The case of Diane Reden. In *Pain as human experience: An anthropological perspective,* edited by M. J. DelVecchio Good, P. Brodwin, B. Good, and A. Kleinman. Berkeley and Los Angeles: University of California Press.

Brody, Howard. 1988. *Stories of sickness.* New Haven, Conn.: Yale University Press.

Browner, Carole, and Ellen Lewin. 1982. Female altruism reconsidered: The Virgin Mary as economic woman. *American Ethnologist* 9:61–75.

Bruner, Jerome. 1990. *Acts of meaning.* Cambridge, Mass.: Harvard University Press.

Bury, Michael. 1982. Chronic illness as a biographical disruption. *Sociology of Health and Illness* 4:167–82.

Cassell, Eric. 1982. The nature of suffering and the goals of medicine. *New England Journal of Medicine* 306:639–45.

Chavez, Leo, F. Allan Hubbell, Juliet M. McMullin, Rebecca G. Martinez, and Shiraz I. Mishra. 1995. Structure and meaning in models of breast and cervical cancer risk factors: A comparison of perceptions among Latinas, Anglo women, and physicians. *Medical Anthropology Quarterly* 9:40–74.

Dreifuss-Kattan, Esther. 1990. *Cancer stories: Creativity and self-repair*. Hillsdale, N.J.: Atlantic Press.

Einhorn, Lawrence, Barry Lowitz, and Dennis Casciato. 1988. Testicular cancer. In *Manual of clinical oncology*, edited by D. Casciato and B. Lowitz. 2d ed. Boston: Little, Brown.

Erwin, Deborah Oates. 1984. Fighting cancer, dying to win: The American strategy for creating a chronic sick role. Ph.D. diss., Southern Methodist University.

Finkler, Kaja. 1991. *Physicians at work, patients in pain: Biomedical practice and patient response in Mexico*. Boulder, Colo.: Westview Press.

Fishbain, David, H. L. Rosomoff, R. B. Cutler, and R. S. Rosomoff. 1995. Secondary gain concept: A review of the scientific evidence. *Clinical Journal of Pain* 11:6–21.

Foster, George. 1967. *Tzintzuntzan*. Boston: Little, Brown.

Frankenberg, Ronald. 1986. Sickness as cultural performance: Drama, trajectory, and pilgrimage root metaphors and the making of social disease. *International Journal of Health Sciences* 16:603–26.

Garro, Linda. 1990. Culture, pain and cancer. *Journal of Palliative Care* 6 (3): 34–44.

———. 1994. Chronic pain and the construction of narratives. In *Pain as human experience: An anthropological perspective*, edited by M. J. DelVecchio Good, P. Brodwin, B. Good, and A. Kleinman. Berkeley and Los Angeles: University of California Press.

Goldwert, Marvin. 1982. *Psychic conflict in Spanish America: Six essays on the psychohistory of the region*. Washington, D.C.: University Press of America.

Good, Byron. 1994. *Medicine, rationality and experience: An anthropological perspective*. Cambridge: Cambridge University Press.

Good, Byron, and Mary-Jo DelVecchio Good. 1982. Toward a meaning-centered analysis of popular illness categories: "Fright illness" and "heart distress" in Iran. In *Cultural conceptions of mental health and therapy*, edited by A. Marsella and G. White. Dordrecht: Reidel.

Good, Mary-Jo DelVecchio, Byron Good, Cynthia Schaffer, and Stuart E. Lind. 1990. American oncology and the discourse on hope. *Culture, Medicine and Psychiatry* 14:59–79.

Good, Mary-Jo DelVecchio, L. Hunt, T. Munakata, and Y. Kobayashi. 1992. A comparative analysis of the culture of biomedicine: Disclosure and consequences for treatment in the practice of oncology. In *Health and health care*

in developing societies: Sociological perspectives, edited by P. Conrad and
E. Gallagher. Philadelphia: Temple University Press.

Good, Mary-Jo DelVecchio, T. Munakata, Y. Kobayashi, C. Mattingly, and B. J.
Good. 1994. Oncology and narrative time. *Social Science and Medicine*
38:855–62.

Gordon, Deborah. 1990. Embodying illness, embodying cancer. *Culture, Medicine and Psychiatry* 14:275–97.

Gutmann, Matthew. 1996. *The meanings of macho: Being a man in Mexico City.*
Berkeley and Los Angeles: University of California Press.

Haes, J. C. J. M. de. 1988. Quality of life: Conceptual and theoretical considerations. In *Psychosocial oncology,* edited by M. Watson, S. Greer, and C. Thomas. Oxford: Pergamon Press.

Hunt, Linda M. 1992. Living with cancer in Oaxaca, Mexico: Patient and physician perspectives in cultural context. Ph.D. diss., Harvard University.

———. 1993. The metastasis of witchcraft: The interrelationship between traditional and biomedical concepts of cancer in southern Mexico. *Collegium
Antropologicum* 17:249–56.

———. 1994. Practicing oncology in provincial Mexico: A narrative analysis.
Social Science and Medicine 38:843–53.

———. 1998. Moral reasoning and the meaning of cancer: Causal explanations
of oncologists and patients in southern Mexico. *Medical Anthropology Quarterly* 12:298–318.

Jackson, Michael. 1989. *Paths toward a clearing: Radical empiricism and ethnographic inquiry.* Bloomington: Indiana University Press.

Kagawa-Singer, Marjorie. 1993. Redefining health: Living with cancer. *Social
Science and Medicine* 37:295–304.

Kaufman, Sharon. 1988. Toward a phenomenology of boundaries in medicine:
Chronic illness experience in the case of stroke. *Medical Anthropology Quarterly* 2:338–54.

Kleinman, Arthur. 1988. *The illness narratives: Suffering, healing and the human condition.* New York: Basic Books.

Kleinman, Arthur, and Joan Kleinman. 1991. Suffering and professional transformation: Toward an ethnography of interpersonal experience. *Culture,
Medicine and Psychiatry* 15:275–301.

Lewis, Oscar. 1963. *Life in a Mexican village: Tepoztlan revisited.* Urbana: University of Illinois Press.

Limón, José. 1994. *Dancing with the devil: Society and cultural poetics in
Mexican-American south Texas.* Madison: University of Wisconsin Press.

Lowitz, Barry, and Dennis Casciato. 1988. Psychosocial aspects of cancer care.
In *Manual of clinical oncology,* edited by D. Casciato and B. Lowitz. 2d ed.
Boston: Little, Brown.

MacIntyre, Alasdair. 1981. *After virtue: A study in moral theory.* Notre Dame,
Ind.: University of Notre Dame Press.

Martin, Emily. 1987. *The woman in the body: A cultural analysis of reproduction.* Boston: Beacon Press.

Mathews, Holly, Donald Lannin, and Toni Mitchell. 1994. Coming to terms with advanced breast cancer: Black women's narratives from eastern North Carolina. *Social Science and Medicine* 38:789–800.

Mattingly, Cheryl. 1994. The concept of therapeutic "emplotment." *Social Science and Medicine* 38:811–22.

———. 1998. *Healing dramas and clinical plots: The narrative structure of experience.* Cambridge: Cambridge University Press.

Mattingly, Cheryl, and Linda Garro. 1994. Narrative representations of illness and healing: Introduction. *Social Science and Medicine* 38:771–74.

Monks, Judith, and Ronald Frankenberg. 1988. Being ill and being me: Self, body and time in multiple sclerosis narratives. In *Disability and culture,* edited by B. Ingstad and S. Reynolds Whyte. Berkeley and Los Angeles: University of California Press.

Ong, Aihwa. 1987. *Spirits of resistance and capitalist discipline: Factory women in Malaysia.* Albany: State University of New York Press.

Ortner, Sherry. 1995. Resistance and the problem of ethnographic refusal. *Comparative Studies in Society and History* 37:173–93.

Panourgia, E. Neni K. 1990. Death by cancer: Local and unlocal knowledge. Paper presented at the annual meetings of the American Anthropological Association, New Orleans.

Patterson, James T. 1987. *The dread disease: Cancer and modern American culture.* Cambridge, Mass.: Harvard University Press.

Paz, Octavio. 1961. *The labyrinth of solitude: Life and thought in Mexico.* New York: Grove Press.

Rosaldo, Renato. 1993. *Culture and truth: The remaking of social analysis.* Boston: Beacon Press.

Rubel, Arthur. 1966. *Across the tracks: Mexican-Americans in a Texas city.* Austin: University of Texas Press.

Sahlins, Marshall. 1976. *Culture and practical reason.* Chicago: University of Chicago Press.

Saillant, Francine. 1990. Discourse, knowledge and experience of cancer: A life story. *Culture, Medicine and Psychiatry* 14:81–104.

Schoen, Marc. 1993. Resistance to health: When the mind interferes with the desire to become well. *American Clinical Hypnosis* 36:47–54.

Scott, James C. 1985. *Weapons of the weak: Everyday forms of peasant resistance.* New Haven, Conn.: Yale University Press.

Shedlin, Michele, and Paul Hollerbach. 1981. Modern and traditional fertility regulation in a Mexican community: The process of decision-making. *Studies in Family Planning* 12:278–96.

Sontag, Susan. 1977. *Illness as metaphor.* New York: Random House.

Strauss, Anselm, and Juliet Corbin. 1984. *Chronic illness and the quality of life.* St. Louis: Mosby.

Turner, Victor. 1969. *The ritual process: Structure and anti-structure.* Ithaca, N.Y.: Cornell University Press.

Uzell, Douglas. 1974. *Susto* revisited: Illness as strategic role. *American Ethnologist* 1:369–78.

Van Gennep, Arnold. 1960. *The rites of passage.* Chicago: University of Chicago Press.

Weisman, A. D. 1979. *Coping with cancer.* New York: McGraw-Hill.

Williams, G. 1984. The genesis of chronic illness: Narrative re-construction. *Sociology of Health and Illness* 6:175.

Williams, G., and P. Wood. 1986. Patients and their illnesses. *Lancet,* December 20/27: 1435.

FIVE

Physician Autobiography

*Narrative and the Social
History of Medicine*

DONALD POLLOCK

Medicine is a narrative art, and physicians are inveterate storytellers. In forms ranging from the clinical accounts physicians construct for each other (Hunter 1991) to essays and popular fiction—as an occupational class medicine has produced an extraordinary catalog of novelists—physicians have always practiced the craft of narrative as a central feature of professional practice. In this chapter I examine one particularly interesting form of physician narrative, the autobiography. I examine a number of American physician autobiographies from the twentieth century to illustrate how these narratives constitute sources for a social history of medicine: how they offer a privileged account of medicine from an inside, experience-near perspective that constructs a public representation of medical practice and culture. I base this account on the assumption that "medicine" as a social field is not limited to the restricted knowledge that physicians learn in exclusive settings, but comprises as well the broader public realms in which physicians and nonphysicians meet; autobiographies, usually written for public consumption, are one such realm.[1]

MEDICAL AUTOBIOGRAPHY: NARRATIVE AND SOCIAL HISTORY

Autobiography as a Western literary genre relies upon a breach of what Hayden White called the legitimacy of canonical behavior (1981); for an individual's life story to be worth recounting, it must deviate somehow from the commonplace and ordinary.[2] The lives of physicians have often been constructed in such terms. Cultural stereotypes that include the heroism of the doctor, the drama of the medical setting, and the physical and intellectual challenges of disease and its cure have long been exploited by physicians in autobiographical form.

Medical autobiographies possess two characteristics that provide the general framework for this account. First, like all biographies, they are forms of narrative, and as such conform to the essential features of narrativity. Second, autobiographies are social acts of representation that are part of the public construction of the domain of medicine; while the life stories of physicians may appear simply to describe medicine, they are forms of the constitution and reproduction of medical domains in ways that are highly sensitive to historical changes in the social system and "culture" of medicine. These two features are not unrelated. The narratizing of such representations is a powerful form of referential practice, conveying a profound sense of experientially based truth that can be exploited politically.

Several features of narrative are critical to a theory of autobiography. First, as Bruner (1991) has noted, the sequential, diachronic order of narrative is only one device for representing events; when coupled to the episodic quality of life histories, the narrative structure imposed on physician autobiography subtly shapes both the author's and the reader's conception of human events as storylike and temporally bounded, and often as tokens of generic moral lessons. Moreover, an autobiography, like any narrative, requires that events or episodes be selected from among the vast range of all possibilities in the flow of experience and then be presented in an order that itself intentionally or unintentionally conveys significance. Autobiographies are also one of the privileged domains of what I call "narrative referentiality": an autobiography purports to describe some reality separate from and independent of the text itself, yet autobiographical "truth" is often a matter of verisimilitude rather than verifiability (Pascal 1960), a function of narrative strategies that convey a kind of basic believability that Labov has called "hermeneutic composability" (Labov 1982). Again, these are not so much aspects of experience itself as of the representation of experience in narrative form.

The nature of the power of narrative to convey this kind of believability need not detain us here, except to acknowledge its forms. Linear narrative stories, as Sartre noted, take place from the perspective of the ending ([1938] 1965: 62) and thus may combine repetition with linearity to enhance verisimilitude. For example, physician autobiographies often possesses the kind of structure that Lévi-Strauss attributed to myth: they develop through both a temporal, syntagmatic dimension—an unfolding story of passage through a series of ordeals, rituals, lessons intellectual and moral—and an episodic, paradigmatic dimension in which similar ordeals and rituals recur, and thus the authors' lessons (and the reader's) are driven home through their repetition (cf. Segal 1984, 1988). The irony in such a poetics is, as Brecht noted, that it reveals the politics of representation through the same devices that are employed to increase their believability (1976:79).

Autobiographies are also particular kinds of narrative. While "scientific texts" rely on propositional structures, and fictional narratives invite what Ruthrof calls a "concretizing transformation" that reduces a text to a shared, coded experience (1981:13), autobiographical narratives are something in between: they are narratives that elicit from the reader both the weight of propositional response and the light of shared experience. Autobiographies thus rely on a pragmatics that refers beyond the text, but they would be dryly propositional if they did not also incorporate a poetics of self-referentiality that we conventionally regard as the essence of "textuality." Or, recalling Labov's "danger-of-death" narratives, one might say that autobiography relies upon a set of narrative framing strategies that announce that a story or experience is worth attending to. At the same time, the use of these narrative strategies—the rhetorical modes that make an experience tellable—restricts the content of the narrative by limiting the range of acceptable developments in the drama, attending to closure, maintaining the integrity of the ending, and so on (Leitch 1986:43, 63, 126). While I cannot explore the full range of such rhetorical strategies in a brief chapter that is primarily concerned to illustrate possibilities in the social history of the genre, the opening lines of J. Kenyon Rainer's book give some feeling for one of the common medical narrative techniques that is intended to grip the reader: "Yellow brain oozed like toothpaste from the right ear. Warm blood dripped from the left ear down the earlobe and puddled onto a sheet under the patient's head" (Rainer 1987:3).

Physician autobiographies must also be understood as social acts that respond to—and reproduce—the social and cultural conditions of medicine, as well as the social position and values assigned to physicians by readers. Thus my interest here is not simply in a literary history of autobiography (see, e.g., Spengemann 1980), but in the social history of a form of literary act. Narratives are not "unsponsored texts"; auto-biographies are motivated, so to speak, by factors that include political, economic, and even religious agendas on the part of authors, publishers, and readers. In this brief chapter my focus is the narrative representa-tion of the social conditions of medical practice, rather than the specific narrative strategies through which such representations are constructed and gain salience.

Memoirs and autobiographies have been published by American physicians for at least two hundred years, of course, but I have limited the cultural and historical scope of this paper to the twentieth century. While there has hardly been a period in the history of American medi-cine that has not been dynamic, twentieth-century physician autobiog-raphies offer several advantages to a brief essay such as this. First, myr-iad changes demarcate nineteenth- and twentieth-century medicine. In the twentieth century medical schools adopted a science-based curricu-lum, often attributed to the impact of the Flexner Report in 1910;[3] med-ical research began to discover and develop a wide range of effective pharmaceuticals; diagnostic technology leaped in sophistication; and the political economy of medical practice assumed much of its current form as physicians consolidated their social power. The latter point, in particular, resonates in interesting ways with medical organization in the 1990s: both periods are marked by physician concern about the ad-verse effects of corporatization, by a discourse of medical practice that foregrounds socially palatable physician concerns about "quality" while backgrounding the political economy and power struggles within which physicians work.

Second, the increase in literacy rates in the United States during the twentieth century has meant that a larger portion of the U.S. population has been able to consume books—and thus indirectly shape their con-tent—than in previous periods of the nation's history. I consider else-where the shape of physician autobiographies in earlier centuries, when such books were written for a different audience, one that distinguished itself in part by its very ability to buy and read such books.

I examine briefly two popular genres of physician autobiography in this chapter, to suggest how reading them against the history and social organization of medicine might offer insights into both these autobio-graphical forms and the representation of medicine.[4] "Genre" is a prob-lematic concept in some realms of contemporary literary criticism, but I employ it here out of a profound sense that twentieth-century American physician autobiographies almost intentionally reproduce a small set of fairly well-defined categories. I say "intentionally" in recognition of the forces that shape the form and content of autobiographies, both for authors who find models in existing narratives and for publishers who seek to locate markets using past experience. There are, as an effect, striking similarities among the autobiographies that I have categorized together, and one of my reading strategies has been to try to decode the cultural significance of those categories composed of numerous individual autobiographies, using specific texts as tokens of the categorical type.

I consider first a series of autobiographies written by women, with the simple question of how issues of gender in medicine have been perceived and represented by women physicians. Although women have been trained as physicians in the United States only since Elizabeth Blackwell entered medical school in the mid-1800s, by World War I women physicians were no longer a novelty. By the 1970s, autobiographical narratives written by women physicians were likely to background gender issues in the practice of medicine and to focus instead on training in medical schools and residencies. This fact introduces an examination of a second genre of physician autobiography: the training tale. Training narratives are interesting for the manner in which they comprise a species of morality tales that can comment on changes in medicine that their authors (and quite likely the reading public) find disturbing and problematic. I have written on the broad genre of training tales previously (Pollock 1996) and here focus on training tales written by psychiatrists. The link that I find between these two genres is that both deal with deviance, though in ways that are inversions of each other. Psychiatrist training tales are invariably organized, in part, around the question of how behavioral deviance is to be understood; autobiographies by women in medicine are organized, in part, by the problem of their own "deviant" status in a profession (and, later, in specialty fields) dominated by men and by masculine values.

There are, of course, numerous other genres of physician autobiography in the twentieth century. Medical scientific and technological advancements often lead innovating physicians to write memoirs that celebrate discovery and progress. Denton Cooley's autobiography (1973, authored by Harry Minetree) is subtitled "The amazing career of the world's greatest surgeon" and focuses almost exclusively on his development of surgical techniques. Morris Fishbein's autobiography (1969) is more comprehensive and focuses less exclusively on his own achievements; however, his narrative is a series of stories about medical advancements that conveys a similar triumphalist message. William

McClenahan's narrative (1971) is justified on the strength of creating the first intensive care unit in an American hospital. A number of physicians have adopted this theme through a kind of inversion, writing about rural practice in which the lack of access to technological marvels and sophisticated science forces innovation and creativity of a low-tech kind (Campbell 1993; Hertzler 1938; Macartney 1938; Searcy 1961); the theme celebrates technological advances through their absence, and the creativity of physicians who must do without.

Physicians to the famous, especially to presidents (McIntire 1946; Travell 1968; White 1971), write autobiographies that are explicitly written from the "end," and provide an account of how particular physicians' careers can be read as rehearsals for the events to come. Authors in the "wounded physician" genre write with a similar strategy, foreshadowing events of a more tragic nature in which the physician becomes a patient, or otherwise suffers. Authors of both are inevitably ennobled by their brushes: with the famous, with death, or with disability. Genres multiply, though not indefinitely.[5]

WOMEN AT WORK

Autobiographies by women in medicine often present explicit commentaries on feminist issues, and through them one can begin to read the historical emergence and development of such issues in medicine. Two themes that shape the history of the genre of "women in medicine" are worth mentioning here, both addressing the issue of sexism and discrimination in medicine, but from somewhat different perspectives.[6] The genre reminds us that the (auto)biographical narrative constructs forms of subjectivity that rely upon the illusory security of axiomatic categories of identity, such as gender.

During the first half of the twentieth century, women physicians tended to write about professional lives that overcame initial *public* suspicions of their capabilities as physicians. In these autobiographies, specifically professional medical bias against women physicians is often present but is typically backgrounded. Medical bias might appear briefly during training; often a single paradigmatic incident is recounted from later interactions with medical colleagues. The theme frequently appears in accounts of practice in rural setting, as in Kaiser's series of James Herriot–like vignettes of family practice among Amish and Mennonite farmers in Pennsylvania (1986), where, it is implied, suspicion of a woman physician itself marks this as a rural and thus somewhat unsophisticated community. Similarly, Mary Dole, whose medical career included microbiological research at the Pasteur Institute as well as small-town practice, alludes to bias against women in medicine only at the outset of her work in Shelburne in western Massachusetts (1941).

Indeed, such vignettes have a common thematic structure; they open with the initial suspicion (typically lay but occasionally professional) of the female physician, leading to a critical incident in which she displays superior knowledge or skill, followed by her complete acceptance by patients (and colleagues). Kaiser attended her first labor and delivery amid community doubts of her ability, which evaporated with the successful birth: "Naomi beamed. 'It was great to have a woman doctor. I'll always want a woman now.' . . . I drove home . . . drenched in victory" (1986: 54–55). And Dole's comment is found in one form or another in virtually all such autobiographies: "After that experience, I could never feel that the best men doctors were unfair to me" (1941:88).

Janet Travell's autobiography (1968) is notable in this regard as well. Travell, whose narrative is actually structured more by the thematic requirements of the "physician to the famous" genre—she treated John F. Kennedy before and during his presidency—writes in what appears to be an almost complete absence of professional gender bias. Travell's father was a physician, and she attended Wellesley College, enjoying both parental encouragement and role models for her career, and a supportive woman's college in which to begin. She graduated from Cornell Medical College in 1926, and during her training and practice in New York she appears to have met with little except professional praise and support. Nonetheless, her career included two decades in both the first half and the second half of the twentieth century, and on the cusp of that midcentury mark she was handed an editorial from the *Westchester Medical Bulletin,* from August 1949. In that editorial, a poll of some one hundred male physicians revealed their belief that female physicians were emotionally unstable, that they neglected medicine if they became pregnant and had families, and so on (Travell 1968:246). Travell's professional standing and her social milieu—a fairly privileged social set that included both male and female professionals—surely insulated her from the kind of occupational gender issues that were expressed in the Westchester survey, and she discusses no overt professional bias leveled directly against her at any point. But her mention of this survey is a sober reminder that, while women physicians writing about their experiences in the first half of the twentieth century were conscious of the need to prove themselves *individually* capable, women physicians writing about their experiences in the second half of the twentieth century are more likely to find themselves being treated as mere tokens of a *class* against which discrimination is overt.

In particular, and almost paradoxically, Travell's, Kaiser's, and Dole's autobiographies (re)present women in medicine before the emergence of the women's movement of the 1960s and the growth of a different form of consciousness of sexism and "patrism" (Turner 1984). Women physicians who trained in the period since the beginning of the women's movement have written about more widespread and systemic forms of bias and discrimination at an explicitly professional level. Moreover, as the focus of autobiography in recent years has narrowed to describe briefer, more discrete phases of a life, women physicians have more often pursued the theme of institutionalized professional bias, often within specific medical specialties, during training or the early years of practice. Elizabeth Morgan, for example, is sensitive to the small details that constantly remind her that her surgical residency is highly male-dominated, from surgical garb that is too large to the value placed on aggressive, domineering personalities among surgeons (1980, 1982). Like Else La-Roe (1957) years before her, she ultimately chooses plastic and reconstructive surgery as her subspecialty, finding less professional resistance to the notion of a women surgeon engaged in the beauty business.[7] Marie-Claude Wrenn quotes a female obstetrician-gynecologist who said, "I wanted to go into general surgery in 1950 . . . but unless you had some real pull, there were no general residency programs in that field available to women" (1977:5). Her story of Alison Merrill is organized largely around the trials of women in medicine in the 1970s: biased admissions to medical school, sexual taunting in classes, restrictions on access to residencies and advancement. By the end of her first residency in surgery, which was terminated against her wishes, Merrill is uncertain if her progress up the pyramid system of training in her surgical residency was stopped because of her gender, but she can only speculate about other possible reasons (1977:234–40).

Moreover, in the second half of the twentieth century, gender issues are more likely to emerge within specific specialties, such as surgery, which have been dominated by male physicians and in which supposedly masculine personality traits and values—aggressiveness, decisiveness, egocentrism—are cultivated and valued. Corresponding thematic shifts in autobiographies by women in medicine perhaps reflect several intertwining changes during this period. While there has been no period in U.S. history when women's participation in medicine has been met with unalloyed enthusiasm, the nature of bias and discrimination against women in medicine has taken different shapes and expressed different themes over time. In the twentieth century, these autobiographies suggest, one such shift has been from a period of qualified professional acceptance of individual women physicians—but some public doubts about the competence of women in medicine—to a period of greater perceived professional bias against women physicians as a class but considerable public acceptance of women in medicine. It is as if the public and professional views had reversed themselves after World War II, and professional bias began to take a more generalized quality.

The apparent paradox lies in the possibility that such shifts in the autobiographical works of women physicians reflect their very success in joining the medical profession. Travell, who graduated from medical school in 1926, and Beulah Parker, who graduated from Columbia University's College of Physicians and Surgeons in 1943 (Parker 1987), both attribute their successful entry into medicine in large part to their privileged social background, at a time when many medical schools had policies barring women (as well as Jews and other minorities) from admission. However, their early careers illustrate different aspects of the history of women in medicine in the twentieth century. Travell entered medical practice at a time when women physicians were rare enough that their competence was assessed individually; twenty years later, Parker found herself the victim of such pervasive gender stereotyping that she struggled for some years to establish her professional competence; women in medicine, and perhaps in other professions as well, had become the generic "other" against which male physicians defined competence. The reasons for this shift lie in the political economy of medical practice that emerged during and after World War II.

As Parker notes, her success in securing a residency, and even a chief resident position, as well as her first professional position, was a function of the domestic shortage of male physicians toward the end of the war. Male physicians returning from wartime service were concerned that the very women who kept medical care available to the American public during the war would displace them following their return home. Two related trends have converged in the past twenty-five years. First, women have been entering medicine in increasing numbers, constituting as much as 50 percent of entering classes in some medical schools in the past few years. Second, during this same period concerns have been raised about a physician "glut": the overproduction of physicians in the United States, or the maldistribution of physicians, particularly specialists who cluster in urban areas and high-income communities.[8] A report by the American College of Surgeons (1975), for example, suggested that the surgical needs of the country could be met for several decades by surgeons then in medical school and residency pipelines. For women trying to enter this last bastion of male-dominated medical practice, the sheer oversupply of surgeons was barrier enough, without the added factor of historical bias against women in this field. In short, the recent position of women in medicine may resemble the backlash against women in other professions that Marvin Harris identified: in a context of (perceived) oversupply, the entry of women into medicine in large numbers may be resisted by male physicians who develop a sense of competition for increasingly scarce resources.

I should note, partly to reinforce this point, that autobiographical narratives written by women physicians in traditionally female-friendly medical specialties rarely discuss this kind of gender bias in any context. For example, Claire McCarthy's 1995 narrative of her training in medical school and a pediatric residency in Boston scarcely hints at gender issues for women, and not at all for women in pediatrics. Similarly, Perri Klass's two training narratives (1987, 1992) reveal no concern with gender issues in her pediatric training. Michelle Harrison's story of her obstetrics-gynecology residency is particularly interesting in this regard (1982). Harrison identifies herself explicitly as a feminist who entered medicine with hopes of improving the treatment of women at a time of heightened ideological regard for feminist issues. She became a family practitioner after graduating from medical school in 1967 but entered an OB-GYN residency after several years of practice. Her narrative is an explicit indictment of the treatment of women—both women patients and women physicians—by obstetrics and gynecology. Her story does not contradict the point; rather, it underscores the extent to which the specialty was still heavily male dominated. Moreover, she reserves her most serious critique for gynecological surgery: here again, a field shaped largely by masculinist values, even one located within a broader specialty in which many women physicians participate, can be read through a critically feminist lens.

TRAINING TALES: PSYCHIATRISTS IN THE MAKING

As I have noted, autobiographical narratives written by physicians in recent years are likely to focus more narrowly on their training, as students or residents, even on a single year of that process (cf. Conrad 1988;

Poirier 1987; Pollock 1996; Stoeckle 1987). These training tales are a particularly interesting form of physician autobiography for several reasons. First, their appearance is recent and rather sudden. Perhaps the first such training tale was *Intern* by "Dr. X," published in 1965. By the 1970s a number of training narratives began to appear, and in the 1980s numerous training tales were published. The trend has continued into the 1990s. Understanding why training tales first appeared when they did, and quickly came to dominate the physician autobiographical form, is an interesting aspect of the social history of physician narrative. Second, there is no obvious reason that a reading public would embrace the accounts of training told by medical students and residents. On the contrary, the authenticity of training tales often seems undercut by the very inexperience of the author. In an older genre, senior physicians reflected back over years of medical work and history in narratives that possessed experiential depth and reflexive weight. Training tales, by contrast, often seem shallow and unreflexive, a kind of raw, unprocessed report of an experience that the student or resident has not really had time to digest or understand. Moreover, by adopting a largely critical position toward contemporary medicine and medical education, training tales deliver an uncomfortable message that might appear to undercut confidence in the profession. Nonetheless, they proliferate and, apparently, sell.

Psychiatrist training tales offer an interesting comparison to training tales from physicians in physical medical specialties. Consider the story told by Mark Warren, a 1979 graduate of the Johns Hopkins Medical School, who did his residency in psychiatry in a Boston hospital (Warren 1986). Like several other examples of the genre, his book is devoted to the first year of that residency, a typically overwhelming experience of too many patients, too much pathology, too few effective treatments, and too little time. He describes the usual response, a sense of drowning in a sea of craziness, lacking the knowledge and skills to make headway against the tide that sucks him farther and farther out. His only guide is a chief resident who seems less interested in treating patients successfully than in managing the unit.

Warren's narrative introduces several themes that I want to pursue here. It goes without saying, of course, that he outlines a fairly common process, a rite of passage by a series of ordeals that one can find in almost any account of professional training. But Warren opens with an issue that has special salience for medicine in the late twentieth century. In his orientation lecture on the first day of his residency, he is troubled to hear the following: "You are all looking forward to being therapists . . . but first you will learn to be administrators." Warren thinks: "Administration? I'm here to be a doctor. Not an administrator. What does this man mean?" (Warren 1986:2–3).

And though he is relieved to find that "administration" means "the working out of a treatment plan for each patient," his dismay returns as he discovers that a "treatment plan" is structured as much by bureaucratic issues—insurance, the availability of beds—as by therapeutic concerns. Throughout his first year—and his book—Warren struggles with the problem of balancing the institutional demand of bureaucratic management against the clinical imperatives that led him to medicine.

Warren organizes his account of this first year through a series of patient encounters, each patient representing a kind of ideal type of common psychiatric disorder: Simon is manic-depressive; Catherine has borderline personality disorder; Shirley is schizophrenic; Eve is a violent sociopathic patient who punches Warren and gives him a black eye. The second theme I want to note is the ambiguous benefits of the medical technology available to treat such patients.

Warren's first patient is Simon, who is manic-depressive. Warren is reluctant to treat Simon's illness chemically, for reasons that first appear to have more to do with Warren's general discomfort with chemicals, artificial additives, and environmental pollutants than with the efficacy of pharmacology. Psychotherapy seems to Warren a more natural therapeutic option, and so long as there are no bureaucratic barriers to Simon's talking treatment, his chief resident is willing to give Warren enough rope to hang himself with this experience. There are two dimensions to this theme. First, Warren makes it clear that the "technology" of pharmacological therapies is only ambiguously beneficial. For example, looking at the *Index Medicus,* he ponders: "So what to read up on? There are many great topics. Like 'Eighty-seven different new drugs to cure depression.' Or 'Eighty-seven new side effects from drugs that treat depression.' How about 'Stress and the psychiatrist'?" He sympathizes with patients who feel that their medications are making them stupid, sluggish. He hates the need to warn patients of the side effects of the drugs he prescribes, some of which, such as tardive dyskinesia (a movement disorder caused by certain antipsychotic medications), are difficult to avoid and impossible to reverse. Second, the ambiguity of such therapeutic benefits underscores the ambiguous nature of mental disease itself. Warren describes in disparaging tones the senior psychiatrist who assures him that "all people need is a little less dopamine. Or a little more of something else. . . . It's all in the chemicals, you see. The molecules tell you what to do. Mental illness is simply a disorder of the neurochemical pathways." The senior psychiatrist's neurochemistry, Warren observes, makes him very slick. Warren objects: "But they have so many problems and issues they have to straighten out. They still have so much to deal with, even when they're medicated to the gills." The senior psychiatrist is not impressed: "That's not their illness; that's their life. . . . Cure the disease; the rest is society's problem." By the end of his first year Warren is still struggling with this ambiguity: "How," he asks, "do I train a scary illiterate tattooed woman with no income or job prospects to succeed in the world?"

These themes are, in fact, the building blocks of medical training tales, in physical medicine as much as in psychiatry. They chart one dimension of the paradoxical quality of the public representations of medicine in the late twentieth century. On the one hand, physicians, often senior physicians, have written extensively about the miracles of technological advancement in medicine: diagnostic technology, pharmacological treatments, surgical breakthroughs. Oliver Sacks revealed to the public the miracle of L-dopa. Weissman, Klawans, and a host of others have written expansively on medical advances. In thinking about the social role of training tales, usually written by young physicians, sometimes while still in the midst of training, I have asked what is the nature of their authority? What is the source of interest in narratives written by neophytes, narratives that are distinguished by the very typicality of the experience they describe? Perhaps our interest in such narratives lies precisely in the counterpoint they offer to the extravagant, almost science-fiction-like promises of the medical essayist who extols technology and science. Mark Warren possesses a kind of innocence that allows him to respond with a "yes, but . . ." at each technological, scientific promise that psychiatry offers him.

Working backward a bit in time, I turn to David Viscott's training narrative, *The Making of a Psychiatrist* (1972). Viscott attended Tufts Medical School in the 1960s and also did his psychiatric residency in Boston, but published his autobiography in 1972. The fifteen or more years between his training and Mark Warren's make little difference to the basic structure of their stories. Like Warren, Viscott is impressed by the power of psychiatric medications, but he hesitates to prescribe powerful tranquilizers such as phenothiazines for fear of their irreversible side effects. He struggles constantly with senior psychiatrists who are portrayed as rather jaded and interested primarily in controlling patients rather than treating them, and who have completely abandoned the hope of curing them.

Viscott's themes, like Warren's, are standard stories in psychiatry training narratives. Most focus on the first year of the psychiatric residency, with tales that pit the innocent resident who pursues his patients' well-being against the institution, which is concerned only with management and bureaucratic issues, or with brain chemistry rather than lived experience. Stephen Seager, who left a practice in emergency medicine to start over as a psychiatrist, went through the same experiences in 1988 (Seager 1991). He characterizes medicine as a whole: "Everything . . . is done by someone else with an expensive machine in another building. Bills are computerized. Charts audited. Discharge decisions made by insurance company formulas. . . . Doctors and patients . . . are separating from one another at an ever-increasing velocity" (1991:89).

Donald Light, in his sociological study of psychiatric training, suggests that the issues I have mentioned in these training narratives are typical of the first year of the residency (Light 1980). He notes, for example, that the tension between management and therapy is sharpened rather than resolved, that first-year residents are reluctant to use drugs, even when impressed by their efficacy, but that they become disappointed when psychotherapeutic efforts fail to produce much effect. As Light says, the problem is not that psychotherapies are ineffective, but rather that first-year residents tend to use them on the wrong patients in the wrong settings. By the end of even the first year, he suggests, psychiatric residents are able to distinguish, and are becoming more comfortable with, the limits of therapy and their own limits, management and therapy, and the often ambiguous line between craziness and normalcy, even in themselves.

It is perhaps significant, then, that of the psychiatric training narratives I've consulted, none pursues the author's development beyond that first year. In other words, readers are left with the rather critical impression of psychiatry constructed by these authors, even though these authors surely knew by the time they wrote these books that they had undergone continuing development, that their attitudes had presumably changed, and that, quite possibly, they had themselves become the managing, chemical-reductionist biological psychiatrists they deplored during their first year. And here, perhaps, lies the importance, and the paradox, of the training narrative in medicine. Its function is largely moral rather than sociological or scientific. It constructs itself as a moral alternative to the triumphalist histories of medical advancement that one finds in the memoirs and autobiographies of so many senior physicians, including psychiatrists. These training tales do not deny the truth of psychiatric advancement; they offer an alternative truth.

I have elsewhere asked how is it that training narratives in medicine appear for the first time only in the 1960s, and rapidly proliferate in the 1980s: Viscott's 1972 autobiography is the earliest I know of that focuses exclusively and at length on psychiatric training, and the others with which I am familiar were all written in the 1980s. One possibility is obvious and is almost always explicit in these training narratives: a profound sense that in the 1960s and 1970s the social organization of medicine and psychiatry changed radically, and that these changes have largely been negative. In these training tales it is the resident who enters that first year with unlimited optimism, only to find his or her hopes dashed on the bureaucratized, technologized, dehumanizing forms of practice and patient management they are asked to learn. As I have commented elsewhere, training tales are usually, in effect, heroic tales of students' and residents' ability to withstand the forces that compromise medicine, forces to which one's fellow students or residents often succumb (Pollock 1996). Psychiatrist training tales offer a small variation on this theme: they are more sensitive to the fact that it is *institutions* that impose barriers and restraints, and that all personnel within these institutions are potential victims of these bureaucratic and oppressive constraints. The author's fellow residents are typically not a part of the problem but are struggling against it as well.

Perhaps the most obvious change in psychiatry that most commentators identify during the period of these training tales is deinstitutionalization, as thousands of hospitalized patients were discharged on medications that theoretically would allow them to function adequately outside of the institution. But psychiatric training tales, curiously enough, tend not to focus on deinstitutionalization. On the contrary, while there is a widespread assumption that deinstitutionalization has increased the use of harmful antipsychotic drugs and has spilled hundreds of patients into the streets to become the new urban homeless, psychiatric training narratives are more likely to emphasize the positive benefits of releasing patients whose medications offer the only possible hope, at this point in history, of leading a remotely normal or independent life. Rather, I am struck by the extent to which a variety of changes constituting increased bureaucratization are blamed by psychiatry residents for the trials and tribulations they experience in their first year of training.

Bureaucratization here includes a range of institutional changes, from complicated insurance issues to informed consent, in which instrumental rationality imposes a conceptual form of iron cage, to use Weber's metaphor, trapping the novice psychiatrist as much as the patient and other staff. Mark Warren expresses his suspicions of the *Diagnostic and Statistical Manual of Mental Disorders,* which seems too recipe-like, too pat but also too ambiguous. Reading the list of diagnostic criteria for borderline personality disorder, he suspects that many of his friends would fit the criteria from time to time. Seager finds the bureaucracy inserting itself between the patient and physician, certainly not a metaphor appropriate to his earlier career in emergency medicine.

In reflecting on the training tales of physicians in other specialties and in medical school, I have suggested that public interest in these narratives might derive from the confluence of several factors (Pollock 1996:355). Popular interest in medicine has increased the access of the lay public to traditionally restricted forms of medical knowledge, and the training tale offers a form of access to medicine that is especially detailed and explicit, constructed, indeed, to conform to public stereotypes. Training tales offer this access in the form of vicarious experience, as the reader easily identifies with the novice physician. But we may still wonder why physicians elect to tell such stories, particularly if, as I suspect, they do so at a point in their development when they realize that their impressions were colored and shaped as much by their inexperience as by the "reality" of their training. As I noted earlier, it appears almost as if a broad lay public had "authorized" these physicians to provide precisely these kinds of critical accounts of medicine and psychiatry, to construct a moral discourse in which patient welfare and patient rights are central to clinical work, and in which the bureaucratic barriers to care that have plagued patients for years are finally acknowledged and resisted by physicians themselves. Indeed, one suspects that within medicine as a whole, such training narratives are approved of as a kind of professional conscience to which novice physicians can give voice, while similar themes from senior physicians would be met with less comfort by the medical profession (cf. Stoeckle 1987). Psychiatrist training narratives accomplish this moral effect by posing precisely the conflicts that shape the profession and its public representations: the ambiguities of mental and behavioral disorders; the tensions in the psychiatrist role vis-à-vis other medical specialties; the ethical dilemmas of medication.

Physician autobiography is, then, a rich source of insight into the resonating ways in which physicians and the public understand medicine and agree to represent it. Physician autobiography can serve as a token of widespread social issues, as in the ways in which women physicians construct a kind of social history of feminism that mirrors the struggles of women in other professions in the twentieth century. Or physician autobiography can serve as a kind of projective screen against which authors can help to cast images of anxiety and uncertainty about medical science and bureaucracy. The power of autobiography to convey such images and messages lies in the quality I have called narrative referentiality, that combination of narrative form and verisimilitude that elevates experience to a moral level. It is in this way that "medicine" is a socially constructed field whose representations are as important as its science. Physician autobiography, as I hope I have suggested here, is an especially privileged site for the production and consumption of such representations.

ACKNOWLEDGMENTS

Research for this chapter was supported by a grant from the National Endowment for the Humanities. I am grateful to Cheryl Mattingly for helpful suggestions on this essay and on the subject of narrative in general. An earlier version of this chapter was read at the 1997 meetings of the Society for Medical Anthropology, in a session organized by Sean Hagberg and myself, "On Psychiatry."

NOTES

1. Hawkins (1993) has examined a fascinating complementary source of the public representation of medicine: the "pathography," stories that patients tell about their illnesses (see also Brody 1987; Kleinman 1988). There is, of course, a parallel genre of physician pathography that blends themes of the two forms of autobiography.

2. This section is drawn largely from my article on training tales (Pollock 1996:341–42).

3. The Flexner Report was a Carnegie Foundation–sponsored study of medical education that recommended the science-based model pursued in urban university medical schools over the apprenticeship models found in rural areas of

the country. However, it appears that changes in medical school licensing were equally or more important in the widespread adoption of new curricula (cf. Starr 1982).

4. Sharon Kaufman's study of twentieth-century medicine through the stories told by seven physicians (1993) is a creative effort to read the history of medicine through the stories told by her physician informants. My interest in such narratives is also to read such stories through the history of medicine, a complementary tactic.

5. I must also stress that, although I have written about physician autobiography from an anthropological perspective (Pollock 1996), this essay makes no pretensions to anthropological insight. In particular, by isolating genres and contexts, I elide cultural issues that would provide a richer, though inevitably longer and more complicated, account. Moreover, the notion of "narrative" itself collapses issues that anthropologists are more likely to consider within the framework of discursive strategies, pragmatics, and metapramatics: autobiographies as forms of inscriptional practice in the micropolitics of subjectivity and power.

6. I have called this genre "women in medicine" and not "women physicians" to emphasize its feminist themes; women physicians also write autobiographies in which gender issues do not play an explicit, organizing role, though they are rarely absent.

7. LaRoe's autobiography is included here, though she emigrated to the United States in the 1930s to escape Nazism in Germany. Like Travell's career, LaRoe's spanned the middle of the twentieth century in the United States.

8. I cannot resist repeating a commonly heard joke from 1996: What does one call a neurosurgeon in southern California? "Waiter!"

REFERENCES

Brecht, Bertold. 1976. *Aesthetics and politics.* London: New Left Books.

Brody, Howard. 1987. *Stories of sickness.* New Haven, Conn.: Yale University Press.

Bruner, Jerome. 1991. The narrative construction of reality. *Critical Inquiry* 18: 1–21.

Campbell, Robert E. 1993. *Vignettes by a village doctor.* New York: Vantage.

Conrad, Peter. 1988. Learning to doctor: Reflections on recent accounts of the medical school years. *Journal of Health and Social Behavior* 29:323–32.

Doctor X. 1965. *Intern.* New York: Harper and Row.

Dole, Mary P. 1941. *A doctor in homespun.* Privately printed.

Fishbein, Morris. 1969. *Morris Fishbein, M.D.: An autobiography.* New York: Doubleday.

Haas, Scott. 1990. *Hearing voices: Reflections of a psychology intern.* New York: Dutton.

Harrison, Michelle. 1982. *A woman in residence.* New York: Random House.

Haseltine, Florence, and Yvonne Yaw. 1976. *Woman doctor.* Boston: Houghton Mifflin.

Hawkins, Anne Hunsaker. 1993. *Reconstructing illness: Studies in pathography*. Lafayette, Ind.: Purdue University Press.

Hertzler, Arthur E. 1938. *The horse and buggy doctor*. New York: Harper.

Hunter, Kathryn Montgomery. 1991. *Doctors' stories: The narrative structure of medical knowledge*. Princeton, N.J.: Princeton University Press.

Kaiser, Grace H. 1986. *Dr. Frau: A woman doctor among the Amish*. Intercourse, Pa.: Good Books.

Kaufman, Sharon R. 1993. *The healer's tale: Transforming medicine and culture*. Madison: University of Wisconsin Press.

Klass, Perri. 1987. *A not entirely benign procedure: Four years as a medical student*. New York: Putnam.

———. 1992. *Baby doctor*. New York, Random House.

Kleinman, Arthur. 1988. *The illness narratives*. New York: Basic Books.

Labov, William. 1982. Speech acts and reactions in personal narrative. In *Georgetown Round Table on Languages and Linguistics 1981*, edited by Deborah Tannen, 219–47. Washington, D.C.: Georgetown University Press.

Labov, William, and Joshua Waletzky. 1967. Narrative analysis: Oral versions of personal experience. In *Essays on the verbal and visual arts*, edited by June Helm, 12–44. Seattle: University of Washington Press.

LaRoe, Else K. 1957. *Woman surgeon*. New York: Dial.

Leitch, Thomas. 1986. *What stories are: Narrative theory and interpretation*. State College: Pennsylvania State University Press.

Light, Donald. 1980. *Becoming psychiatrists: The professional transformation of self*. New York: Norton.

Macartney, William. 1938. *Fifty years a country doctor*. New York: Dutton.

McCarthy, Claire. 1995. *Learning how the heart beats: The making of a pediatrician*. New York: Viking.

McClenahan, William U. 1971. *G.P.* Philadelphia: Dorrance and Co.

McIntire, Ross T. 1946. *White House physician*. New York: Putnam.

Minetree, Harry. 1973. *Cooley: The amazing career of the world's greatest surgeon*. New York: Harper Magazine Press.

Morgan, Elizabeth. 1980. *The making of a woman surgeon*. New York: Putnam.

———. 1982. *Solo practice: A woman surgeon's story*. Boston: Little, Brown.

Olney, James, ed. 1988. *Autobiography: Essays theoretical and critical*. Princeton, N.J.: Princeton University Press.

Parker, Beulah. 1987. *The evolution of a psychiatrist: Memoirs of a woman doctor*. New Haven, Conn.: Yale University Press.

Pascal, Roy. 1960. *Design and truth in autobiography*. Cambridge, Mass.: Harvard University Press.

Patterson, Jane, and Lynda Madaras. 1983. *Woman doctor: The education of Jane Patterson, MD*. New York: Avon.

Poirier, Suzanne. 1987. Ethical issues in modern medical autobiographies. *Perspectives in Biology and Medicine* 30:278–89.

Pollock, Donald. 1996. Training tales: U.S. medical autobiography. *Cultural Anthropology* 11:339–61.

Rainer, J. Kenyon. 1987. *First do no harm: Reflections on becoming a brain surgeon*. New York: Willard Books.

Rosenbaum, Edward. 1988. *A taste of my own medicine*. New York: Random House.

Ruthrof, Horst. 1981. *The reader's construction of narrative*. London: Routledge and Kegan Paul.

Sartre, Jean Paul. [1938] 1965. *Nausea*. New York: Penguin.

Seager, Stephen B. 1991. *Psychward: A year behind locked doors*. New York: Putnam.

Searcy, Harvey B. 1961. *We used what we had*. Birmingham, Ala.: Colonial Press.

Segal, Daniel. 1984. Playing doctor, seriously: Graduation follies at an American medical school. *International Journal of Health Services* 14:379–96.

———. 1988 A patient so dead: American medical students and their cadavers. *Anthropological Quarterly* 61:17–25.

Spengemann, William. 1980. *The forms of autobiography*. New Haven, Conn.: Yale University Press.

Starr, Paul. 1982. *The social transformation of American medicine*. New York: Basic Books.

Stoeckle, John D. 1987. Physicians train and tell. *Harvard Medical School Alumni Bulletin* 61 (winter): 9–11.

Tambling, Jeremy. 1991. *Narrative and ideology*. London: Open University Press.

Travell, Janet. 1968. *Office hours day and night*. New York: World.

Turner, Bryan. 1984. *The body and society*. New York: Blackwell.

Viscott, David S. 1972. *The making of a psychiatrist*. New York: Arbor House.

Warren, Mark. 1986. *The making of a modern psychiatrist*. New York: Doubleday.

Wheeler, John Brooks. 1935. *Memoirs of a small-town surgeon*. New York: Frederick A. Stokes.

White, Hayden. 1981. The value of narrativity in the representation of reality. In *On narrative*, edited by W. J. T. Mitchell, 1–23. Chicago: University of Chicago Press.

White, Paul Dudley. 1971. *My life and medicine*. Boston: Gambit.

Wrenn, Marie-Claude. 1977. *"You're the only one here who doesn't look like a doctor": Portrait of a woman surgeon*. New York: Crowell.

SIX

"Even If We Don't Have Children [We] Can Live"

Stigma and Infertility in South India

CATHERINE KOHLER RIESSMAN

PROLOGUE

It began in 1994 in a coastal fishing village in Kerala, South India, where I was interviewing women that a village informant had identified as childless. Drawn to Kerala because of the advantaged position of women there, I had completed fieldwork in an infertility clinic of a government hospital since arriving the year before. I had also interviewed, together with my Malayalee assistant, Liza, several dozen women in urban and rural areas throughout Kerala about being childless, and its consequences for their lives. On this particular day, we were meeting "Celine." Dressed in a polyester sari (the fabric preferred by village women), she was waiting for us by the door of her concrete (*pucca*) house in a grove of coconut palms. Twenty-six years old and married eight years to a fisherman, Celine had expected to conceive right after marriage but had not, and she was deeply sad. A visit from "Dr. Catherine from America" (how I was introduced, because my last name was unpronounceable for Malayalees) may have carried hopes of a cure, despite the introduction: I was a sociologist studying childless women, not a gynecologist.

As we entered the house, escaping the scorching heat, various family members emerged from the darkness of the interior: Celine's husband (Rajiv), her parents, and several adolescents who, we learned, were her sister's children. A family member offered us a cool drink: a coconut punctured with a plastic straw. Celine's parents asked questions of Liza (Was she married?) and of me (Where was my husband? How many children did I have?). Eventually we moved into the formal interview. Family members expected to be part of any conversation about infertility—a family tragedy in the Indian context. Our desire for a confidential interview with Celine was not understood.[1] As Liza questioned Celine in Malayalam and, from time to time, translated her brief answers for me, family members volunteered information. After several interruptions when neighbors came to listen, Liza asked if there was a private space. Celine led us into a small bedroom hung with laundry, with a door that closed. The conversation continued with the three of us sitting on a hard platform—the marital bed. Our seclusion proved critical: narratives emerged in the private space, including the one that follows my essay (Story 1, on pp. 134–35).

Infertility is not an illness, but, nonetheless, infertile women in India construct narrative accounts to make meaning of their disrupted lives (Becker 1994). In this chapter I analyze Celine's narrative to explore problems of interpretation and meaning in context. The work is part of a larger theoretical project on stigma—its manifestations and management—and resistance to stigma in South India (Riessman 2000 and in press). My methodological approach here draws on sociolinguistic traditions of narrative analysis that have been used to illuminate a variety of health topics. These include urban violence (Labov 1982), coherence in schizophrenic discourse (Gee 1991), presentation of self in chronic illness (Riessman 1990b), experiences of women exposed to diethylstilbestrol (DES) during their mothers' pregnancies (Bell 1988, 1999) and breast cancer survivors (Langellier in press), and doctor-patient communication (Mishler 1984; Clark and Mishler 1992). Although diverse in topic and method, all these investigations relate meaning to the structure of discourse, in contrast to other narrative approaches that examine primarily the content of talk. My analytic approach, in addition, examines the interactional production and performance of narrative in social contexts (Mishler 1986a, 1986b, 1995, 1999; Langellier 1989 and in press; Peterson and Langellier 1997; Riessman 1993).

Close textual analysis requires systematic transcription of interviews, and attention to the role of audiences (interviewer, translator, and reader) in the construction of meaning. The approach attends to contexts (local, cultural, and historical) in the interpretation of personal narratives. Here, for example, I attend to the locality of Kerala, which provides possibilities for women not easily available in other parts of India, along with constraints. The approach leads to insights about lives in context and the workings of oppressive social structures—not portraits of an "authentic" subject or "true" self, as critics have claimed (Atkinson and Silverman 1997).

The investigator examines the way a story is told—how it is put together, the linguistic and cultural resources it draws on, and how its performance persuades a listener of authenticity. In previous work (Riessman 1990a, 1990b), I have examined how narrators craft their tales together with listeners using specific cultural discourses, linguistic devices, and narrative genres. Here I move away from close, text-based analysis because the interview with Celine was conducted in Malayalam and subsequently translated, transcribed, and edited for an English-speaking audience.[2] Attention to certain formal aspects of language— precisely *how* something is said and lexical choice—requires verbatim materials in the speaker's language. Instead, I create structures from the interview texts to convey the sense I've made. A kind of textual experimentation, I use poetic stanzas (groups of lines about a single topic) and other units of discourse (Gee 1986) as rhetorical devices to make my analysis of the organization of a story clear for the reader (Mishler 1991). I also attend to the sequence and contexts in which topics appear in the interview, how they are talked about, and my shifting understandings of them.

The translated materials (which initially seemed daunting) have, in fact, opened up the narratives to multiple readings, a possibility that narrow structural approaches tend to foreclose. Work with translated narratives—precisely because of ambiguities of language and meaning—makes visible interpretive problems that all narrative analysts face, whether native speakers or not. In interview studies as in ethnography, we "translate" the experiences of others, cross borders, and confront our double or multiple attachments (Clifford 1997). "If language constructs as well as describes a society, the figure of the interpreter/translator must come from behind the shadows" (Temple 1997:607).

Turning to my substantive topic, infertility is not rare in India,[3] but the reproductive issue remains invisible. The dominant discourse of the Indian government (and the international agencies on which it depends) concerns overpopulation; there is little social research on infertility in India (Unisa 1999; Riessman 2000), and the situations of individual women remain hidden. Yet narratives of childless women could inform population policy, if only by demonstrating the strength of the motherhood mandate and the stigma faced by those who cannot conceive.

The institutional importance of motherhood in India cannot be overestimated, even as family life is undergoing rapid change. Despite regional variation in the status of women, the normative biography for an Indian woman mandates childbearing after marriage; culturally, it is a master narrative. Motherhood is a woman's sacred duty—a value enshrined in religious laws for Hindus, Muslims, Sikhs, and Christians alike. Bearing and rearing children are central to women's power and well-being, and reproduction brings in its stead concrete benefits over the life course: a child solidifies a wife's often fragile bond with a spouse in arranged marriage and improves her status in the joint family and larger community; with a child, a woman can eventually become a mother-in-law—a position of considerable power and influence in the Indian family. In old age, women depend on children (particularly sons) for economic security in a country with few governmental social welfare programs, and, upon death, a son makes possible essential rituals for Hindus. For families with significant property or wealth, sexual reproduction allows for social reproduction—the orderly transfer of privilege through inheritance to the next generation of kin. Motherhood, in sum, serves critical cultural functions in India's hierarchical society (rigidly stratified by gender, caste, and class) that are masked by psychological or sentimental discourses (e.g., it is "natural" to want to bear a child). Indian women are keenly aware that their reproductive capacities are an important source of power, especially when they lack it from other sources (Dube 1986; Lateef 1990; Jeffery et al. 1989; Stone and James 1995; Uberoi 1993). A married woman who is childless exists in a liminal state—socially betwixt and between. Given these cultural realities, how do women find ways to resist the master narrative of childbearing, and what resources aid the process?

Theoretically, my research builds on recent scholarship on women and reproduction (detailed later) and on the work of Erving Goffman.

He articulates how bodily signs that depart from the "ordinary and nat-ural" are deeply discrediting: the person is reduced "from a whole and usual person to a tainted, discounted one" (1963:3). One of the few In-dian studies of women who visited an infertility clinic reveals consider-able self-blame: "There is something wrong with me" was a common statement (Jindal and Gupta 1989; Jindal and Dhall 1990). Biological reproduction is fused with women's bodies in cultural representations around the world (Ginsburg and Rapp 1995); fertility problems are con-sequently seen as women's failings—a view often shared by childless women themselves.

It seems that childlessness, like breast cancer, carries an ancient stigma for women: it is "a culturally marked illness, a dominant societal symbol that, once applied to a person, spoils radically the individual's identity and is not easily removed" (Kleinman 1988:22). Unlike breast cancer, however, childlessness is not a disease but a social status. Unlike a disease, some women may desire it, though others may view it as a chronic disability. The very meaning of childlessness is ambiguous—be-twixt and between classification—a contested terrain with oppositional definitions possible. Even when childlessness is involuntary, however, re-search assumes that the absence of fertility, like many disabilities, can re-main "secret" and invisible to view, and consequently resistant to soci-etal judgment (Miall 1986).

Stigma theory contains many Eurocentric assumptions in its repre-sentations of social life. It assumes, for example, that disclosure is an in-dividual strategy. An "invisible" and potentially stigmatizing attribute (such as not having children) can remain hidden; the actor chooses whom to disclose to and when. She can pass as normal. In India, selective dis-closure is rarely possible. It is common knowledge in Celine's village, for example, that she cannot conceive, and she is constantly reminded of her "spoiled identity" (Goffman 1963): "Neighbors, they ridicule me. When I go out and all they call me 'fool without a child,' like that." Identity work in the face of stigma involves a different process for South Indian women than for Western women, and concepts that privilege the in-dividual, and assume privacy and mass society, have limited use (Riess-man 2000).

Scholarship on women provides a useful corrective to some of the problematic assumptions of stigma theory by calling attention to agency in the face of difficult conditions. Women with disabilities, for example, confront and resist dominant views (Fine and Asch 1988). Demography is beginning to explore women as real demographic actors who monitor their activities and modify their reproductive lives as the need arises (Greenhalgh 1995). Women grapple with their position as victims of their culturally constructed subordinate status, at the same time as they search for creative ways to resist subordination (Fisher and Davis 1993; Franz and Stewart 1994; Mahoney and Yngvesson 1992).

Narrative accounts offer a unique window into these processes and reveal the biographical work women do to position themselves in the social world (Riessman in press). Kristin Langellier articulates the importance of narrative in studies of women's lives: "Women have always opposed their oppression in myriad ways, even while lacking the social power and authority to make their meanings 'stick' in institutional practices. Narratives of personal experience open up a discursive space in which individual women can resist dominant subject positions by articulating the contradictory meanings in their experience" (1989:1–2). Because personal narratives are not "fixed texts" but change with each telling and may be interpreted differently by different audiences, narratives of resistance, Langellier argues, must consider the performative element: the conditions under which stories are told and other situated narrative practices (Langellier in press).

This brief summary of concepts suggests some of the narrative challenges Celine faces. Her account is part of a larger corpus from fieldwork in South India.[4] I selected hers for analysis because of its theoretical significance and power: the stigma she faced because of infertility was the harshest and most punishing we encountered during fieldwork, and yet she found ways to fight back. She is an active subject, at the same time as she is constrained by a discourse of compulsory motherhood in India. My selection and analysis of excerpts were guided by several questions: When does Celine tell stories[5] in the context of our interview conversation? How are they performed, in collaboration with an audience of two women? How can the stories be interpreted, and what different readings of them are possible? Broadly and thematically, what do the stories reveal about how an Indian woman contests stigma and subordination, and what cultural resources aid her?

Based on these guiding questions, I transcribed several stories in the interview for closer analysis. I also include nonnarrative (question-and-answer) segments as context for the stories, and information from other places in the interview. Beyond the structural and interactional features noted previously, I explore the content of the stories—the events to which language refers. But I do not assume an easy correspondence. Meanings are problematic and ambiguous, most obviously because of translation. "If there is no one meaning to a text, then there can be no one translation of it" (Temple 1997:610). Celine's account is also shaped in major ways by the particular interactional context that produced it. She develops her narrative of the past from a position in the present. To further problematize meaning, my position relative to the stories has changed over time, and my interpretations of them have shifted—a reflexive process I include in the analysis.

A brief word about transcription: I have numbered the lines for ease of reference, and grouped lines into stanzas and couplets to visually represent my understandings about major units of meaning. Breaks in a speaker's stream of speech are noted with a dash ("—"). The texts represent my translations of materials translated from Malayalam.[6] I have included the interviewer's questions and comments in the excerpts, which represent a conversation that involves three women—Celine, Liza, and me (noted as "C," "L," and "CR"). Although "messier" than a conventional transcript, the representation of talk here allows me to explore how a narrative is jointly produced (in this case by a teller and two listeners/ questioners) and to discuss my shifting "translations" of meaning.

As we talked in the bedroom hung with laundry, Celine told several stories about spending large amounts of money on medical care when she did not conceive, and about a relative's bad experience with a formal adoption, before telling the particular story represented here. In other words, it emerged nearly an hour after the interview began, as we were nearing the end, and after we had covered a great deal of ground. Liza asked, "Has being childless affected your married life?" which was from an interview checklist of possible effects (marital, social, religious, financial). Celine seized the question as an opening for a story that relates physical and psychological abuse at the hands of her husband and in-laws. Neither Liza nor I was prepared for what she said.

STORY I

01   Liza: Has being childless affected your married life?

02   Celine: (lowers voice almost to whisper)
03   Initially very much.
04   Because of not having children
05   he has beaten me.

06   L: During the initial years, I see.

07 C: Since five years—
08 when we started going to hospitals
09 and even then didn't have children.

10 Initially, for six months after marriage,
11 I stayed with my husband's family.
12 Then for them—
13 what they are saying is because I don't have children
14 I should be sent away.

15 My husband's father, mother, and siblings
16 they won't talk to me and all that.
17 Since I don't have children, they asked him to leave me.
18 His father and mother said that he should again marry.

19 (lowers voice). After that I quarreled with them
20 and am living in this house [her family's home].

21 L: How long have you been here?

22 C: After the marriage I stayed there for only six months.

My first reading of the narrative fitted my Western precommitments (and the mind is never free of precommitment, as Bruner [1987] says). I saw Celine as a victim of violence: her husband beat her when she failed to conceive after six months of marriage. Although his physical abuse of her and the harassment by his family were the most extreme we encountered during fieldwork, the response is consistent with a pattern reported by other village women, and it contrasts with the subtler forms of stigma affluent childless women face (Riessman 1995b, 2000). Affluent women confront persistent intrusive questions about their fertility at social events (*vishesham*), which most find "insulting," but they have latitude in the timing of pregnancy, especially if they are professionals. They are criticized, however, if they elect to remain childless (rare in Kerala). Poor women have little choice in timing, their family situations are visible to all, and if they do not conceive shortly after marriage, they are harshly judged by neighbors who gossip, taunt, and ridicule them, even in cases where the "failing" is the husband's (e.g., no sperm). Like other village women, Celine was deemed worthless—a farm animal that did not reproduce (*machi*).

Information from other parts of the interview forced me to consider additional meanings beyond abuse, suggesting other provisional interpretations of Celine's marital experience. Her biography is, in many ways, typical of the life course of young women from the rural areas of Kerala, arguably the most progressive state in India. Celine was educated for ten years in the village school, although she did not successfully complete the secondary school exams and could not go on to further education. Her family, though poor and from the *pulaya* (formerly slave) caste, is not destitute. Both parents are employed (her mother as a day laborer and her father as a fisherman), and they own land. Celine's marriage was arranged when she was eighteen. After marriage she moved into her in-laws' house in a village some distance from her natal home. Somewhat atypically, the marriage was arranged despite religious differences between the families (hers is Christian, his is Hindu). Celine is dark-skinned in a country where "fair" skin is valued in women, and perhaps it was difficult to arrange a marriage for her. Rajiv, who was twenty-one and a fisherman, had less education than Celine and poor economic prospects. His parents pressured him into marriage, apparently because of the size of the dowry. His family's economic status was threatened because of several bad harvests, and the dowry—an instrument that preserves and perpetuates class position (Stone and James 1995)—promised to secure their situation. The marriage, however, did not make things better: his family developed further financial problems, and meanwhile the total dowry promised did not materialize. His "backward" family (Celine said) thought the new bride had brought misfortune—poverty and illness—on the family; in this context, unhappiness with Celine grew, including displeasure with her "nature" and lack of fertility. When she had failed to conceive after six months, the in-laws refused to talk to her. They pressured their son to abandon her, hoping perhaps that he would get another wife and another dowry.[7]

Celine's experience is consistent with my general findings regarding women living in poverty: infertility is typically assumed to be *her* problem, and it has its harshest meanings when other things go wrong too, such as dowry promises (Riessman 2000). A Western imagination might read an ending to her biography in the form of a violent death at the hand of displeased in-laws, in a "suspicious kitchen fire" perhaps—the bride burnings that the Indian media report (mostly in urban areas of North India, and unheard of in Kerala). With the recent influx of foreign goods into India and increasing consumerism, coupled with high unemployment, dowry has become a way for families to imagine having more.

But the story does not end with violence, or even abandonment. Nor does Rajiv follow his parents' directives, leave his wife, and remarry. There are hints of another story—growing independence from his family's coercion. Celine, instead of continuing to submit to harassment and violence, contests her subordination. In the turning point of the story, she says:

19 After that I quarreled with them
20 and am living in this house [her family's home].

The couplet represents the coda of the story (i.e., it signals the end by returning the perspective to the present). But the couplet relates events that certainly are not routine in the life of an Indian family. Celine refers to actions against powerful gender conventions and age hierarchies. She says she dared to "quarrel" and challenge the expectation of silence and subservience to in-laws. She leaves the joint family and returns to her natal village and home. It is not clear from the sparse story whether she accomplished these actions on her own or with her husband's consent. Later, however, she states that he supported her, perhaps even taking the initiative after the quarrel ("We'll go to your house because things are so bad here"). She also relates later that she never accompanies her husband on occasional visits to his family ("They don't like me so I don't go").

In view of the contextual information, my initial reading of the text— a story of abuse—seems incomplete. Although Western women readers are accustomed to seeing victimization in stories of domestic violence, the ending of this one calls for additional interpretation. How Celine chooses to end it is not trivial: narrators plan discourse, including the "point" they wish their listeners to retain. As Celine constructs the sequence of the story, and its resolution, she suggests a second reading that emphasizes resistance and agency—gaining freedom from oppressive conditions.

There is a third provisional reading: the story sets up the problem of an arranged marriage gone awry. But it is surviving. Like many stories, this one is told with its end point in mind—the couple are living together, following physical abuse and family rejection. The sparse story does not work out the family conflicts set forth in the plot. It leaves the listener/reader uncertain about how the marriage has survived.

Looking beyond referential content, are there cues in the interview interaction that aid interpretation? Collaboratively, the account gets structured narratively, and the story assumes a near-classic form: it presents a problem (Rajiv's abuse), its context (his family), and actions that resolve the problem—or a turning point (her quarrel and departure). To examine more precisely how the story is collaboratively performed, I shift the angle of vision to the relationship between teller and audience. Viewing the text as a collaborative performance (a *narrative* event) brings into view aspects of Celine's situation that are missed when the *narrated events* alone—referential content—are considered.[8]

Story 1 is a dialogic performance involving Celine (the teller) and Liza (the audience). Liza begins with a question about "married life," and Celine narrates about her infertility in the context of the arranged marriage and joint family. Although lines 4 and 5 could have become an abstract for a story to follow—about beatings because of infertility— the story does not get developed that way. The topic of physical abuse does not surface again. There are several ways to make sense of the shift. Perhaps because the topic was so unexpected, Liza backs away from the beatings and comments on their timing ("during the initial years"), which, in turn, prompts Celine to give a chronology of the initial years of the marriage and to end with her decisive action to leave the joint family. Embedded in the tight temporal sequence are several stanzas that emplot the family's response to her. Liza does not respond specifically to the family drama, which the stanzas describe, but instead after the coda asks again about time ("How long have you been here?"). The performance of the story gets shaped by the audience: Liza mediates the way the story begins and ends, how it gets structured narratively around time and place, and what themes get developed. The audience permits certain facts to come to the fore and get included in the drama, while others remain outside—momentary visitors who leave the stage when they are not given a part. Celine's husband, for example, has no role after the beginning because Liza does not respond to Rajiv as a major character in the drama. Like all members of an audience, Liza tries to make sense of what she is hearing, and locating the events in narrative time and space aids her meaning-making process.[9]

Perhaps a story of wife abuse is more than Liza can hear. Liza is a twenty-six-year-old woman (the same age as Celine) whose own marriage is about to be arranged.[10] Liza asks about the marriage and, in this context, Celine and Liza collaborate to develop the theme most salient to both of them—the evolution of an arranged marriage from inauspicious beginnings. The ensuing story presupposes shared cultural knowledge about gender and family relations. In the performance of narrative, meanings are constituted, enhanced, and contested (Langellier 1989) in a reciprocal process that involves teller and audience.

Other performance features, which enhance the narrated events and intensify meanings, aid interpretation of the story. Celine alters markedly the volume of her voice at two key places: as she opens the story, and as she moves to close it (lines 2 and 19). Lowering her voice almost to a whisper signals meaning and importance: these are unspeakable events, unknown perhaps to her family in the next room.[11] Given the privacy of the setting and the many topics that had been touched on in the hour interview, she decides to reveal the abuse and her actions against it—between women. Talk about family problems to strangers is not customary in India. Speaking out to Liza and me challenges social conventions, just as Celine's "quarrel" with her in-laws and departure from their home defied conventions in the Indian family. The performance of the story supports a reading involving a woman's resistance to oppressive circumstances. At the same time, it leaves open another interpretive possibility: a story about the transformation of a marriage from an abusive one to something different.

Shortly after Story 1, our interview was interrupted by Celine's sister, who brought us tea and snacks, and then by Rajiv. He came into the room to tell Celine he was going out and when he would be back. I watched their solicitous interaction. After he left, we ate food the family provided as people wandered into the room and asked more questions of Liza (Since she is twenty-six, why isn't she married?) and of me (Why did Madam come to India? Had she diagnosed Celine's problem yet?). We answered all questions, and again said I was not a gynecologist. I was reminded of the unresolvable complexities of research that Estroff describes (1995): my presence had a different meaning in the lives of my informants than I experienced or intended. Issues of informed consent, responsibility, and authority are compounded when the ethnographer works in another culture.

While we had tea, Liza used the break from the formal interview to inquire about how the marriage was arranged, given religious differences between the families—a topic of obvious personal interest (she, like Celine, is Christian). We learned how the marriage was held in Celine's village, "since they [his family] are Hindus." After she moved to their village, religious harassment began: they would not let her go to church and pressured her to attend their temple, which she refused to do. Meanwhile, her family had difficulty amassing the dowry promised, so they gave property instead of gold. Liza listened intently to Celine's descriptions and, as the tea things were collected, moved to complete the formal interview. She quickly summarized the preceding conversation for me ("She had a problem with not giving adequate dowry. After six months she's come back and stayed here").

I was puzzled about the husband's place in the narrated events, specifically his reaction to his parents' directive to abandon Celine and marry again. Contradictions in Story 1 further puzzled me: he beat Celine but also accompanied her after she quarreled with his family. His behavior to her during our visit was kind and attentive. Earlier, I had asked Liza to clarify the structure of the household; the couple was living permanently with her family, not his as is more common. I now sensed something further, and very unusual for a South Indian family: he is distant from his natal family and allied with his wife. My puzzlement stimulated a question-and-answer exchange, and an embedded second story, linked to and expanding the first.[12]

STORY 2

01 Catherine: But now her husband is with her. Is that right?

02 Liza: I'll ask her.
03 [in Malayalam] Is your husband here always?

04 Celine: Yes.

05 L: For the past eight years?

06 C: When they scolded him,
07 told him he should marry another girl,
08 their son used to hurt me a lot at first
09 [unclear] now he won't abuse me

10 L: So your husband is staying here always?

11 C: Yes, yes, he is staying here.

12 L: He doesn't go to his house?

13 C: No.

14 L: What is your husband's reaction about remarrying?

15 C: I told him
16 since we don't have children,
17 "remarry,"
18 then when he remarries he will get children.

19 L: You said that to your husband?

20 C: So that it won't be so hard for him,
21 he will get children when he remarries, right?

22 So he asked me, "Will you stay like this?"
23 I told him, "Yes, it's no problem for me.
24 I'll stay here,
25 you marry again and I'll stay."

26 But then he doesn't leave.
27 Even if we don't have children, can live.

1 L: [in English] She tells her husband that he should marry again.
2 So that he may have children, but he doesn't want to do that.

The narrated events in the second story raise questions about meaning in the first story. Some uncertainties regarding Celine's situation get resolved, but others remain. It is clear that Rajiv has distanced himself from his parents physically, and from their "scolding." Relatedly, perhaps, he has stopped abusing Celine.[13] My first reading of Celine's narrative (and life) as one of victimization at the hands of husband and family because of infertility is clearly inadequate. Similarly, the second story renders my earlier interpretation of Celine's agency somewhat problematic—a woman acting (implicitly alone) to resist the stigma of infertility. Events reported in the second story require that Rajiv be included in any analysis of resistance. He supported her actions against oppressive circumstances. Both partners—separately and together—have challenged dominant discourses and social conventions, and are remaining married despite the disappointment of infertility and social stigma. It appears that Celine and Rajiv have a committed union, although what sustains their marriage (with no children or tie to his family) remains unclear.

Closer attention to the narrative event—the performance of the story—adds meanings and opens up further questions. The performance of Story 2 is a "trialogue" involving a narrator (Celine), translator (Liza), and investigator/interpreter (CR), who, working together as narrator and audience, shape the performance of the story, including the events, plot, and characters allowed onstage. Rajiv, a shadow figure in the first story, returns as a central character in the second, prompted by audience puzzlement (Paget 1983)—my explicit instruction to Liza to inquire about Rajiv. Similarly, his response to his parents' directive to remarry (central to the plot of the first story, and introduced again in the second) is resolved because Liza explicitly asks about it (line 14). Celine's performance of a conversation with Rajiv about remarriage is particularly meaningful:

15   I told him
16   since we don't have children,
17   "remarry,"
18   then when he remarries he will get children.

Whatever a reader might think of remarriage as a "solution" to infertility, Celine voices the recommendation here, not his family as in the first story, to get rid of her. She is the active subject, not the victim of others' views of her worth. Liza seems to be a bit taken aback by the assertiveness, if not the message ("You said that to your husband?"). In the lines that immediately follow, Celine suspends the plot to explain herself in evaluation (Labov 1982), indicating how she wants Liza to interpret the marital conversation: she made the suggestion to relieve him of a difficulty—he will get children if he remarries.[14] She engages in a kind of "reflexive monitoring and rationalization of a continuous flow of content" (Greenhalgh 1995:19). Here she is not a passive object of stigma and abuse—acted upon by others—but an agent of her own life. I wonder whether Celine's statement to Rajiv to have a child with another woman can be read as an act of love. So, too, perhaps can his decision to leave his family and come to live in her village.

Having explained herself to the audience, Celine returns to the plot, and again her agency is palpable:

22   So he asked me, "Will you stay like this?"
23   I told him, "Yes, it's no problem for me.
24   I'll stay here,
25   you marry again and I'll stay."

Celine represents a conversation with reported (reconstructed) speech—a way of telling that achieves effects other ways of telling do not. Often strategically used by narrators to evoke sympathy and build credibility

(Riessman 1990a), the narrative device may serve here to convince Liza, who is an incredulous listener, of the veracity of the marital conversation. It "really happened" just as Celine represents it. Celine voices the recommendation of remarriage from a position of greater power than when it was put forward by her in-laws earlier. It is altogether different if she proposes the "solution," instead of others. Circumstances, too, have changed: she is now in her village, living with her parents. Even if Rajiv leaves her to remarry, she will have family.

But he does not leave. The second story, like the first, ends with a coda, but the conflicts put forth in the story are not entirely resolved. There is considerable ambiguity in the last line, made more so by translation: "Even if we don't have children, can live." I have presented the line exactly as translated, and a key pronoun is missing (not uncommon in Malayalam). Celine's wording in the final clause suggests two possibilities: "I can live" or "we can live"—statements that carry very different meanings.[15] Relatedly, it is not clear from the performance who is speaking the last line of the story. Is remaining childless (the solution suggested) voiced by Celine or Rajiv? If it is her line, she is again challenging stigma and social convention—life is possible even for a South Indian village woman who does not have children. If it is his line (and it is strategic and effective for a narrator to give the evaluation of a narrative, and the last line of a performance, to another character), the message carries additional tender meanings: he views their life together as important, even without progeny. He is willing to face stigma himself by permanently remaining with a wife who cannot conceive. Could the last line be hinting at a love story?

I have explored several provisional readings of a South Indian woman's narrative about marriage and infertility. Like all stories, Celine's have ambiguities and relative indeterminacies. The texts are sparse, there are gaps and uncertainties, and they leave considerable room for reader response. Those who read the stories enter them and participate in constructing their meaning. Readers can even imaginatively rewrite the narrative (Iser 1978).

My readings have been guided by a theoretical interest in how a woman, facing stigma, violence, and rejection when she cannot conceive, operates "stealthily in the interstices of power" (Martin 1987:182) in a South Indian family. Another reader might view the text as an instance of the victimization of women who live in poverty. There is some support for such a reading, but, I have argued, it is insufficient. The structure of the text sets up a series of cues and interpretive questions, and it rules out others (Gee 1991). Like other stories of women's resistance and survival, the oppositional practices in this tale include an active rather than a passive heroine, and the depiction of strategies against male violence and stigmatization (Maclean 1987). The narrative represents a gendered telling, listening, and reading. The analysis also reflects my changing position regarding the narrative—my visions and revisions of its meaning.[16]

Multiple readings are potential in all narrative work. The problem becomes highly visible when investigators work with narratives in another language, and those that appear "strange" in other ways. Translation can open up ambiguities of meaning that get hidden in "same-language" texts. When we have a common language with our informants, we tend to easily assume that we know what they are saying, and alternative readings tend to get obscured, or even ignored, because of the methodological and theoretical assumptions we bring to the work. Misunderstandings can also get obscured when working with same-language narratives (Behar 1993; Riessman 1987). Future research in other cultures and languages is important for fuller understanding of the topic. Temple suggests some of the issues:

> The use of translators and interpreters is not merely a technical matter that has little bearing on the outcome. It is of epistemological consequence as it influences what is "found." Translators are active in the process of constructing accounts and an examination of their intellectual autobiographies, that is, an analytic engagement with how they come to know what to do, is an important component in understanding the nature and status of the findings. When the translator and the researcher are different people the process of knowledge construction involves another layer. (1997:614)

Other dilemmas of particular relevance for narrative research include problems of translation and meaning for English-speaking audiences, story structures in different languages and how to represent them, and issues of the written representation of translated materials (e.g., translating a translated narrative). There is a creative element in all translations and in all representations of the spoken word.[17]

Extending the insights of Goffman (1963), my representation and interpretation of the narrative has emphasized women's agency in the face of stigma. Yet it is clear that Celine did not act alone. She cannot resist the master narrative for women in India by herself. Her husband's place in her resistance process cannot be ignored, even if uncertainty remains about his precise role. Nor does she state how her family's responses may have enabled her actions. Narrative analysts never have the whole life story; we work with fragments.

To emphasize women's agency is not to minimize social structural factors. Research participants—investigators, translators/interpreters, and subjects—are constituted by the cultural and structural frameworks available to them, which provide the only way they have of interpreting their lives (or research materials). I have suggested some of the ways in which my social location and precommitments, and Liza's, influenced our respective interpretive processes and relationships with informants. Celine, too, has resources at her disposal to aid interpretation and action. As Sen (1999:xii) argues, "There is a deep complementarity between individual agency and social arrangements."

Kerala—the regional setting for Celine's narrative and life—is unique in India (even South India). Women there have freedoms, notably higher status, relative to women in other parts of India. Kerala has invested in primary and secondary education for both girls and boys, even in remote rural areas. Consequently, Celine is literate—far surpassing the majority of Indian women in educational attainment. Schooling enlarges comprehension of public health information and the ability to interpret destructive elements in the environment, and it encourages social participation—taking action. Education increases women's capabilities, self-concept, and bargaining power in marriage. Celine's narrative (especially the second story) suggests a degree of gender equality in marriage, and a social position impossible in areas of India where girls are not educated beyond primary school. Kerala's history provides another resource, specifically a traditional model of matrilineal family organization among a dominant caste, which benefits women, compared with patrilineal patterns, and moderates the impact of childlessness. Although matrilineal traditions have changed, it is still expected that the wife's closeness to maternal kin will continue after marriage, and it is not uncommon for married women to go back to the mother's house for various purposes. (This is generally true in South India, but more common in Kerala.) Cross-cousin marriage patterns (also common in the region) further cement closeness to natal kin. Nucleated families are not unusual in the contemporary period, and typically couples live where economic circumstances are best. Thus Celine and Rajiv can escape harassment and oppressive circumstances in the joint family and reside in her natal home, choices not open to other Indian women. Pressure to have children is less great in Kerala, too, with the acceptance of small family norms.

The development policies of Kerala empower gender relations—

through education and credit availability for women, and land reform and political voice more generally.[18] Although progressive aspects of Kerala's political economy do not necessarily translate into jobs for women, they do offer freedoms for women that they use in marriage to become "active agents of their own reproductive destinies" (Greenhalgh 1995:25).

EPILOGUE

Several weeks after interviewing Celine, I chanced upon her again. Walking down the path to the beach, I passed her house. She was squatting over a stone, grinding spices for the family's fish curry, perhaps. Spotting me, she motioned for me to come and sit with her under a coconut palm. We communicated as best we could—gestures, my bits of Malayalam, her bits of English (all Malayalees study English, among other languages, in the village school). She stroked my arm, examined my "white" skin (heavily tanned by the hot sun), and seemed curious about my moles. It felt as if the usual fixed divide in fieldwork between Self and Other, subject and investigator, had blurred, but not because of an essential, cross-cultural sameness between us. Our "womanhood was only a partial identity" (Abu-Lughod 1995:377). There was a profound difference in our sameness—nationality, language, education, religion, social class, motherhood—that gender could not erase.

Rajiv emerged from the house, and, still holding my hand, Celine called out for her husband to join us and pointed to a cluster of coconuts high above our heads. Rajiv smiled, shimmied up a tree, knocked down several nuts, cracked open several green ones with his machete, and carefully scooped out the gelatinous interior. We shared the moist fruit.

Coconuts, like narratives, are abundant in Kerala, and as intimate parts of the culture, they carry many meanings and uses—material, religious, medicinal. There is even a suggestion of fertility motifs. Here the offer of a coconut was a sign of hospitality from a family that was poor but not destitute, an intimate invitation to me to join their lives.

As we ate the glistening fruit, I remembered Celine's narrative about the early years of her marriage: stigma and rejection when she did not conceive, beatings, the threat of abandonment. I looked at Celine and Rajiv now laughing, performing a love story that invited me into their relationship. Although I was tempted to construct a Western ending to my narrative of their marriage ("They lived happily ever after"), I was reminded of depressed feelings Celine had expressed at points in our interview regarding not having children.

But the couple would enter their thirties soon. In the ebb and flow of adult relationships (I had learned from fieldwork), urgent pressures for children become attenuated. An ideational change was possible: they could transform their biological "failing" and construct a social family. As we ate the coconuts together, I sensed I might be witnessing a performance of the coda: "even if we don't have children, [we] can live."

ACKNOWLEDGMENTS

I thank "Celine," Liza George, and other women who taught me during fieldwork. I am grateful for critiques of earlier versions from Elliot Mishler, Sara Dickey, Joan Mencher, Margareta Hydén, Lars-Christer Hydén, Vicky Steinitz, an anonymous reviewer, and my philosophy study group. The Indo-U.S. Subcommission on Education and Culture, Council for the International Exchange of Scholars provided financial support for fieldwork.

NOTES

1. On family interviews in Turkey where one member had epilepsy, see Good and Good (1994).

2. Malayalam is a member of the Dravidian family of languages, which are spoken in South India. Pronominal reference and verb tense are often ambiguous, and must be inferred from the surrounding discourse. Regarding the interviews, my representation of the translated talk has benefited from conversations with Liza while I was in India, and with India specialists since my return to the

United States. Liza conducted the interviews, translated and transcribed most of them, and checked the others. Her insights about meaning have been incorporated into my translations and editing of the narratives, but I also differ with her interpretation at a key point (see note 10).

3. The World Health Organization notes that high fertility rates may, in fact, mask infertility in the same country. Worldwide 8 to 12 percent of couples experience some form of infertility during their reproductive years (World Health Organization 1991), and rates for developing countries are higher (Wasserheit 1989; Berer 1999; Okonofua and Snow 1999).

4. For a reflexive account of the research, see Riessman (1995a, 2000).

5. I use *story* and *narrative* interchangeably in this chapter (but see Riessman 1990b). My use suggests a more restricted definition than other authors do: a particular kind of discourse that is organized structurally and sequentially (temporal or otherwise). There is considerable disagreement among scholars about the precise definition of narrative (Riessman 1993), and how one locates the boundary between text and context (Peterson and Langellier 1997).

6. For example, I typically inserted pronouns in the English texts where they are assumed in Malayalam (pronominal reference was often absent in the initial translations; see note 2). I edited syntax that was a direct translation from Malayalam to make it less awkward in English. The transformation of spoken language into written text is an interpretive practice, regardless of the language spoken (Mishler 1991). As Derrida argues, translation creates the "original" text: it depends for its existence on translation, and different versions are possible (cited in Temple 1997).

7. Dowry transactions have been illegal in India since the Dowry Prohibition Act of 1961, but they continue, and demands have inflated with India's market, cash economy. Dowry murders have apparently risen as well (Stone and James 1995). Feminist organizations in India are currently active in the antidowry movement.

8. On the distinction between narrated event and narrative event, and their interdependence, see Bauman (1986).

9. See Riessman (1987) on the typical use of chronological time to establish sequence in personal narratives, and the potentials for misunderstanding when narrators use other forms of organization.

10. There is evidence for my interpretation here. As we were walking away from the house after the interview, Liza told me it was the "saddest case she has heard so far," and her translation to me stressed "abuse" (her lexical choice). She was clearly upset by the interview, and in subsequent discussions of the research (and related conversations about women's position in Indian society), she often referred to the "sad case." Liza's "translation" of Celine's experience differs from mine, a consequence no doubt of our contrasting positions, biographies, nationalities, and gender ideologies (Temple 1997).

11. There is another place later in the interview when Celine lowers her voice in a similar way: she says Rajiv spends money "for immoral ways . . . [prostitutes] because of the thought of not having children." Like the physical abuse, I suspect his "immoral ways" remain a secret from her family, hence the whisper. Or it may be that they know, but because it is a contentious and shameful issue,

Celine doesn't want them to think about it, or to overhear her telling outsiders about it.

12. See Bell (1988) on linked stories in interviews.

13. But there is ambiguity about timing here: in the first story Celine suggests the abuse may have continued for five years, yet the move back to her village happened six months after the marriage.

14. It is not at all clear from material elsewhere in the interview that the infertility is her problem. Both partners have seen doctors, and the source of their difficulty is ambiguous.

15. I lean toward the second reading, which explains the title for the chapter. In Malayalam, pronominal reference is often ambiguous, and requires the listener to fill in (see note 2). Missing pronouns typically imply the previous one is understood, which supports the second reading.

16. An anonymous reviewer offered an alternative reading of the material: "The husband has chosen to live with his wife's family because it is in a much better financial state than his own. As a son-in-law he may also gain certain advantages—he is treated well and, in addition, given the opportunity to lead a somewhat independent social life with enough money to visit prostitutes—conditions perhaps not available in his family of origin." In the absence of information from Celine's husband, this alternative male-centered interpretation must remain speculative. Not a text-based reading, it is at odds with the structural approach to narrative research developed in the paper. As Temple (1997) argues, there are constraints "placed on the reading of a text by the need to make sense of it on its own terms, and thus while there may be many versions of the 'truth' of a text, each must be made possible by something *within the text, by its logic, syntax and structuring resources*" (p. 609, italics mine). The autobiographies of translators/interpreters (and in this case readers) obviously enter into what's "in the text."

17. For a thoughtful presentation of some of these issues that compares Tamil and English translations of narratives, see Dickey 2000.

18. On the political economy, special ecology, and unique circumstances of Kerala, see George 1993; Gulati, Ramalingam, and Gulati 1996; Jeffrey 1993; Mencher 1965, forthcoming; Nag 1988; Sen 1999; Visvanathan 1993.

REFERENCES

Abu-Lughod, L. 1995. A tale of two pregnancies. In *Women writing culture,* edited by R. Behar and D. A. Gordon. Berkeley and Los Angeles: University of California Press.

Atkinson, P., and D. Silverman. 1997. Kundera's "Immortality": The interview society and the invention of self. *Qualitative Inquiry* 3:304–25.

Bauman, R. 1986. *Story, performance, and event: Contextual studies of oral narrative.* Cambridge: Cambridge University Press.

Becker, G. 1994. Metaphors in disrupted lives: Infertility and cultural constructions of continuity. *Medical Anthropology Quarterly* 8:383–410.

Behar, R. 1993. *Translated woman: Crossing the border with Esperanza's story.* Boston: Beacon Press.

Bell, S. E. 1988. Becoming a political woman: The reconstruction and interpre-

150

Catherine Kohler Riessman

tation of experience through stories. In *Gender and discourse: The power of talk,* edited by A. D. Todd and S. Fisher. Norwood, N.J.: Ablex.

———. 1999. Narratives and lives: Women's health politics and the diagnosis of cancer for DES daughters. *Narrative Inquiry* 9 (2): 1–43.

Berer, M. 1999. *Reproductive Health Matters* 7 (13) [entire issue devoted to living without children].

Bruner, J. 1987. Life as narrative. *Social Research* 54:11–32.

Clark, J. A., and E. G. Mishler. 1992. Attending to patients' stories: Reframing the clinical task. *Sociology of Health and Illness* 14:344–72.

Clifford, J. 1997. *Routes: Travel and translation in the late twentieth century.* Cambridge, Mass.: Harvard University Press.

Dickey, S. 2000. Mutual exclusions: Domestic workers' and employers' narratives on labor, class and character in South India. In *Home and hegemony: Domestic service and identity politics in South and Southeast Asia,* edited by K. M. Adams and S. Dickey. Ann Arbor: University of Michigan Press.

Dube, L. 1986. Seed and earth: The symbolism of biological reproduction and sexual relations of production. In *Visibility and power: Essays on women in society and development,* edited by L. Dube, E. Leacock, and S. Ardener. Delhi: Oxford University Press.

Estroff, S. E. 1995. Whose story is it anyway? Authority, voice, and responsibility in narratives of chronic illness. In *Chronic illness: From experience to policy,* edited by S. K. Toombs, D. Barnard, and R. A. Carson. Bloomington: Indiana University Press.

Fine, M., and A. Asch. 1988. Disability beyond stigma: Social interaction, discrimination, and activism. *Journal of Social Issues* 44:3–21.

Fisher, S., and K. Davis. 1993. *Negotiating at the margins: The gendered discourses of power and resistance.* New Brunswick, N.J.: Rutgers University Press.

Franz, C. E., and A. J. Stewart, eds. 1994. *Women creating lives: Identities, resilience, and resistance.* Boulder, Colo.: Westview Press.

Gee, J. P. 1986. Units in the production of narrative discourse. *Discourse Processes* 9:391–422.

———. 1991. A linguistic approach to narrative. *Journal of Narrative and Life History* 1:15–39.

George, K. K. 1993. *Limits to the Kerala model of development: An analysis of fiscal crisis and its implications.* Trivandrum, South India: Centre for Development Studies.

Ginsburg, F. D., and R. Rapp, eds. 1995. *Conceiving the new world order: The global politics of reproduction.* Berkeley and Los Angeles: University of California Press.

Goffman, E. 1963. *Stigma: Notes on the management of spoiled identity.* Englewood Cliffs, N.J.: Prentice-Hall.

Good, B. J., and M. J. DelVecchio Good. 1994. In the subjunctive mode: Epilepsy narratives in Turkey. *Social Science and Medicine* 38:835–42.

Greenhalgh, S., ed. 1995. *Situating fertility: Anthropology and demographic inquiry.* New York: Cambridge University Press.

Gulati, L., Ramalingam, and I. S. Gulati. 1996. *Gender profile: Kerala.* New Delhi: Royal Netherlands Embassy.

Iser, Wolfgang. 1978. *The act of reading: A theoretical aesthetic response.* Baltimore: Johns Hopkins University Press.

Jeffery, P., R. Jeffery, and A. Lyon. 1989. *Labour pains and labour power: Women and childbearing in India.* London: Zed.

Jeffrey, R. 1993. *Politics, women, and well-being: How Kerala became "a model."* Delhi: Oxford University Press.

Jindal, U. N., and G. Dhall. 1990. Psychosexual problems of infertile women in India. *International Journal of Fertility* 35:222–25.

Jindal, U. N., and Gupta, A. 1989. Social problems of infertile women in India. *International Journal of Fertility* 34:30–33.

Kleinman, A. 1988. *The illness narratives: Suffering, healing, and the human condition.* New York: Basic Books.

Labov, W. 1982. Speech actions and reactions in personal narrative. In *Analyzing discourse: Text and talk,* edited by D. Tannen. Washington, D.C.: Georgetown University Press.

Langellier, K. 1989. Women's personal narratives: Strategies of resistance. Paper presented at the annual meeting of the Speech Communication Association, San Francisco.

———. In press. "You're marked": Breast cancer, tattoo and the narrative performance of identity. In *Narrative and identity,* edited by J. Brockmeier and D. Carbaugh. Amsterdam and Philadelphia: John Benjamins.

Lateef, S. 1990. *Muslim women in India.* London: Zed.

Maclean, M. 1987. Oppositional practices in women's traditional narrative. *New Literary History* 5:37–50.

Mahoney, M. A., and B. Yngvesson. 1992. The construction of subjectivity and the paradox of resistance: Reintegrating feminist anthropology and psychology. *Signs* 18:44–73.

Martin, E. 1987. *The woman in the body: A cultural analysis of reproduction.* Boston: Beacon Press.

Mencher, J. 1965. The Nayars of South Malabar. In *Comparative family systems,* edited by N. N. Nimkoff. Boston: Houghton Mifflin.

———. Forthcoming. The Nayars of Kerala. In *Encyclopedia of Indian studies,* edited by K. David.

Miall, C. E. 1986. The stigma of involuntary childlessness. *Social Problems* 33: 268–82.

Mishler, E. G. 1984. *The discourse of medicine: Dialectics of medical interviews.* Norwood, N.J.: Ablex.

Mishler, E. G. 1986a. The analysis of interview-narratives. In *Narrative psychology: The storied nature of human conduct,* edited by T. R. Sarbin. New York: Praeger.

———. 1986b. *Research interviewing: Context and narrative.* Cambridge, Mass.: Harvard University Press.

———. 1991. Representing discourse: The rhetoric of transcription. *Journal of Narrative and Life History* 1:255–80.

———. 1995. Models of narrative analysis: A typology. *Journal of Narrative and Life History* 5:87–123.

———. 1999. *Storylines: Craftartists' narratives of identity.* Cambridge, Mass.: Harvard University Press.

Nag, M. 1988. The Kerala formula. *World Health Forum (Geneva)* 9 (2).

Okonofua, F. E., and R. C. Snow. 1999. *African Journal of Reproductive Health* 3 (1) [entire issue devoted to infertility and woman's reproductive health in Africa].

Paget, M. A. 1983. Experience and knowledge. *Human Studies* 6:67–90.

Peterson, E. E., and K. M. Langellier. 1997. The politics of personal narrative methodology. *Text and Performance Quarterly* 17:135–52.

Riessman, C. K. 1987. When gender is not enough: Women interviewing women. *Gender and Society* 1:172–207.

———. 1990a. *Divorce talk: Women and men make sense of personal relationships.* New Brunswick, N.J.: Rutgers University Press.

———. 1990b. Strategic uses of narrative in the presentation of self and illness. *Social Science and Medicine* 30:1195–200.

———. 1993. *Narrative analysis.* Qualitative Research Methods Series, No. 30. Newbury Park, Calif.: Sage.

———. 1995a. Locating the outsider within: Studying childless women in India. *Reflections* 1 (3): 5–14.

———. 1995b. Women searching for fertility in South India: Narrative representation of experience. Paper presented at the annual meeting of the American Anthropological Association, Washington, D.C.

———. 2000. Stigma and everyday resistance practices: Childless women in South India. *Gender and Society* 14:111–35.

———. In press. Positioning gender identity in narratives of infertility: South Indian women's lives in context. In *Interpreting infertility: Childlessness, gender, and the new reproductive technologies in global perspective,* edited by M. C. Inhorn and F. van Balen. Berkeley and Los Angeles: University of California Press.

Sen, A. 1999. *Development as freedom.* New York: Knopf.

Stone, L., and C. James. 1995. Dowry, bride-burning, and female power in India. *Women's Studies International Forum* 18:125–34.

Temple, B. 1997. Watch your tongue: Issues in translation and cross-cultural research. *Sociology* 31:607–18.

Uberoi, P., ed. 1993. *Family, kinship and marriage in India.* Delhi: Oxford University Press.

Unisa, S. 1999. Childlessness in Andhra Pradesh, India: Treatment-seeking and consequences. *Reproductive Health Matters* 7 (13): 54–64.

Visvanathan, S. 1993. *The Christians of Kerala: History, belief, and ritual among the Yakoba.* New Delhi: Oxford University Press.

Wasserheit, J. N. 1989. The significance and scope of reproductive tract infections among Third World women. *International Journal of Gynecology and Obstetrics,* suppl. 3:145–68.

World Health Organization. 1991. *Infertility: A tabulation of available data on prevalence of primary and secondary infertility.* Geneva: World Health Organization.

SEVEN

Broken Narratives

*Clinical Encounters and
the Poetics of Illness Experience*

LAURENCE J. KIRMAYER

Language doesn't only build bridges into the world, but also
into loneliness.

Paul Celan

Contemporary medical anthropology has put increasing emphasis on
narrativity in accounts of suffering and healing (Good 1994; Kleinman
1988). The analysis of narrative seems to give us a way to understand
how personal and cultural constructions of illness become stabilized, re-
ified, and socially embodied through stories told to self and others. But
narratives are not the only constituents of experience. Indeed, in acute
illness, narratives are often fragmentary or undeveloped; where narratives are most coherent, they also may be formulaic and distant from
sufferers' experience. Prior to narratization, salient illness experiences
are apprehended and extended through metaphors (Kirmayer 1992).
These metaphors may subvert the project of narrative and come to dominate the sense of self (Kirmayer 1994a).

For many illness episodes, narrative represents an end point, not a beginning. In psychotherapy, we try to construct coherent narrative out of
symptoms and behaviors that make no sense or struggle to revise mis-
prisoning stories that make hurtful sense. Sufferers are encouraged to discover new narrative possibilities latent in their own metaphors of self
and illness (Kirmayer 1993b). For classical psychoanalysis and other
forms of therapy devoted to uncovering "genetic" or historical truth, the
goal of therapy is the retelling of hidden (suppressed or repressed) narratives, either as an end in itself (insight is a virtue that confers status on
its holder within the psychoanalytic community) or to trade in for a new
story, a revisioned account of the self as victim, survivor, and author of

its own heroic journey (Spence 1982; Schafer 1992). Work in cognitive and developmental psychology—and on the philosophical underpinnings of psychoanalytic interpretation—has challenged the historical veracity of the accounts produced in psychotherapy and shown how such accounts are shaped by narrative templates given by the theory itself.[1] This self-confirming process, however, does not vitiate the potential therapeutic benefit of such narratives. Indeed, solution-oriented, strategic psychotherapies, growing out of the work of Milton Erickson and subsequent generations of family therapists (Kirmayer 1988b), embrace this circularity and have moved toward storytelling and interpretation ("reframing") as ways to remoralize patients and restore a sense of meaning and coherence that can support new patterns of behavior (see, e.g., Gilligan and Price 1993). Similarly, many cognitive psychotherapists have come to emphasize the basis of psychopathology in self-injurious narratives and seek solutions through constructing new narrative accounts of self and others that can sustain more successful social behavior (Neimeyer and Mahoney 1995). For all such constructivist therapies, the goal is to weave the narrative strands of self into a tapestry, a seamless whole or at least a cognitively and socially workable and rhetorically powerful account.

Through narrative we construct a morally valued and conceptually coherent identity and sense of self (Bruner 1990; Freeman 1993; Kirby 1991; McAdams 1991).[2] Narrative conventions serve to stabilize and authorize stories, including those that make up personal history, through direct effects on remembering (narrative conventions guide semantic encoding and reconstruction) and through effects on social acceptance (narrative conventions determine what is considered a credible, coherent, complete, interesting, moving, and morally sound story). Through reconstruction, narrative exerts effects that move backward in time to reshape memories to fit conventions (Bartlett 1932; Neisser 1994; Young 1995). This effect can be therapeutic or pernicious according to the psychological and moral consequences of rewriting the past (Kirmayer 1996).

A corollary of this synthetic function of narrative is that identity can become fragmented through ruptures in narrative. These ruptures can occur because of pathologies including discontinuities in attention (e.g., dissociation; cf. Kirmayer 1994b) or cognitive developmental delays that impair the sense of continuity of self (Chandler and Lalonde 1995). Even where cognition and attention are intact, mundane experiences may undermine our efforts at self-construction. A minimal list of these threats to the narrative coherence of the self would include intrusions of bodily distress; cognitive dissonance that makes us unable or unwilling to assimilate unpleasant but necessary facts about our self; and a wide range of social constraints, including outright sabotage by others with conflicting goals.

Narratives are important for codifying, representing, and remembering experience, but other knowledge structures may be more common— for example, action-schemas, image-schemas, metaphors, and other figures of thought and speech (Gibbs 1994; Lakoff 1993; Turner 1996). Just as fragments of poetry can be written with no overarching narrative, or only the briefest strand hinted at, so can we articulate our suffering without appeal to elaborate stories of origins, motives, obstacles, and change. Instead, we may create metaphors that lack the larger temporal structure of narrative but are no less persistent and powerful. Such fragments of poetic thought may be the building blocks of narrative: moments of evocative and potential meaning that serve as turning points, narrative opportunities, irreducible feelings and intuitions that drive the story onward.[3]

As Ricoeur (1977) has shown, metaphor is literary work "in miniature." Metaphors present narrative possibilities and can be extended to create more complex stories. Even the few words of an isolated trope invoke a whole conceptual space or world. Indeed, metaphor involves the blending of two or more different conceptual spaces (Lakoff 1993; Turner and Fauconnier 1995). A similar process underlies the creation of meaning in more extended narratives like parables, which are structured in terms of core metaphors (Turner 1996).

At the same time, the meaning of metaphor itself depends on a larger narrative context that may exist prior to or independently of the specific metaphor. This overarching narrative can generate divergent metaphors. Metaphors then may function as gestures toward a story that is not taken up and completed or as reminders of a story that is already authoritative (even if it remains implicit or untold). Metaphor therefore occupies an intermediate ground between embodied experience and the overarching narrative structures of plots, myths, and ideologies (Kirmayer 1992, 1993b).

Although the notion of narrative in medical anthropology has borrowed heavily from literary theory, the metaphors of reader, writer, and text obscure essential features of clinical storytelling. The act of telling one's story, no less than the act of "reading" implicit in diagnosis and therapeutic interpretation, occurs in a social context radically different from that of the writer carefully composing a text for publication. Everyday stories are more fragile, inconsistent, and incomplete than a self-consciously constructed text. The clinician, as reader, is heavily constrained by the institutional context and the necessity to act based on his reading of the situation.

A more apposite rendering of the clinical situation would borrow from another field of criticism, that of rhetoric. If we think of rhetoric as the verbal art of persuading others, we see it at work in clinical conversation and interaction as patient and healer try to influence each other to reach a mutually satisfying conclusion or way to continue. Studies of rhetoric suggest that much argument and effort to influence others rests on the poetic/evocative use of language (Perelman 1982). The task for a discourse poetics of the clinical encounter, then, is to understand how patient and clinician fashion a conversation that embodies experience, gains them rhetorical power, and both challenges and contributes to larger narrative structures, including both the patient's life narratives and the textual authority of medicine.

While this chapter is concerned with the poetics of discourse, I approach discourse not from the model of linguistics as a self-contained structural system but from pragmatic and anthropological viewpoints as a culturally mediated human encounter in which active agents struggle to negotiate meaning with materials given to them by the cultural surround—a milieu into which they must then take any meaning they have managed to construct. Thus the interpretive system I use appeals to cultural knowledge about the intentions of actors and the larger institutional ideologies and practices that inform and constrain their individual agendas.

These considerations of rhetoric and pragmatics point to the limitations of the metaphor of narrative as text. *Enactment* offers a better—because broader—notion than writing for how clinical narrative comes into being. Patient and clinician are actors engaged in conversation; although they need each other to tell and enact their stories, at the same time they wrestle with each other to see whose version of the story will be lived. This wrestling itself may become part of the final version of the story, or it may be suppressed to construct an authorizing genealogy. Once authorized and accepted, a story is retold and so persists, becomes stabilized, and influences future stories. This account points to the limitations of literary theory to address what, for medical anthropology, are the central problems in analyzing illness narratives: the relationships of narrative to bodily experience and to social power (Kirmayer 1992; Lock 1993).

In this chapter, I want to examine the elements of illness experience as they are enacted in a clinical encounter to show how different narrative possibilities are tendered but not fully carried out because of cross-purposes between clinician and patient. What exists in place of an overarching integrative narrative, or even two side-by-side texts, is an intercutting of many voices, a heteroglossia, and, ultimately, the mutual subversion of accounts. This subversion leads to the failure to construct a shared narrative on which joint action can proceed. In offering this example, I hope to show that by focusing on narratives in their discursive context, with attention to rhetorical aims, we can identify those situations of flawed reality construction[4] that are among the most significant examples of clinical impasses. These situations of conflict and contestation can reveal structural problems and ideological conflicts in medical care (Waitzkin and Britt 1993); at the same time, they provide important opportunities for the creation of new meaning.

A FIRE INSIDE

The following passages are taken from a transcript of an interview of a patient referred to a psychiatric screening clinic. This twenty-three-year-old woman was referred by a general practitioner concerned that her somatic problems were related to personal difficulties or stress. The interviewer is an experienced clinical psychiatrist at an academic general hospital psychiatry department. The interview was videotaped originally for teaching purposes, to display an exemplary clinical evaluation interview in which the basic goal is to make an assessment and disposition for appropriate treatment or psychotherapy.[5] As such, a crucial part of the clinician's task is to construct a definition of the problem that either identifies it as amenable to psychiatric treatment or sets it clearly in the category of what is unnecessary or impossible to treat within the local mental health care system. For her part, the patient seeks to have her troubles understood, explained, and, most importantly, alleviated.

In the first segment, at the start of the interview, just after the interviewer has told the patient how long the interview will last and that at the end he will give her "an idea of what we can do for you," she explains:

P: OK. I have suddenly, I have been having a tremendous amount of . . . of stomach and heartburn and chest pains, I've been to two gastroenterologists, I've been to St. Elizabeth's Hospital, I've been taking antibiotics, I've had all sorts of X rays, from gastrostropic to large and small intestine. They have mentioned . . . these gastroenterologists, they've mentioned that it's merely a case of nerves, acidity, anxiety, mainly, that wraps it up. And it's very discomforting, very aggravating. I have this burning sensation within my chest and within my stomach. They've given me all sorts of antibiotics, Ativan, to relax my stomach and etcetera, antibiotics, antacids, all sorts of things, and . . . up until now, up until now, it's been five months, five months and a half, close to six months, absolutely nothing.

T: Six months.

P: More or less, between five to six months, yeah.

T: That sounds miserable.

P: More or less, yes. I go to bed, I wake up in the middle of the night with that burning sensation. It's greatly, greatly centered in my stomach area and within my chest.

T: And there's no ulcer

P: They have found absolutely nothing, absolutely nothing. With all the tests that I've taken, absolutely nothing. I've been to Doctor, Doctor Digby, he had referred me to you and they have mentioned that I should go see a psychiatrist to see if it is a case of nerves. But personally, myself, it is not. Because I feel inside that burning sensation where . . . it's discomforting, very aggravating, very, very aggravating. Now . . .

T: Yes.

P: Can you say, personally, is this a case of nerves?

T: Well, why don't we try to find out more about you and see.

In this opening account, the patient clearly sets out her dilemma. First, there is a "tremendous amount . . . of stomach and heartburn and chest pains." Two gastroenterologists, numerous diagnostic tests, and treatment with medication all have been to no avail. The doctors now say it is "merely a case of nerves, acidity, anxiety." While that "wraps it up" for the doctors—an ironic comment on the limits of the clinicians' understanding—it leaves her with the burning pain, the aggravation, and "absolutely nothing" by way of satisfactory explanation or treatment. She then throws down the gauntlet: "Can you say, personally, is this a case of nerves?"

The patient has already given indications that she does not find "nerves" a sufficient explanation. So this question is a challenge to the clinician: Will he repeat the same reductionistic explanation she has already encountered? By asking him to speak "personally," she seems to

ask for his authentic response at the same time as she indicates her reluctance to receive yet another expert opinion founded on the authority
of medical texts.

The clinician is quickly engaged by the question of whether this is "a
case of nerves." Although presented as a technical diagnostic question, at
root this is a problem of social legitimation: of certifying *real* disease versus imaginary or self-engendered, and humiliating, "nerves." "Nerves"
is a common idiom of distress in everyday discourse used to comment
on a wide range of personal and social troubles (Low 1994). In the clinical context, the metaphor becomes contested ground, since it implies a
measure of personal culpability (Kirmayer 1988b, 1994a). By joining in
the patient's quest for legitimation through resolving the causal or ontological status of the problem, the clinician has allowed the encounter
to focus on a question on which the clinical negotiation will ultimately
founder—for if "nerves" for the patient lead outward to social predicaments, for the doctor "nerves" lead inward to intrapsychic conflict or
personality traits assessed against a normative model of psychological
development and family structure.

The patient presents the psychiatrist with two conundrums that challenge his authority on the basis of the failure of the doctors she has already seen: (1) everything has been done to diagnose this problem, but
it remains unnamed; (2) despite treatment, it persists. The doctors have
attempted to explain away her problem as excess acid caused by nerves.
Despite naming it "nerves," the patient can identify no area of tension
or anxiety sufficient to account for the symptoms; if it was "merely
nerves," naming the problem and doing something for "nerves" should
be sufficient to make the pain disappear. The intractable burning pain,
present and irrefutable in her body, is opposed to the explanations about
"nerves" offered by physicians based on textual authority.

After some discussion of her heavy workload of the past semester and
her part-time housekeeping job, the patient introduces a problem in her
social world that doctors have already linked to her distress: a disap-
pointing love affair with a man, an immigrant from the Middle East,
which ended in anger and recriminations. She was attracted to him because he was cultured, refined, and polite, spoke beautifully, and was in-
tellectually her superior. He was "masterful," but different expectations
for heterosexual relationships led to her being "pushed around." The relationship that was "loving" and "full of everything" at the start became
an arena of conflict and misunderstanding. The relationship ended just
one month prior to this consultation:

T: You broke up.

P: Sure, I had to, because . . .

T: When was that?

P: Just recently, the month of November. I had to because I was becoming very aggravated and I couldn't take it anymore, I still had the, the sensation within me, now, I really can't pinpoint if this, surely, this did begin in July, but I guess it also was the cause of my relationship, too. I must admit, but not fully, fully. And they have mentioned that, these gastroenterologists have mentioned that all the tension and the aggravation and the anxiety that you have taken from him . . .

T: He was giving you a stomachache. That's, that's the hypothesis.

P: More or less, more or less. I have reached to a conclusion that yes, he did give me what I had inside but why is it still continuing? If . . .

T: OK, that's a good question.

P: Why do I still have the sensation, why do I feel that I have more than a case of nerves? Why . . .

He gave her what she has inside—the burning pain, but also the emptiness she feels. Now she wants to be "free and liberated," no longer subservient to a man who made increasing demands for acquiescence and obedience. But since she has thought her way free of this confining relationship, why does the burning continue? Working the causal connection backward, she alludes to one possible explanation: she continues to think of him, so he continues to be present in her.

T: Are you worried about him? Since you've broken with him?

P: To tell you very frankly, there are times where all those very good, and those loving memories flash right by me, but there are plenty times where I have those aggravating moments and those bad mem . . . , bad memories that I have flash by me, too. Deep in my heart, there is usually, after a relationship, there are little spots in the heart where you still feel that you love him. But I've turned out to be so bitter inside because I guess he made me suffer at the very last minute, the last point, and he's made me very aggravated. Now, I don't know if his aggravation is leading to my stomach and chest pain, burn, pain, that, I'm trying to find out. But there are times that I wake up and I'm crying, that I do feel lonely and very hurt, used.

T: Angry, still?

P: More or less, yes. More or less.

The burning pain is a residuum of her relationship, an active bodily process through which she remains connected to her boyfriend. This is clearly a sort of psychosomatic explanation, but the clinician fails to explore her epistemological grounds for this connection. Following a common folk and professional psychological notion that links anger with stomach acid (and, perhaps, searching for the emotion that is downplayed in her self-presentation), the clinician ignores her mention of crying, feeling lonely and hurt, and picks up on the theme of anger implicit in her mention of aggravation.

The patient's family did not approve of the relationship because of differences in ethnicity, religion, and citizenship. The breakup coincided with the intensification of her symptoms (they worsened even though the stress of schoolwork was over for the semester), and her family responded with solicitous concern—a point which the interviewer, eager to find evidence of secondary gain,[6] immediately picks up on:

T: So your symptoms have made your mother fuss over you more.

P: She's very worried, very, very, very worried and, more or less, we've reached a point where we're both fed up. I'm . . . I've reached a point where I'm tired, because what's inside of me is very discomforting, like, at the present moment now, I have, I have a lit fireplace inside of me, which is very terrible, very, very discomforting. They've also mentioned that, you know, I produce too much acid inside of me, which, I have my meals, my stomach burns.

T: Does your mother have to make special meals for you?

P: Oh yes.

The burning is a "lit fireplace," a discomfort that goes on and on, tiring both the patient and her mother, who must prepare special meals to avoid aggravating her daughter's condition. For the patient this is simple comfort; for the clinician it is evidence of reinforcement of the sick role and, perhaps, of pathological enmeshment of mother and daughter.

After discussing the patient's relationship to her mother and father, the interviewer turns the conversation back to the relationship with her boyfriend, as someone who challenged her parents' expectations for her. He also reviews her school career, determining that she took longer than average to finish high school. Finally, he inquires about her larger social world:

P: To tell you very frankly, I'm very closed and very reserved, I'm very quiet, I'm to myself. There are times where I wake up, there are times at work, if I got out, I'm very closed, I'm very quiet, very lonely inside, very lonely, very depressed . . . I do have a couple of friends, but at the present time now, I'm very closed and I'm very reserved because I, inside I feel very hurt, very used. And at work, I just feel like crying because I

> feel left out. A friend has suggested that it's all in my mind. Is it all in
> my mind, is it myself?

Again, the ontological question: "Is it all in my mind?" Yet there is a
pain inside her, in her stomach, and a feeling of sadness "deep inside."
The depth of this feeling makes it hard to talk about, hard to understand
and express.

Telling her story, she has arrived back at a place of loneliness and isolation. Some rupture in her sense of self has occurred: "I saw myself as
a young, respectable lady. . . ." Something has challenged her self-
respect, and she has retreated from a relationship that might have taken
her out of her family of origin, a relationship that, in her choice of boyfriend, already constituted a challenge to her parents' expectations. The
relationship did not work out, and she is left with the dilemma of her
anger and frustration, which are directed not only at the partner who let
her down but, presumably, also at family members who hoped for the
relationship to fail and who are now relieved to have her firmly back in
their orbit.

The patient's narrative of self is sketchy and conventional. There is no
complicated story about who she was and will be, no obstacles to be
mastered, only an effort to reach developmental milestones in a way
appropriate for her chronological age. This uncomplicated life trajectory—which amounts to a lack of plot—is found also in her recollections of childhood; after a few brief recollections of family vacations and
meals, she runs out of stories:

P: That's about it, but I've never, my mom has never really told me
     specifically about my childhood. She told me that I was quite quiet,
     I wasn't . . .

T: How come your mom has to tell you, how come you can't remember
     yourself?

P: I never really looked back in my childhood very specifically, you know,
     point by point, I never really . . .

T: Do you ever think that something was missing in your childhood?

P: No, no, oh no, no, no. As I've reached, now, you know, as a young lady,
     I'm not missing anything.

The interviewer believes he has found unusual lacunae in the patient's
memory that indicate psychological defensiveness, and he challenges this
to see how well she might engage in a psychotherapeutic conversation
oriented toward recollection and reconstruction of her childhood expe-

riences. She resists his effort to elicit dissatisfaction with her childhood and family and emphatically rejects the possibility that something was missing in her childhood. Finally, the clinician uncovers evidence of friction in the family:

T: But what's the re . . . , what's your, the reaction of them to your illness?

P: They're blaming me because of this young gentleman that I've been out with.

T: I see, they say it was your fault for making the mistake.

P: Exactly, exactly.

T: I see.

P: They have mentioned that I could have been more brighter, more wiser, more intellectual, more open-minded, but I guess at that time, love was very blind. Love was very blind and I must admit, yes, I did make a very grave, grave mistake, a terrible mistake. That I must endure . . .

"Love was very blind," and led by it she reached an impasse. This appeal to the conventional metaphor of "blind love" ratifies the authenticity and simplicity of her love and allows her to acknowledge a sense of naïveté but to attach it to "love" rather than to her self.

Having collected information on past and present relationships that allows him to understand the problem as a developmental conflict, the interviewer makes a "trial interpretation" that emphasizes the patient's dependence on her family and the difficulties in finding a partner as a step toward separating from them. Her reaction to this will indicate her ability to make use of insight-oriented, psychodynamic psychotherapy, which would proceed in essentially the same way:

T: Can I suggest to you the following possibility and let's see what you think about it.

P: OK.

T: All your life you've been very close to your mother.

P: Yeah.

T: And, and, in moving outside of that orbit, so to speak, you're kind of unsure of your ground, not quite sure what to look for in a man. Looking for somebody, perhaps, who was older, more sure of himself, could kind of take care of you, and perhaps that has something to do with the fact that in the family, you were your mother's special little girl, maybe had less to do with your father and your brothers, and perhaps didn't know men well enough.

P: Exactly, exactly. My parents want to see me married to a nice, respectable gentleman who will take care of me, not have another relationship like I've had and really put me into pain and sorrow. They just want to see me very happy and healthy, that's all. Like any parents want for their children, happiness and health. More or less.

The clinician leaves uninterpreted the more provocative notion that the choice of a partner from a different ethnic background might also express some opposition to and anger toward her family (cf. Paris and Guzder 1989). After this first sally, however, she turns away from her anger toward the young man and avoids any potential hostility toward her family. The interviewer tries a second interpretation, this time proposing a causal mechanism linking suppressed anger to burning in the stomach:

T: I think you're very angry.

P: Yes, that I know, yes.

T: And, but the anger has nowhere to go, it's going, it's becoming physical because it's like you can't scream, you can't shout, the anger is kind of all bottled up inside.

P: Bottled up.

T: Yeah.

P: OK, all right.

T: And maybe you've always been like that. To some extent.

P: More or less, yes.

T: Yeah.

P: I'm very to myself. There were times where, I remember when I began to love him, I couldn't tell him, face him, I had to write it on paper. There were many times where I had so many things to tell him, I just bottled it up, and he always taught me, my dear, say it, say it, say it. I guess I just felt afraid and just so unsure not to tell him. I'm, as I've mentioned, I'm very closed and very reserved. I usually don't like to say my feelings, depending what situation and what circumstance, more or less. Yes, I am angry because of this relationship that, you know, I have been through, but I'm mainly, mainly aggravated with what I have inside because it's, like I, as I have mentioned, very discomforting, very, very, very painful.

The psychiatrist introduces the metaphor of anger as a fluid under pressure "bottled up inside." This is a conventional metaphor for anger (Lakoff 1987) that has wide currency (Hollan 1988), probably because it reflects experiential qualities of the sort of bodily arousal that accompanies anger (increased heart rate, blood pressure and pulse pressure, facial flushing). Yet while she understands the experiential basis of this metaphor and agrees that her anger is bottled up, she sees it only partially as a result of her loss of relationship and mainly as a consequence of her frustration with persistent stomach pain. Certainly, she does not view the burning pain as a reflection of half-hidden conflicts over autonomy and dependence within her family.

Trying to increase the patient's motivation for psychotherapy, the interviewer makes pessimistic predictions, amplifying the anger metaphor to drive home his point:

T: I don't think your pain is going to go away until you're over this whole thing psychologically, and you're not . . .

P: So you're saying, more or less, psychologically, this is related to what I have inside of me. So, just, it's really a case of nerves.

T: I would say you're boiling over with rage and hurt, actually.

P: OK.

T: And I think that hasn't, that can be like a burning fire inside.

P: OK, all right. Because my mom has also, and I myself, I was thinking if this was not a case of nerves, I wanted to, like, try another top specialist at University Medical Center.

T: Well, OK, well, that's a key question right now because . . .

P: OK.

T: . . . we're going to, we're coming to the end of the, of our interview, we have to decide what to recommend.

P: OK, exactly.

T: And if you're still going to be looking for a physical answer, there's no point to see the psychiatrist, is there? But, are you sufficiently convinced that this is psychological, that you'd be willing . . .

P: I really cannot say, as . . . , what you have explained to me, yes, it is psychological, but I'm also looking for the physical inside of me, because I've also been through a lot of, more or less, internal bleeding, and hemorrhage. I've had, I've broken a vein on the side of my leg, on the left side of my leg . . .

The psychiatrist is hoping for a joint decision ("*we* have to decide what to recommend"). He introduces strongly dualistic thinking (the problem is either psychological *or* physical), then tries to soften the dichotomy. This "either-or" presents a narrative bifurcation into two potential narratives: one that assimilates her pain to "psychological" issues, and the other that treats the pain as evidence of physical injury. Forced to choose, the patient opts for the independence—and hence authenticity and seriousness—of her physical problems. She returns to her bodily affliction by mentioning broken blood vessels, but the psychiatrist does not see the connection between her leg and her stomach. What is salient for him is not the fact of bleeding or some general bodily vul-

nerability but the specific anatomical site of the lesion. In the face of her
insistence on a physical dimension to her problem that demands a physical explanation and solution, the psychiatrist returns to the metaphor
of resistance:

T: Maybe you'd rather not talk about it right now, maybe you're feeling
      like you're too hurt to even discuss it.
P: Depending on who I'm speaking to. Surely, you know, you're in a very,
      you know, educational field and I, I have to respond to you. To others, a
      stranger or someone that, who's going to have a one-to-one correspon-
      dence to me, maybe I will, but I don't want to be, at home, my parents
      and others will bring up his name and himself, there are times where
      I'm still speaking to my parents, pardon me, to my mom, about him.
      But I try to close the case as much as I can. Because . . .
T: Yeah, I guess we're suggesting reopening the wound, in a way.
P: But if this is going to reopen the wound, is it really going to . . .
T: Sometimes you have to reopen the wounds to make them heal.
P: So true. Very logical. But I don't know if I have a wound inside to be
      healed, I don't know, I really cannot say if it's going to be healed.
T: Well I can't give you a guarantee either.
P: Yeah, very true.

Despite all the time they have spent in the interview talking about the
social world, she insists her body needs more attention, that her physical health really is at stake. She acknowledges that talking about her
difficulties helps her emotionally but that she needs physical help as well.
Ironically, despite the fragmented or truncated nature of her story, the
patient is more able to acknowledge the situated nature of her speech
("depending on who I'm speaking to"), and the many directions it might
take, than the psychiatrist, who is determined to follow one line of explanation. The irony grows as she notes that his appeal to the metaphor
of reopening wounds is logical—of course, it is not logical but rhetorically effective because it is a powerful figure—but perhaps neither em-
pirically true nor efficacious.

The psychiatrist again presents the patient with an either-or in the
form of a logical implication: if she insists on seeking more medical
opinions and investigations about her pain, then she is not ready for psychotherapy. Only when she is ready to give up the search for a physical
cure can she begin to focus productively on the psychological dimensions of her problem. She is not convinced that psychological help will
eliminate her physical problem, although the psychiatrist thinks it will.
He interprets her reluctance to give up the search for physical cure and

commit to a purely psychological approach as resistance to dealing with emotional issues:

T: But you're afraid it might even be worse if we get into this. You might end up . . .

P: More or less, yes.

T: We might kind of like . . .

P: Pin . . .

T: Blow, blow the fire even hotter.

P: Pin, pin the point on the donkey, more or less.

T: That's a risk, but I guess you'd have to feel that . . .

P: Because that's what . . .

T: Yeah.

P: As you've noticed, I'm looking at a physical side, mainly. I don't know why, but I'm just looking at that too.

T: I would suggest the reason you're looking at it is because the other side scares you.

P: Are you telling me that emotionally, I'm a little mixed up?

T: I would say, I would say that you probably have never . . .

P: What do you see me . . .

T: [I would say . . .

P: [right now at the point?[7]

T: I would see you as a person who has never had the opportunity to think through her emotions very clearly. I don't know if anyone has ever helped you with that.

P: No, no, no, no. That's very true, I've, true, the emotions that I have are mainly, just, out, unlearned, straightforward, that's all.

T: OK. Anything else you want to ask me before we stop?

P: No, not really.

T: OK. So you're going to give me a ring.

P: More or less, yes, and I will give you, I'll let you know.

Not surprisingly, she does not return for follow-up at this clinic. The psychiatrist has presented her with a Hobson's choice: give up on physical diagnosis and treatment even though I can give you no definite alternative diagnosis and little assurance that psychological treatment will make things better.

While the patient has given him stretches of narrative about the vicissitudes of a relationship and its unhappy end, about stress and anger causing stomach acidity and burning pain, and about a mother and father reacting to her illness with concern, she presents these as unrelated narrative strands. For his part, the interviewer has elicited bits of historical information and interpreted them in terms of his own preexisting theoretical schema to construct a competing narrative that integrates the separate strands:[8] she has been overprotected or enmeshed in her family of origin; she chose someone from a markedly different background than her family to try to distance, differentiate, and ultimately separate from her mother. This motivation biased her mate selection in a way that undermined the possibility of finding an appropriate partner. Having had the relationship fail, she is now firmly back in the orbit of her family. She chafes at this dependence, but the effort to preserve self-respect and family harmony makes her unable to name or face that component of her anger that is directed at family members.

The interviewer's theory-driven hypothetical narrative provides a larger story in which he inserts and contextualizes her account. He then makes tentative interpretations intended to get her to acknowledge this larger story. She fails to do this, returning to elements of the story that she describes as disconnected or related only through the persistence of the burning pain. The failure to endorse the connections the psychiatrist has made is then interpreted as evidence of defensiveness or a lack of psychological-mindedness. As a result, he judges her as less suitable for psychotherapy and gives her a test in the form of a choice that, on the evidence of the preceding interview, she is bound to fail. Her failure to follow through for referral then confirms his hypothesis that she is unable, unwilling, or unready to pursue psychotherapy.

Still, we have to ask why—when she is able to use the psychosomatic schema given to her by the doctors (and very close to popular notions of nerves and ulcers as responses to stress)—she ultimately rejects the prescription of psychotherapy. Why does this schema of psychosomatic causation not provide a coherent framework for a story that would prompt a search for a psychological cure? The conventional psychiatric account of this failure to endorse a narrative of psychosomatic causation rests on the notion that the patient has a personality structure or defensiveness that precludes living with the evident connections between her emotional conflicts and her bodily distress. A sociological view would understand this failure in terms of the stigma associated with psychosomatic explanation or as a consequence of the extent to which doctor and patient use different communicative codes that reflect their respective social positions and reference communities.

But the structure of the clinical conversation also reveals more basic bodily and cultural reasons for this failure to agree on an explanation. At the level of bodily experience, the failure of the psychological narrative reflects its limitations before the power and insistence of somatic distress. In illness we have the breaking through into consciousness of nonnarratized, inchoate experience that resists narrative smoothing and containment. At a social level we have the conflicting interests of doctor and patient, who take up each other's metaphors for different ends. This play of cross-purposes tears apart the fragile world of shared experience. Examining this failure to construct a mutually satisfying joint narrative, we can begin to catalog the many ways that narratives are broken.

VOICES IN THE CLINICAL ENCOUNTER

This account illustrates the heteroglossia characteristic of all clinical encounters. Doctor and patient are attempting to communicate, but their conversation is heavily constrained by the demands of the situation and their efforts to present an appropriate face to each other. Each speaks from a different position, which includes awareness of both the interactional context and its relationship to larger social spheres. Each speaks with the voice of the self but invokes the voices of others. Indeed, we can understand this conversation not simply as an exchange between two conversational partners but as the antiphony of many voices in the wings.

At various moments in the conversation, we have the voice of the body, the voice of medical authority (which is both temporal and textual), and muffled voices of the family. Each voice carries a particular form of authority and conviction for the partners in this exchange. These voices should not simply be identified with doctor and patient: both participants invoke (and speak on behalf of) different versions of the same voices.

The clinical conversation occurs as an exchange of temporary metaphoric constructions that draw from bodily experience and textual or institutional authority. To authorize an interpretation, each participant in the exchange invokes the authority of the voices of the body (physical experience in its privacy, immediacy, and implacability) and the text (technical knowledge, codified norms, institutional procedures).

Bodily experience reflects both the lived functions and physiology of the body and the physically embodied aspects of the social world. The patient returns consistently to the brute facts of bodily distress. The authoritative voice of her body undercuts the technical authority of the physicians, who explain it as "all in her head." The psychiatrist tries to elide her physical body, to move the conversation from stomach pain to the area of his expertise: psychological conflict and family interaction.

In his attention to her social world, he invites her to let other voices speak through her, but the social body of the family is not present, and its voices remain muted and indistinct.

The clinical conversation also draws from myths or models, overarching narratives that are invested with moral significance and more or less unquestioned truth. Medical authority is part of the mythic world of the patient as well as the physician. But this authority does different work for each. The patient uses accounts of the authority of medical opinion to try to convince the doctor that her problem is physical and intractable, that her problems with her boyfriend are separate from those of her stomach, and that she has no problems with her family. For her, medical authority has created a problem of loss of face by implying that her problem is rooted in her own psychological conflicts. She must manage this assessment interview to save face. She does this both by ironic comments on the inability of physicians to explain or alleviate her symptoms and by appeals to the authority of her own bodily experience to trump the psychiatrist's psychosomatic explanations.

The psychiatrist has a similar problem, since the patient's persistent symptoms and rejection of a purely psychological explanation cause him to lose face. He is merely another in a long line of experts who have failed. Her skepticism about his offer of treatment not only devalues his expertise but also challenges his rhetorical ability to provide a convincing explanation and promote psychotherapy as a solution.

In the middle ground, each participant tries to turn the conversation to his or her advantage—to have his or her point of view taken up by the other, to validate it against shared and implicit cultural values and norms, to save face that is threatened both by the power asymmetries in the relationship and by the recalcitrance of the medical problem. Tentative and shifting metaphors are used to negotiate meaning. Each metaphor delivered into the middle ground can be taken up by the other participant and used for different rhetorical purposes.

This view of conversation as strategic self-presentation—as an effort to protect and promote one's social face or self-depiction—ascribes consciousness and agency to the actors. But conversation presents narrative possibilities, at the level of metaphoric models and figural extensions, that actors are never fully aware of. So, the interaction is more than the fencing of two agents; it occurs within and against a social and cultural background that—no matter how much we wish to acknowledge and empower the autonomy of individual actors—heavily conditions and constrains their vision, rhetoric, and action (Berger 1995).

HOW TO THICKEN A PLOT

In the clinical encounter we find narratives that are broken by the intrusions of symptoms, the incomprehensibility of illness, the inattention
and discounting of powerful interlocutors (like physicians), or the de-
bilitating effects of illness on creative and integrative cognitive functions.
In chronic illness, coherent narratives eventually emerge, but in acute illness we often have a situation where narratives have not yet been constructed or where multiple tentative accounts coexist and compete. Both
the absence and the plurality of narrative raise questions of meaning and
authority—questions that are urgent insofar as patient and clinician
want a satisfactory end to suffering and to their encounter.

Psychodynamic theory argues that gaps in narrative may mask or
hide a deeper narrative that is repressed or denied because of its painful
substance. But the fractures of narrative may also reflect the inchoate nature of illness represented as islands of reason, fragmentary stories, narrative strands, and, above all, poetic evocation through bursts of figural
language (Kirmayer 1992). This emphasis on figures and fragments
rather than extended narratives reflects a basic view of everyday thinking as rooted in poetic refigurations of the world. Research on the central role of metaphor in language and thought supports this view of the
quotidian mind as poetic (Gibbs 1994; Lakoff 1993; Turner 1996).[9] The
structure of narrative itself is built on a scaffolding of tropes just as abstract thought is built up out of sensorimotor and emotional experience
(Johnson 1987; Lakoff 1987, 1993).

Time and space are used to metaphorically structure narrative as
travel along a trajectory (strand, thread, line) or across a landscape (plot).
Below this level of abstraction, there are endless metaphors for narrative
drawn from the terrain of social life. These metaphors for narrative have
implications for or links with cognitive and social theories of psychopathology and for the corresponding processes of psychotherapy.[10]

The notion of trajectory provides one view of narrative structure that
fits the metaphor of life as a journey and behavior as the motion of the
self through space and time. The strong sense of temporal ordering this
gives can be contrasted with the metaphor of narrative as emplotment,
the creating of a larger field or context in which the story is embedded.
In Eco's (1994:33–34) distinction, *story* is narrative with linear progression, *plot* has looping back in time and so violates the ordinary, uni-
directional flow of time through foreshadowing, flashbacks, and other
structural innovations that create new levels of meaning by relating past,

present, and future in spatially ordered ways. From a psychological perspective, what plot adds to the simple narrative of story is teleological structure, usually given by human goals and intentions. Emplotment turns a narrative in which events simply follow one another by contiguity into a narrative that is organized and driven forward by causality.

While the causal structure of narrative can take many forms, Todorov (1981:43ff) distinguishes two broad types: (1) *mythological,* in which the minimal units of causality enter into an immediate relationship with each other; and (2) *ideological,* in which the minimal units of causality do so only by the intermediary of a general law of which they happen to be the illustrations. In mythological narrative, the causality is that of the irreducible agency of the "actants" (i.e., the actors or, in the case of psychological narratives, mental states), while in ideological narratives, the actants are merely exemplars of laws or processes of action, relationship, and transformation, whether these be political, sociological, or physical. Both religious and scientific narratives, including psychiatric explanations, may be either mythological or ideological. In mythological narratives, the various states and agents are granted causal power and autonomy; in ideological narratives, they have power but no real autonomy. In fact, their power can be analyzed in terms of hidden dependencies rather than autonomy.

Much of psychiatric diagnosis and therapeutic interpretation—as we have seen in the case study presented here—involves efforts to turn the patient's acausal story or mythic narrative into an ideological account. This turning of myth into ideology serves three simultaneous functions: (1) it gives a specific kind of coherence to the story; (2) it gives the clinician technical control over the interpretation and continuation of the story; and (3) it reinforces the reality of the ideology from which it draws its structure. These effects will be helpful for the patient only if one of these three consequences are useful to her, that is: (1) the cognitive and social coherence of ideology is superior to the coherence obtained by the mythic narrative; (2) the technical control underwritten by the ideological narrative can somehow alleviate suffering; or (3) the overarching ideology is also invested in by the patient so that its reinforcement is a boon.

The resources that both patient and clinician use to construct an ideological narrative include epistemologies based on specific root metaphors (e.g., psychic causation; personal, family, and social meanings of bodily distress); conventional narrative forms (e.g., models of developmental or moral schemes); and sheer professional authority (i.e., the power to discount, suppress, distort, or reinterpret alternative accounts—in the present instance, the physician's power to diagnose).

The reluctance of the patient to have her story subsumed, redirected, and/or reinterpreted by the clinician is termed "resistance" in psychoanalysis on analogy to broader political resistance to oppression or hegemonic control. Notwithstanding the manifestly unequal power of doctor and patient, we ought to recognize the symmetry in this situation in which the doctor, too, resists the patient's story and tries to overcome it with his own version in which certain hypothetical links (psychological or interactional processes) derived from a therapeutic ideology count for more that the events (symptoms, experiences) themselves. In this sense, the doctor is arguing at once for the metaphorization of suffering and for the concretization or literalness of his metaphors; the patient, for her part, insists on the literal nature of her experience but reserves the right to assert the polysemy of metaphor in her own exploration of the illness. To insist on this symmetry points to a semiotics quite different from that evoked by the metaphor of reader/text. When we reintroduce the real world of asymmetry, it is the use of power (not merely of temporal sequence, perspective, or position) that gives authority to the production and reception of texts, behaviors, and experience.

People do not tell their stories in a vacuum. They must fight (be good rhetoricians or debaters) to tell their story and to have it heard and more or less accepted, authorized, or taken up by others. They try to control the circumstances of its hearing and, to some degree, its interpretation. But the telling is an interaction in which audience (or interlocutor) actively shapes the telling and the teller—indeed, in which more than one story(teller) is active at once, and each shapes the other in an ongoing exchange or contest.

In the end, the patient is not allowed to tell her story, but neither is the clinician able to advance his interpretation as the master narrative, since she fails to return for treatment. To the extent that the master narratives of psychiatry claim healing efficacy, this failure to follow up on treatment and be cured constitutes a threat to its authority. This threat is neutralized by pathologizing the patient—she does not come for treatment because she is not psychologically minded or otherwise not yet ready to hear the truth.

But where does this truth come from? Although psychiatry, like the rest of biomedicine, lays ideological claim to a scientific basis for its interpretations of human action, in practice, the meaning of the actions and experiences of an individual patient are always underdetermined by any existing body of scientific knowledge (Kirmayer 1994a). In place of the scientific truth of strong causal explanation, the clinical ascription of symptom and illness meanings invokes both poetic and narrative forms of "truth." Some interpretations (diagnoses, explanations) are true by virtue of the coherence of the story judged not so much on grounds of logical consistency but in terms of how well it conforms to the overarching narrative forms of myth or ideology; in this context specific metaphors serve a subsidiary function, shoring up an argument or advancing the plot (Spence 1982). Other clinical interpretations are true by virtue of the evocative force of a single image or metaphor in and of itself. In this case a poetic fragment creates its own context of meaning and truth through the associations and actions it evokes (Kirmayer 1993a, 1994a).

The issue of poetic versus narrative truth is important for understanding this patient's experience because she can be viewed either as evasive or as putting forward her own version of the truth. Her poetic truth resides in "the burning," which is held like an eternal flame in the hearth of her belly ("He gave me what I had inside") and, equally, in the epistrophe of her frequent statements "more or less," which mark her doubt and reserve her the right to add something more to or take something less from the psychiatrist's authoritative narrative of her affliction.

CONCLUSION

Medical anthropology is concerned with the interaction of social and personal constructions of illness meaning. In recent work, these constructions are commonly understood as narratives generated by patients, clinicians, and other actors drawing from cultural beliefs and practices to further a specific project of self-presentation or social positioning. However, as a result of structural and ideological constraints (as well as the intrinsic qualities of much illness experience), the narratives presented in clinical contexts are often fragmentary and contradictory, taking the form of potential stories or tentative metaphors. In this chapter I have tried to show how the play of metaphors unfolds in one type of clinical encounter, a screening evaluation for a psychiatric clinic where what is at stake is the very definition of the clinical problem. Analysis of the bodily, psychological, and social embedding of this discourse reveals the ways in which metaphoric constructions are presented by both patient and clinician and either stabilized or subverted on the basis of the differential power and rhetorical skill of the participants. Although there is an effort in the clinical encounter to construct a shared narrative, this often fails when patient and clinician are at cross-purposes. Narrative accounts of suffering and healing can then be understood not as coherent social constructions received ex cathedra but as locally produced and contested essays of meaning that require shifts in the conceptual models and relative social position of actors to pursue.

This perspective gives us a way to enter into the making and breaking of narrative: (1) attend to what is unfinished, incomplete, and tentative—the myriad forms of "nonnarrative" communication; (2) attend to the voices of others who speak through those who are present; and (3) attend to potential stories—those that are hinted at (or assumed) but not told. How can we know what stories are not told, potential or elided? We need a theory or a model that tells us what is expected in the situation. Psychodynamics provides one such account, but knowledge of the social world provides other, largely independent, versions.

We are able to understand the meaning of the tropes and narrative forays of clinician and patient by determining their probable communicative aims or intentions. We understand these intentions vis-à-vis a backdrop of information about the larger myths, ideologies, and institutions that govern the beliefs and practices of clinician and patient. This is the fundamental shift that an anthropological perspective brings to what would otherwise be a purely structural, semiotic analysis of the stylistic turns and rhetorical power of discourse. With attention to the power structures and givens of the social world on one side and the insistence of bodily experience on the other, we are prepared to explore the evocative power, surplus meaning, and narrative potential implicit (embodied) in and through clinical discourse.

The doctor's overall aim in the clinical encounter is to subdue or settle the issue, seeking coherence. The patient's aim is to break through, seeking relief. The problem of efficacy—and the corresponding question posed to discourse poetics—then is: Under what circumstances does one person's coherence become another person's relief? The answer must be sought not in a structural poetics of discourse but in cognitive and social analysis that traces metaphor both inward to its physical embodiment and outward into the world where it functions as part of a rhetoric that confers social power (Kirmayer 1992, 1993b). Close attention to metaphor in lived experience, social interaction, and cultural performance can yield an account of the efficacy—and failures—of healing that goes beyond stylized renderings of literary power or dramatic effect.

Talk of poetics risks aestheticizing illness experience. Yet the use of figural language to evoke images and feelings and to persuade others of the seriousness of one's suffering is central to the play of meanings in the clinical encounter. Whether this is collaboration or contest depends on both the inner resources of patient and clinician and on the ideological and institutional practices that define their goals and constrain their communication.

ACKNOWLEDGMENTS

I would like to thank Barbara Hayton, Yeshim Ternar, and Farzad Zaré-Bawani for helpful readings of earlier versions of this chapter. This work was supported by grants from the Fonds de la recherche en santé du Québec. An earlier version was presented at the annual meeting of the American Anthropological Association, Washington, D.C., November 16, 1995.

NOTES

1. There is by now a voluminous critique of the epistemological basis and empirical truth of psychoanalytic interpretation; most of these arguments apply to the range of psychodynamic psychotherapies. The classic philosophical treatment is Grünbaum (1984). For a wide-ranging review of the shaky empirical basis of psychoanalytic theory, see Macmillan (1997).

2. "Identity is a life story—an internalized narrative integration of past, present, and anticipated future which provides lives with a sense of unity of purpose" (McAdams 1989:161). Explicit, self-conscious links occur between different stages of a person's life—indeed, such links define the stages—and their absence may signal developmental problems to a clinical ear tuned to conventional life narratives.

3. In recent years, metaphor theory has been elaborated within cognitive science (Gibbs 1994; Lakoff 1987; Ortony 1993), discursive psychology (Edwards 1997), and anthropology (Fernandez 1986, 1991; Friedrich 1986; Wagner 1986).

4. The notion of flawed reality construction is developed by Hilbert (1984).

5. The patient gave informed consent for the use of this tape for teaching and research purposes. The transcription follows Mishler's (1984) conventions. Although essentially a verbatim transcript, details have been changed to protect patient anonymity. Her knowledge that it would be viewed by others undoubtedly colors the interview and made her more guarded. Some of her equivocation and reluctance to discuss personal matters may well reflect this special circumstance. A transcript gives only a very partial sense of what is communicated in the actual interview. There are many idiosyncrasies in this woman's use of language. She speaks in a hushed and solemn voice; she tries to use an elevated vocabulary but at times makes malapropisms; she frequently answers simple yes or no questions with "more or less . . . more or less." Many of these odd locutions

also can be understood in the light of information that comes out later in the interview. She is the daughter of immigrants, the first in her family to attend college. Her father has worked as a janitor, her mother cleaning houses of middle-class people. Her speech style expresses her preoccupation with social status and a conscious effort to elevate herself through more cultivated diction. Her qualified agreement "more or less" may reflect this effort at refined speech, but it also allows her to give only partial assent to statements she does not accept without open confrontation of authority.

6. Secondary gain refers to benefits that accrue to the patient as a result of illness and which, therefore, may be motivations for or reinforcers of symptoms and the sick role. In practice, the assessment of secondary gain depends on circumstantial evidence such as the lack of fit of symptoms with physiological models or the patient's style of clinical self-presentation (Kirmayer 1988a, 1994a).

7. Following Mishler's (1984) notation, the pair of opening brackets indicates that the speakers are talking simultaneously.

8. This account of the clinician's implicit narrative is based on later informal conversations with him.

9. One of the five branches of classical rhetoric, *elocutio*, the study of tropes or figures of speech, came to dominate the subject; but many classical and modern accounts have tended to treat figures as deviant or exceptional modes of discourse in which an effect is achieved by transgressing standard usage. The listener recognizes this transgression and adduces the special meaning and affect achieved by the rhetorical use of tropes. Against this view, Sperber and Wilson (1990), along with many contemporary cognitive scientists, psychologists, and philosophers, argue that tropes are standard usage. They suggest that each type of trope achieves its effect by presenting the listener with information that can be used to construct some set of implications that are relevant to the speaker's implied intentions. For example, metaphor involves speaking loosely about things; out of the many different implications suggested by a metaphoric juxtaposition, the listener generates and selects those that are relevant to the speaker's intentions (as inferred from the context, i.e., the history and ongoing flow of a conversation and wider social knowledge). Irony, to take another trope, involves a different inferential process. An ironic statement employs the common conversational move of "echoing" the other's statements. In so doing, it invites the listener to generate the meaning of this echo, which is typically a way of indicating close listening, understanding, or agreement. Irony works to communicate a different meaning (namely, the speaker's disagreement with, or ability to see beyond, the conventional knowledge expressed in the echoed statement) because it relies on evoking strong norms that implicitly contradict the ironic statement. These norms may be moral notions, common factual knowledge, or specific attitudes and values of the speaker or listener, which the listener can be expected to know and which the ironic statement contradicts.

10. A narrative trajectory can branch, loop or reenter itself, be broken or terminate. We could apply dynamical systems theory to these structures of narrative as potential mental dynamics. This links narrative form with cognitive psychological models of psychopathology. As examples of parallels between psychopathology and trajectories of narrative consider: *branching* as multiply-

ing possibilities with growing uncertainty of how to continue leading to scattered thoughts, inability to act and concomitant anxiety; *looping* as obsessive ruminations, returning endlessly to one spot in a narrative to trod it again and again; *terminating* as the abrupt ending or rupture of story with no idea of how to continue which, in the case of the story of self, is a marker of depression or despair (cf. Chandler and Lalonde 1995). These dynamics may be instantiated as either cognitive or social interactional processes, but in either case they are mediated by metaphors that govern the narrative structure of the story. A change in metaphor therefore may change the plot and, with it, the dynamics of thought, allowing us to escape vicious circles of despair and self-alienation, revealing imaginative possibilities that offer a way to continue.

REFERENCES

Bartlett, F. C. 1932. *Remembering.* Cambridge: Cambridge University Press.

Berger, B. M. 1995. *An essay on culture: Symbolic structure and social structure.* Berkeley and Los Angeles: University of California Press.

Bruner, J. 1990. *Acts of meaning.* Cambridge, Mass.: Harvard University Press.

Chandler, M. J., and C. E. Lalonde. 1995. The problem of self-continuity in the context of rapid personal and cultural change. In *The self in European and North American culture: Development and processes,* edited by A. Oosterwegel and R. A. Wicklund, 45–63. Dordrecht: Kluwer.

Eco, U. 1994. *Six walks in the fictional woods.* Cambridge, Mass.: Harvard University Press.

Edwards, D. 1997. *Discourse and cognition.* London: Sage.

Felstiner, J. 1995. *Paul Celan: Poet, survivor, Jew.* New Haven, Conn.: Yale University Press.

Fernandez, J. W. 1986. *Persuasions and performances: The play of tropes in culture.* Bloomington: Indiana University Press.

———, ed. 1991. *Beyond metaphor: The theory of tropes in anthropology.* Stanford, Calif.: Stanford University Press.

Freeman, M. 1993. *Rewriting the self: History, memory, narrative.* London: Routledge.

Friedrich, P. 1986. *The language parallax: Linguistic relativism and poetic indeterminacy.* Austin: University of Texas Press.

Gibbs, R. W. 1994. *The poetics of mind: Figurative thought, language and understanding.* New York: Cambridge University Press.

Gilligan, S., and R. Price, eds. 1993. *Therapeutic conversations.* New York: Norton.

Good, B. J. 1994. *Medicine, rationality, and experience: An anthropological perspective.* Cambridge: Cambridge University Press.

Grünbaum, A. 1984. *The foundations of psychoanalysis: A philosophical critique.* Berkeley and Los Angeles: University of California Press.

Hilbert, R. A. 1984. The acultural dimensions of chronic pain: Flawed reality construction and the problem of meaning. *Social Problems* 31:365–78.

Hollan, D. 1988. Staying "cool" in Toraja: Informal strategies for the management of anger and hostility in a nonviolent society. *Ethos* 16:52–72.

Johnson, M. 1987. *The body in the mind: The bodily basis of meaning, imagination, and reason.* Chicago: University of Chicago Press.

Kirby, A. P. 1991. *Narrative and the self.* Bloomington: Indiana University Press.

Kirmayer, L. J. 1988a. Mind and body as metaphors: Hidden values in biomedicine. In *Biomedicine examined,* edited by M. Lock and D. Gordon, 57–92. Dordrecht: Kluwer.

———. 1988b. Word magic and the rhetoric of commonsense: Erickson's metaphors for mind. *International Journal of Clinical and Experimental Hypnosis* 36 (3):157–72.

———. 1992. The body's insistence on meaning: Metaphor as presentation and representation in illness experience. *Medical Anthropology Quarterly* 6: 323–46.

———. 1993a. La folie de la métaphore. *Anthropologie et Societé* 17 (1–2): 43–55.

———. 1993b. Healing and the invention of metaphor: The effectiveness of symbols revisited. *Culture, Medicine and Psychiatry* 17:161–95.

———. 1994a. Improvisation and authority in illness meaning. *Culture, Medicine and Psychiatry* 18:183–214.

———. 1994b. Pacing the void: Social and cultural dimensions of dissociation. In *Dissociation: Culture, mind and body,* edited by D. Spiegel, 91–122. Washington, D.C.: American Psychiatric Press.

———. 1996. Landscapes of memory: Trauma, narrative and dissociation. In *Tense past: Cultural essays in memory and trauma,* edited by P. Antze and M. Lambek, 173–98. London: Routledge.

Kleinman, A. 1988. *The illness narratives.* New York: Basic Books.

Lakoff, G. 1987. *Women, fire, and dangerous things.* Chicago: University of Chicago Press.

———. 1993. The contemporary theory of metaphor. In *Metaphor and thought,* edited by A. Ortony, 202–51. Cambridge: Cambridge University Press.

Lakoff, G., and M. Johnson. 1980. *Metaphors we live by.* Chicago: University of Chicago Press.

Lock, M. 1993. Cultivating the body: Anthropology and epistemologies of bodily practice and knowledge. *Annual Review of Anthropology* 22:133–35.

Low, S. 1994. Embodied metaphors: Nerves as lived experience. In *Embodiment and experience: The existential ground of culture and self,* edited by T. Csordas, 139–62. Cambridge: Cambridge University Press.

Macmillan, M. 1997. *Freud evaluated: The completed arc.* Cambridge, Mass.: MIT Press.

McAdams, D. P. 1989. The development of a narrative identity. In *Personality psychology: Recent trends and emerging directions,* edited by D. M. Buss and N. Cantor, 160–74. New York: Springer-Verlag.

———. 1991. Self and story. In *Perspectives in personality,* edited by A. J. Stewart, J. M. Healy Jr., D. Ozer, and R. Hogan, 133–59, vol. 3 (pt. B). London: Jessica Kingsley Publishers.

Mishler, E. G. 1984. *The discourse of medicine.* Norwood, N.J.: Ablex.

Neimeyer, R., and M. J. Mahoney, eds. 1995. *Constructivism in psychotherapy.* Washington, D.C.: American Psychological Association.

Neisser, U. 1994. Self-narratives: True and false. In *The remembering self: Construction and accuracy in the self-narrative,* edited by U. Neisser and R. Fivush, 1–18. New York: Cambridge University Press.

Ortony, A., ed. 1993. *Metaphor and thought.* New York: Cambridge University Press.

Paris, J., and J. Guzder. 1989. The poisoned nest: Dynamic aspects of exogamous marriage. *Journal of the American Academy of Psychoanalysis* 17: 493–500.

Perelman, C. 1982. *The realm of rhetoric.* Notre Dame, Ind.: University of Notre Dame Press.

Ricoeur, P. 1977. *The rule of metaphor: Multi-disciplinary studies of the creation of meaning in language.* Toronto: University of Toronto Press.

Schafer, R. 1992. *Retelling a life: Narration and dialogue in psychoanalysis.* New York: Basic Books.

Spence, D. P. 1982. *Narrative truth and historical truth: Meaning and interpretation in psychoanalysis.* New York: Norton.

Sperber, D., and D. Wilson. 1990. Rhetoric and relevance. In *The ends of rhetoric: History, theory, practice,* edited by J. Bender and D. E. Wellbery, 140–55. Stanford, Calif.: Stanford University Press.

Todorov, T. 1981. *Introduction to poetics.* Minneapolis: University of Minnesota Press.

Turner, M. 1996. *The literary mind.* New York: Oxford University Press.

Turner, M., and G. Fauconnier. 1995. Conceptual integration and formal expression. *Metaphor and Symbolic Activity* 10:183–204.

Wagner, R. 1986. *Symbols that stand for themselves.* Chicago: University of Chicago Press.

Waitzkin, H., and T. Britt. 1993. Processing narratives of self-destructive behavior in routine medical encounters: Health promotion, disease prevention, and the discourse of health care. *Social Science and Medicine* 36:1123–36.

Young, A. 1995. *The harmony of illusions: Inventing posttraumatic stress disorder.* Princeton, N.J.: Princeton University Press.

EIGHT

Emergent Narratives

CHERYL MATTINGLY

Suppose that some stories are not told so much as acted, embodied, played, even danced. On such occasions, time itself takes on narrative shape. Actions acquire some of the formal and aesthetic qualities of the well-told tale: drama, suspense, risk, adventure, surprise, plot, a sense of the whole, and especially that sense that something significant is afoot. Let us call these narrative acts "emergent narratives."

Sacred and secular rituals have provided anthropologists places to contemplate moments like these. By and large, the narrative moments that have caught the attention of anthropologists are culturally defined as "high drama," "times out of time," as Abrahams (1986) puts it. Following Victor Turner's inspiration in particular, anthropologists have emphasized the dramatic and narrative aspects of these ritual occasions. For Turner (1986a, 1986b, 1969), narrative moments are bounded by clear cultural markers that separate such occasions from the ordinary routines of everyday life.

The narrative times I explore in this chapter, however, are not so cleanly marked, and it is not always easy to predict when or where these narrative moments will arise. The emergent narratives I consider are small dramas, rituals of the everyday in the world of Western biomedicine. These dramas are minimally planned or arise quite by accident. They are not traditional enactments of any social charters, not the performance of grand narratives. Nor are they performances of formulaic cultural tales, those sorts of stories that have long interested anthropologists (Leach 1984:361). They may draw from and build upon familiar cultural scripts but are not part of a culture's celebrated public dramas. Rather, my focus is on improvisational "little stories," to borrow a term from Lyotard (1984), impromptu minor plots that easily escape the notice of onlookers. Despite their casual and idiosyncratic qualities, despite their fleeting nature, these emergent narratives may have great cultural resonance and deep phenomenological import. This chapter concerns one such "little story" created by a nine-year-old child and her occupational therapist in a New England outpatient clinic. The clinical session I examine is emplotted in such a way that a healing narrative is created; the session exemplifies a performance of healing in the biomedical world.

This chapter is directed to two primary tasks. One is to outline a conception of emergent narrative that has special relevance for certain healing practices. The second is to rely upon this notion of emergent narrative to argue for the close kinship between narrative and experience despite some powerful arguments that contest such a kinship. Though in the space of a single essay these tasks must be undertaken in an abbreviated form, I elaborate some of them more extensively elsewhere (Mattingly 1998a).

The idea that life itself has narrative shape (in the form of personal life stories and collective histories) or that humans naturally think in narrative terms has been argued persuasively by a number of formidable theorists (e.g., J. Bruner 1986, 1990a, 1996; Ricoeur 1984, 1985, 1987; Carr 1986, 1997; Olafson 1971, 1979; MacIntyre 1981, 1997). But powerful arguments *against* the narrativity of lived experience have also been made by literary theorists and some of those anthropologists most intrigued with narrative. From a number of vantage points and across a broad array of disciplines, it has been contended that there is a deep discontinuity between stories told and lives lived and, furthermore, that much is lost or obscured by trying to understand the one in terms of the other. Two presumptions about the natural correspondence between narratives and human events have come under particularly heavy attack from those holding a "discontinuity view," as the philosopher David Carr (1997) labels it. Critics of mimetic or representational positions have challenged what is sometimes dubbed "naive realism," namely, the idea that the stories we tell simply re-present or imitate (in words) prior actions and experiences. Along different but not necessarily incompatible lines, anthropological critics of semiotic paradigms have also argued the need to abandon the notion of action as (narrative) text. The attention of these latter critics is directed to analytic frames in which lived experience and cultural actions are presumed to play out prior narrative texts or scripts. From a semiotic perspective, rituals (for example) enact myths. Within this semiotic frame, cultural narratives are treated as prior to any particular action, event, or experience. Events, one might say, imitate stories. Such claims—at least when identified with semiotic positions—have been provocatively assaulted from many sides. Especially pertinent to my arguments are the challenges offered by performance-minded anthropologists.

Before setting out my own argument concerning emergent narratives in clinical work, I turn to these contemporary critiques. My question, then, will be, is it possible to speak about the narrative qualities of clinical events in the face of some very compelling objections? Further, what do we learn about healing by seeing it as connected to the narrative shaping of clinical actions—a story created in clinical time?

WHY STORIES DON'T IMITATE LIFE: CRITIQUES OF NAIVE REALISM

In modern, and especially postmodern, times, it is often contended that narratives do not mirror life. The basic argument goes something like this. Life is not like a story for two main reasons. For one, narrative has a plot, and life does not. For another, a story has a narrator, which life as lived also lacks. Plots and authoritative narrators are key to what makes a story work as a story—these are rhetorical tools essential for creating narrative meaning. A basic assumption in this line of thinking is that stories significantly distort the form and shape of lived experience precisely *in order to* achieve their meaning and significance. Correspondence theories, the discontinuity critics complain, miss a great deal of the artifice of narrative; the art of the good story depends upon its capacity to dramatically transform lived experience.

Why doesn't life have a plot? The argument, in brief, is that a plot is a unifying structure that gives, to some stretch of time, a beginning, middle, and end. Narratives are teleological structures; they have a "sense of an ending" (Kermode 1966) that life does not. Although we generally read or tell a story from the beginning to the end, and the beginning is chronologically earlier than the ending, this temporal frame only appears to imitate life. Life also proceeds from some earlier chronological point to some later point. (We were born before we got married, had children, and died, for instance.) This apparent imitation in narrative discourse is a mere "chronological illusion" (Barthes 1975). The illusion is created because a story really begins with the ending. That is, it is the ending that tells the storyteller where to start, what to include, as well as where to stop. While life as lived opens onto an uncertain horizon, the storyteller knows what happened next. The simplest example makes this clear. A person might ask, "Have I ever told you about my narrow escape on the streets of Los Angeles?" "No," you reply. "Well," the narrator says, "I was out in L.A. for a job interview. It was a dark and stormy night . . ." And, from there, a story unfolds. The narrator knows what to include, how to foreshadow, what was irrelevant, all because she knows where the story will end. Because the narrator weeds out irrelevant details, those that do not "add up" to the important events of the story, life in story time appears to have a great deal more coherence than it does when we live it.

Our lives unfold in ways that surprise us, that force us to recognize the uncertainty of things. We live, by and large, with no clear recognition of how things will end, trying to portend the significance of current events in light of a future we can only imagine. "The end," writes literary critic Frank Kermode, "is like infinity plus one and imaginary numbers in mathematics, something we know does not exist but which helps us to make sense of and to move in the world" (Kermode 1966:37). Another highly influential literary critic, Seymour Chatman (1978), has argued that the notions of "beginning," "middle," and "end" apply only to story events as imitated rather than to real actions themselves, simply because such terms are meaningless in the real world. Via the magic of narrative, sequence, or "clock time," as E. M. Forster (1927) once called it, is transformed into a plot. Anthropologists and historians preoccupied with "true stories" have echoed literary theorists in affirming that life as lived lacks coherence and plot. Experience is "unruly" (Clifford 1983), a "flux" (Bauman 1986 quoting Mink 1978), elusive, internal, personal, unavailable to language. When the ethnographer becomes the storyteller, she engages in a language game in which the chaos of fluid experience is translated into a coherent, authoritative text (Clifford 1983; Marcus and Cushman 1982; Marcus 1998; E. Bruner 1986). Experience is "alien, even chaotic," difficult to decipher. The story functions as an overriding sense-maker that shepherds, if not annihilates, this realm of confusion. The ethnographer, in this sense, is a storytelling "trickster" (Crapanzano 1986). The philosopher of history Hayden White (1980, 1987) argues that histories are also artful illusions. A historical narrative is created out of the "chaotic form of 'historical records.'" This narrative is a "wishful fantasy," as though real life actually had the coherence and order that govern the meaning of the historical narrative. In actuality, such a history is a cultural form that imposes the structure of plot on the bare chronicle of events. Life as lived may be incoherent or mere chronology at best, but narrative texts involve the complex orchestration of a plot, which makes a whole out of temporal continuity.

Such complex orchestration requires a narrator's gaze. Literary theorists and many anthropologists are in strong accord on this point, contending, as I have argued elsewhere, that

> the narrator knows the ending. From his retrospective perspective, he is able to select the relevant events and reveal their causal relations because he knows how events unfolded to bring about the particular ending which, narratively speaking, gives meaning to those events. Stories are read backwards. Narratives are . . . ordered around an ending, and it is the ending which has a fundamental role in shaping the meaning of the narrated events (Olafson 1979; Ricoeur 1984). . . . In actual fact, the story's structure exists because the narrator knows where to start, knows what to include and exclude, knows how to weight and evaluate and connect the events he recounts, all because he knows where he will stop. (Mattingly 1998a:38)

The narrator is equipped to narrate because he can survey the entire action landscape from beginning to end and recount the story events in a particular way (one that ultimately gives the story its meanings and morals) from this privileged perspective. It is the narrator's *vision* of events that allows for narrative configuration. When narrative theorists describe narrative as something told rather than lived, they especially have in mind the function of the narrator as discloser and arbitrator of perspective. The narrator has more than knowledge; she also has a moral voice. Aristotle (1970) spoke of plots as moral arguments, and there is a good reason for this. The narrator has the chance to shape the "moral of the story," as we say, through a host of discursive strategies, including the capacity to sequence events in a particular way.

But in real life, we are more like the characters in a story than its narrator. Characters necessarily act from their limited perspective, unable to see ahead to consequences, unable to read the eventual meaning that their actions and experiences will acquire. In everyday life, we are accustomed to the shock of realizing that we have misjudged situations, that events developed in unanticipated ways, that things did not go according to plan. Life, unlike narrative, does not afford us the luxury of the retrospective glance. Narratives are always fictions because "life just isn't like that."

CRITICS OF SEMIOTIC POSITIONS: WHY LIFE
EVENTS ARE MORE THAN IMITATIONS OF STORIES

The rise of a performance-centered anthropology has generated another kind of critique. Here, too, it is argued that "life is not like that," but the chief complaint runs in a rather different direction. The difficulty is not that the artistry of narratives is overlooked. Rather, the contention is that social action is oversimplified and reduced when interpreted in narrative terms. It is important to note that narrative, as treated within this critique, is a different sort of creature and serves a different function than the type literary theorists have in mind. It operates less as a retrospective account of some prior set of (fictional or purportedly true) actions than as a cultural script, a kind of social charter, which guides the behavior and meaning making of cultural actors (Leach 1984).

Thus, from a rather different quarter (but converging on a compatible point), anthropologists have objected to the action-as-text metaphor, which has been so powerful in interpretive and especially semiotically inspired anthropological accounts. The notion that action is a text, contend critics, is fundamentally misleading, for such a metaphor obscures the subtlety and uniqueness of the particular social event, the centrality of context, the phenomenological aspects of social life and the emergent quality of meaning. "There may be a correspondence between a life as lived, a life as experienced, and a life as told, but the anthropologist should never assume the correspondence nor fail to make the distinction," writes Edward Bruner. When Bruner goes on to try to imagine how such a correspondence might occur, he notes that there might be an occasion when a life takes on the shape of a cultural narrative, but this would be an extremely unusual situation, requiring "a remarkable concordance between the ideal and the real, without any out-of-phase incidents. The individual would have to be a letter-perfect copy of his culture, with no discrepancy between outer behavior, inner state, and how he chooses to characterize those behaviors and states in the stories told about them" (1984:7). The problem identified here is not that stories appear to be mere vessels, which simply "tell what happened," but that narratives treated as context-independent texts are all too important; meaning is reductively located in extractable cultural signs and the symbolic systems of which they are a part. Particular actions undertaken in particular situations are seen as mere incidental vessels in which cultural texts (often construed in narrative terms) are played out. The strong critique here is that the meaning of events (including storytelling events) should not be reduced to a reading of their standard cultural meaning, for events are always more than mere enactments of idealized "abstract plot structures" isolated from their situational context (E. Bruner 1984:5).

Quite commonly, a textual analysis is equated with a narrative analysis, which, in turn, is depicted as a sequential and formulaic vision of action. Such an equation is especially prevalent in the study of ritual. Schieffelin, for example, notes that the traditional anthropological focus on ritual describes the "overall narrative ordering of the performance—the succession of its phases, the sequencing of its symbolic enactments" (1996:63), a focus he rejects. An equation of narrative with the merely sequential has its roots, of course, in semiotic and structuralist treatments of ritual. Fernandez, to take another instance, distinguishes his own framework of ritual interpretation, in which the metaphoric properties of ritual action are primary, from narrative analyses, which merely allow a focus on the "surface" of events. He argues that in "a narrative-oriented analysis ... the syntax of the narrative looms large and the agonistic surface arguments and denouncements are primary" (1986:173). He follows Jakobson's distinction between metonym and metaphor and Saussure's distinction between syntagmatic and paradigmatic relations in language which informs his own preference for investigating ritual as providing "organizing images" that "define the inchoate."

A semiotic and narrative framework is recurrently set against constructionist, phenomenological, and situational accounts where the emergent qualities of meaning and experience are emphasized. The introduction to a recent collection of essays on ritual and performance states it clearly: "In this book, ... there is no invocation of Geertz's (1973) interpretation of the Balinese cockfight as Western tragedy. Instead, the contributors renounce the performance-as-text model" (Hughes-Freeland 1998:3). Performance-centered approaches are "concerned with the experience-near aspects of social phenomena: with actions more than with text, with illocutionary rather than with propositional force—with the social construction, rather than just representation, of reality" (Schieffelin 1996:59) A textual approach to analysis is often contrasted with a phenomenological one. Csordas, who has offered some cogent arguments along these lines, declares: "Performance thus invites us—though we do not always accept the invitation—to go beyond the sequence of action and the organization of text to the phenomenology of healing and being healed" (1996:94).

Anthropologists are often wary of narrative for quite another reason—a focus on narrative may blind the researcher to the nonverbal aspects of meaning in cultural action. Particularly in the domain of ritual, anthropologists have looked increasingly to the array of nonnarrative and nonlinguistic aspects of performance: music, dance, smells, visual performances. And many have been unwilling to treat these multimedia, multisensory elements of action merely as a colorful rendition of a script, where the script itself is presumed to hold the key to meaning. They raise the question of how to understand meaning and efficacy, how to build an aesthetic and sensual anthropology that explores these dimensions of human acts without reducing meaning to discursive and linguistic elements (Stoller 1989, 1997; Jackson 1989; Kendall 1996; Laderman 1996; Csordas 1994). Even inanimate objects may serve as the primary carrier of meaning (Hoskins 1998). Silence, too, when artfully deployed, may speak much more loudly than any words, as Wikan (1995) eloquently demonstrates. Performance approaches, with their emphasis on the sensual, embodied, multivocal, constructive, improvisational, and nonverbal, attempt to highlight the aesthetic, imaginative elements of the ritual act that a semiotic narrative treatment may overlook or treat in an overly schematic fashion.

EMERGENT NARRATIVES
AND EMERGENT EXPERIENCE

Might it be possible to avoid both naive realism *and* an "action-as-text" semiotic treatment of social life while preserving the idea that stories and action have a special correspondence? The difficulty is how to bring these two terms—narrative and action—into a close interpretive relationship without reducing either to a pale copy, a "mere" representation or enactment of the other. How do we see narrative in terms of life and life in terms of narrative without loss of richness and complexity, without neglecting the phenomenological complexities of lived experience and the creative artifice of narrative?

As Renato Rosaldo (1986) suggests, one reason to preserve the idea that stories are experience-near is because often our informants presume this to be so. If stories are only distortions (albeit very interesting ones) of action and experience, why (one might wonder) do people bother to tell stories as a way to communicate what happened to them and how it felt? If narrative takes them so far from their lived experience, what is the point? This is especially the case when something unexpected happens. Stories, after all, concern the untoward, events that involve risk, suspense, danger, chance—not a predictable replaying of a usual scenario. They are about life in the breach (J. Bruner 1986, 1990a; Kleinman 1988; Good and Good 1994). People do seem to think, sometimes at least, that they are getting nearer to these experiences when they couch them in stories. Are they just utterly deluded?

Perhaps not. It is true enough that stories necessarily "fictionalize" events and that lived experience is never the mere playing out of a pregiven cultural script. But one need not abandon the exploration of this relationship for fear of losing sight of these central points. Although there are strong reasons to claim that action is one thing but narrative is something else entirely, there are stronger reasons to recognize their kinship. Actions and narratives are intimately bound up with one another because of the nature of social action and human sociality. Any number of arguments have been made that support this claim, from J. Bruner's discussions of narrative as an "idealized form of folk psychology" (1990b:349), to phenomenological and hermeneutic accounts of the narrative structure of human time (cf. Ricoeur in particular), to anthropological analyses of the dramatic structure of a culture's extraordinary times, its ritual occasions. (Here, of course, Victor Turner's work has been seminal.)

My own argument in this chapter calls upon all these lines of thinking. Stories may be created in and through actions even if few words are ever spoken. This is not to say that stories resemble life because they passively re-present it, like so many containers into which life spills. Rather, it is to claim that some moments in life are lit up with those qualities we take to belong to finely wrought narrative. My particular interest is the sort of dramatic moment that lies between the publicly demarcated ritual event and the narrativity that characterizes all experience. The narrative moments I have in mind are not preplanned, and their form is not culturally preordained. They represent a "breakthrough into performance," as Dell Hymes (1975) once put it. Unlike Hymes's narratives, however, the ones I describe are likely to be created with few words; language is not the prime messenger of the story. Like any ritual, they depend upon a range of communicative media, especially kinesthetic ones. What I investigate here, in other words, are improvisational and embodied stories.

The moments I consider arise, in part, because the actors are in search of narrative, in quest of drama. Actors may seek to turn their actions into a definable and vivid form that has its own temporal unity, a dramatic coherence that cannot be reduced to sequence without loss of meaning. To explore this further, I now turn to a concrete case. When and how do these narrative times emerge? What shifts humdrum everyday time into narrative time, characterized by dramas, risks, and the like? What differentiates the quality and form of these dramatic times from more ordinary moments? If these emergent plots are not culturally preordained, such questions are not readily answered.

GOING FOR THE GOLD

Since 1986, I have worked with research colleagues in a series of ethnographic studies of occupational therapists in Boston, Chicago, and Los Angeles, often videotaping and analyzing their work with clients (Mattingly 1991a, 1991b, 1994, 1998a, 1998b; Mattingly and Fleming 1994; Mattingly and Lawlor 1997; Lawlor and Mattingly 1998). I have observed hundreds of sessions and interviewed dozens of therapists. While treatment is not highly standardized in this practice, I have come to recognize certain hallmarks that characterize what most therapists would consider a "good session." Perhaps the three most important qualities are these. First, clients are involved in performing some kind of activity that will improve their capacity to carry out everyday life tasks, despite disability. Second, clients find the treatment activity engaging and see it as connected to their everyday lives. Third, clients willingly "partner up" (Lawlor and Mattingly 1998) with therapists so that treatment activities acquire a particularly social character.

The clinical case I analyze here concerns a single encounter between a pediatric therapist and her nine-year-old client, an encounter that took place in 1991 in an outpatient pediatric clinic in the suburbs of Boston. The treating therapist, Ellen Cohn, is someone I have known for many years. The session was videotaped, though not by me. It is not unusual for therapists, particularly in pediatrics, to videotape sessions. These are sometimes used as teaching aides in which students or novice therapists can examine experienced therapists at work. This is one such tape. Ellen Cohn sent it to me because she thought I might find this session interesting, as indeed I did, for it was clearly one of those "good sessions." And it was highly dramatic as well. It offers a fine example of the creation of a dramatic plot in the midst of quite usual treatment, the sort one might witness in pediatric outpatient clinics throughout the United States. It is not a remarkable encounter, from an occupational therapist's point of view, but it is certainly a successful one.

Ellen is an experienced pediatric therapist. The client in this case, Sarah, suffers from severe vestibular problems, becoming fearful when her sense of balance is disrupted. This session has become, for patient and therapist, a familiar round of treatment activities designed for patients with sensorimotor deficits. Treatment consists in providing structured sensory experiences to "teach the body" to sense the world in a more normal way. This generally involves many sensory movements (touching, swinging, whirling, jumping), which children ordinarily engage in on the playground but which these children avoid and often find extremely uncomfortable.

In the following excerpt, Sarah has just completed one familiar activity. As she is about to embark on the next exercise, she says, "I have an idea. Let's pretend this is an Olympic sport and when if I go through there if I don't touch anything, I get a point. OK?" Therapist agrees, and, in this pretending, what is ordinarily a routine motor activity is transformed into a drama. The actions of child, therapist, and cameraperson all contribute to the development of a plot, one in which the child is not a disabled patient undergoing treatment but a brilliant athlete performing her breathtaking feats for an admiring audience. The ironic joking of patient and spectators recalls the "this is just play" frame but does not undermine the excitement engendered by this storymaking. Routine movements are transformed into episodes that take their meaning as part of an unfolding drama, one in which the ending is in suspense. As Sarah makes repeated jumps through the hoop, the following dialogue ensues:

SARAH: I have an idea. Let's pretend this is an Olympic sport and when if I go through if I don't touch anything, I get a point. Okay?

ELLEN: Who's going to give the points?

SARAH: You!

ELLEN: Okay. One point.

SARAH: This is going to be a snap!

ELLEN: Should I pretend to hold up one of those cards?

Sarah repeats her performance. As the jumps continue and points begin to mount, the therapist acts more and more animated.

SARAH: So that was one point.

ELLEN: Okay.

SARAH: So that was two points.

ELLEN: Ooooooooooo. Four points.

SARAH: Thank you.

ELLEN:	For Miss Sarah . . .
SARAH:	Miles. (Inventing a new last name for herself.)
CAMERA-PERSON:	Going for the gold medal . . .
ELLEN:	. . . Ooooooo, six points for Miles.

Things continue in this fashion, although there are a few frame breaks. Sarah and Ellen make some adjustments to the equipment.

SARAH:	I've got to make this more softer.
ELLEN:	Would you like another crash pad?
SARAH:	No, that's okay.
ELLEN:	Okay.
SARAH:	Hopefully, ah . . . (jumping again) that was more like it.

Ellen then forgets Sarah's invented last name, using her real last name instead, and is sternly corrected by Sarah.

ELLEN:	Six points for Miss Johnson.
SARAH:	Excuse me? (with heavy irony)
ELLEN:	Excuse me?
SARAH:	Miles.
ELLEN:	Miles.
CAMERA-PERSON:	Mistake for the last listing.

Another frame break is initiated by Sarah, who worries her leg has touched and tries to retract points Ellen has enthusiastically awarded.

SARAH:	Uh, uh, my leg touched.
ELLEN:	(Pauses, startled.) It did?
SARAH:	Eight points still.
ELLEN:	Okay.
CAMERA-PERSON:	Eight and a half.
SARAH:	(Trying to explain) Usually I can tell if I touched cuz . . .
ELLEN:	(Ignores her) She's in the starting gate. She's preparing to take off. She's wiping her face, scratching her eyes. And ten points. (Sarah goes through again.)
ELLEN:	She's up, she's thinking about it, she's preparing, she makes fourteen points. Are you getting tired?
SARAH:	No, just resting my head. Oh, I think my leg brushed.
ELLEN:	It did? Did you feel it?

SARAH: I felt something brush, and it was on my leg.

Gradually, Ellen looks to Sarah to tell her the points accumulated.

ELLEN: So what's your score, Sarah?
SARAH: Fourteen points.
ELLEN: Ooooo, very nice. Sixteen for Ms. Sarah Miles.
SARAH: Finally, she gets my name right.
ELLEN: The champion of OT Associates.

Later, still, there is a negotiation about the ending. Originally Sarah had proposed a forty-point goal score, but, beginning to get tired, she requests a change.

SARAH: Couldn't we make it thirty instead?
ELLEN: We can make it whatever you choose.
CAMERA-
PERSON: Or we could do finals; they're for four points.
SARAH: Four points, you think?
CAMERA-
PERSON: Sure, you deserve it!
SARAH: Okay.
ELLEN: What's your score now?
SARAH: Eighteen.
ELLEN: Oooooooo.
SARAH: Twenty-two.
ELLEN: Very nice. Ms. Miles is rearranging the crash pad ladies and gentlemen.
SARAH: Twenty-six.
ELLEN: And she goes for the big thirty.
SARAH: Then I need ten more points.
ELLEN: And she does it. She makes thirty. Ooooooo.
SARAH: Thirty-four.
ELLEN: Very nice.
SARAH: Thirty-six.
ELLEN: Well done.
SARAH: Actually it's thirty-four. My leg brushed.
ELLEN: So you want to give yourself thirty-four?
SARAH: Uh huh.
ELLEN: Okay.
SARAH: Thirty-eight.
ELLEN: Wow, Sarah.

Sarah announces that the end is approaching:

SARAH: Phew, okay, here comes the final jump.

ELLEN: Okay. And she does it!

SARAH: Forty-two points. I've really done it. Can we do the swing now?

FROM SEQUENCE TO PLOT

This clinical session unfolds with a familiar round of activities. The segment of the session just described plays off a customary routine of more or less unvaried actions—jumping through a hoop again and again. Time is not so much chaotic as monotonously ordered; here exactly is that clock time which Forster believed characterized life outside the novel. Time marches on, marked by the piling up of jumps. One, then two, then three. . . . But this regular progression is halted by Sarah, who takes the role of director and initiates the transformation of sequence into plot.

With this interruption, the predictable is converted into a fanciful drama in which the end is playfully held in suspense. Though the client sets the story in motion, all three actors help to keep it going. Improvisational elements are evident everywhere. Even mistakes get folded into the drama. When the therapist forgets the patient's invented last name, this becomes another element in the story, "Mistake for the last listing," the cameraperson says. When Sarah moves out of her play role, from Olympic star to patient, and speaks literally of her error, "Usually I can tell if I touched . . . ," the therapist replies in language more befitting the story they have set in motion, speaking as a sports commentator: "She's up, she's thinking about it, she's preparing." And when Sarah begins to get tired and wants to renegotiate when they can stop (thirty points instead of forty), the cameraperson invents an ending appropriate to *this* particular story, solving the problem of Sarah's increasing tiredness (which the therapist is worrying about) within the story context by doubling the points per jump. "We could do finals," he says. "They're for four points." The therapist provides the appropriate enthusiastic commentary, allowing Sarah to make the point calculations and thereby choose when things will end, which Sarah does by announcing, "OK, here comes the final jump."

Therapy time becomes situated between a past and a future, and temporally situated in more than one sense. The present is not a series of "nows," not a chronicle as Hayden White would have it, but has a threefold structure, what Augustine described as a "three-fold present" where each moment takes its meaning as a kind of middle wedged between past and future. (This picture of human time has inspired any number of theorists [Carr 1986, 1997; Crites 1997; Ricoeur 1984, 1985, 1987]. I explore it in more detail elsewhere [Mattingly 1998a]). The future plays an especially important part in organizing the meaning of any event. A single act (yet another jump through the hoop) acquires significance as part of a larger narrative whole, the one in which Sarah emerges as the victorious athlete.

In this emergent plot there is the "sense of an ending" that Kermode tells us characterizes literary time. The meaning of each jump is (playfully) judged in terms of a gymnast feverishly—and brilliantly—competing for a gold medal, matching her skill against an unstated narrative backdrop in which other talented gymnasts are waiting to perform. Endings guide a literary narrative (or any ordinary well-told story) in the sense that the narrator includes only those events which point toward that final culmination. A narrative "admits no noise," as Roland Barthes once wrote. With this same Spartan logic, guided by an ending which the therapist has already privately determined (Sarah will not be defeated), only those actions that build toward this victory are emphasized. Even the frame breaks engendered by Sarah, who steps out of her role to anxiously report accidental infractions of the hoop-jumping rule, are quickly suppressed by the therapist so that the story can proceed to a happy conclusion. While in one sense the conclusion is foregone (the therapist will ensure a successful finish and, as "judge," is in a good position to do so), this therapeutic drama draws from and evokes the imaginative world of the Olympics, in which suspense is of the essence and no win is a sure thing. That edgy excitement seeps into the session as Sarah is drawn into her own fantasy.

The ending is in suspense in another sense, for more than one plot is sketched in this small exchange. There is the future of the particular exercise. (Will Sarah win the gold?) But, beyond that, this Olympic event is nested between therapies past and therapy times to come. It marks another episode in an unfolding healing narrative. From the therapist's perspective, creative dramas like this one make therapy with Sarah memorable. Ellen remembers Sarah fondly long after treatment has ended. Recalling her work with Sarah some seven years later, Ellen wrote to me, "I truly enjoyed the places Sarah took me to, like the Olympics. I must admit," she went on, "every few years when the Olympics come around and we hear that familiar music and see those well-trained athletes, I think of Sarah."

Most important, there is the past and future of Sarah's life, in which all of therapy is one small moment. When this particular clinical session took place, Sarah was a lonely nine-year-old who was very bright, did extremely well in school, and spent much of her life reading. Her imaginative abilities were obvious, and the therapist readily drew upon them in shaping the clinical session. But because Sarah suffered from severe vestibular problems, becoming very fearful when her sense of balance was disrupted, she did not play with other children on the playground and avoided physical activities. This withdrawal from the physical world and the play world of other children was part of Sarah's life long before she began therapy. She was first assessed by an occupational therapist and diagnosed as having sensorimotor problems when she was five. However, her initial assessment was carried out while her parents were going through a difficult divorce, and no treatment was pursued because it was not clear whether Sarah's problems were related to the emotional upset of the home or were organic. When her motor problems did not lessen over the intervening years, she began treatment.

This Olympic victory takes on meaning within Sarah's unfolding life story, standing in playful and dramatic opposition to the everyday. The playground has been a place of solo wandering for Sarah, her physical difficulties serving to cut her off from involvement with others, but in this session, her physical feats in therapy connect her to the social world. She is the center of a vast audience of admirers. Thus this emplotment carries a contradictory message, one in which physical play connects rather than separates. Sarah anticipates in imagination what she cannot in fact anticipate. She relies upon her imagination to desire endings not realistically possible, and in so doing plays a part in a very different story than the one she more literally lives. She dabbles, for a short while, in being a different sort of person, a great athlete, winner of gold medals.

Sarah has borrowed a script from another cultural scene. This script allows Sarah to place her own struggle within a broader and more culturally dramatic narrative of the athletic elite who also struggle to master their bodies, training them to perform feats that require great effort and concentration. In the story she sets in motion, she can express longings for a future that go far beyond performing well at a clinical exercise. The therapist participates enthusiastically because she, too, cares that Sarah find ways to connect therapy to commitments and concerns that reach deeper than performing a set of therapeutic tasks successfully. Success for the therapist also means moving beyond the literal goals of therapy and helping to create therapeutic experiences that hold cultural power for Sarah, allowing her momentarily to connect her struggles with those of the extremely able-bodied.

These plots do not string along, one after the other, but represent different narrative horizons, all present as part of a single jump through the hoop. Present experience, then, is configured by remembrances and anticipations. Both Sarah and Ellen seek to change their current situations to more desirable ones. Practical imagination guides their perception of unfolding events as they seek to move things along in some directions rather than others. It is not merely that these actors somehow "picture" a future state, which they then try to attain. Such an instrumental and sequential depiction does not do justice to the improvisational play of this pretend Olympics. Rather, as their story line develops, these jumps are transformed into embodied metaphors (Csordas 1994), which evoke story worlds past and future and some never to be lived at all, at least not by Sarah.

THE SOCIAL CONSTRUCTION OF EMERGENT PLOTS

What provides Sarah and Ellen this facility to emplot their time together, to dance effortlessly from sequence to plot? How can they find their way so gracefully into a drama they have never played before and may never play again? They have come to know one another, of course, and this helps them to "read one another." As J. Bruner and others have pointed out, reading other minds is an inherent and fundamental aspect of human sociality, one that begins in infancy, even before the acquisition of language. This "mind reading" is given a great boost because Ellen and Sarah share many cultural resources (Carrithers 1992). They are acquainted with a vast repertoire of cultural scripts that provide models for action.

Clearly culture gives them cognitive tools to apprehend the world through a common stock of stories, enabling them to recognize and take up roles in cultural scenarios with which they are familiar. But this is only part of the picture. Emergent plots involve more than the capacity to play the proper part in a culture's well-rehearsed plot lines. They even require more than having the imaginative facility to transfer scripts associated with one cultural domain (elite athletic events) onto an entirely different cultural scene (clinical encounters). Meaning is not preordained by prior scripts or cultural rules but in some important sense emerges. And it emerges out of a social interaction in which improvisation is prized and cultivated.

Narrative meaning shifts moment to moment as it is socially constructed. There is much subtlety in reading for the plot. Notably, Ellen's
facility at taking up and subtly adjusting the story line is a key aspect of
her therapeutic competence. In this bit of therapeutic storymaking,
Sarah makes the story line explicit and even assigns the therapist her
particular part—as judge. The sensitivity required in a proper "reading" of the story is evident in how the therapist reformulates her role.
She decides that the story Sarah wants to create (or she wants Sarah to
create) is one in which Sarah masterfully executes her Olympian tasks,
not the one in which Sarah falls short of a perfect performance. Therefore, she subtly recasts herself into sportscaster and enthusiastic specta-
tor rather than critical judge recording flaws in the performance. This
recasting was a conscious decision by the therapist, as revealed later in
interview. "Reading" the story Sarah begins involves an active interpretation of the deeper drama Sarah (and the therapist) cares about, one in
which she performs with grace, rather than one in which great exertion
is required just to master skills her peers execute effortlessly. By shifting
her narrative role, the therapist can reinforce a story in which Sarah's
successes rather than her defeats are playfully exaggerated and admired.
While Sarah worries about errors, the therapist brushes over these with
minor comment or ignores them altogether, thus helping to propel a
particular sort of therapeutic story along and discourage a less desirable
one. The grand finale ends in happy accord as Sarah echoes the therapist in assessing her performance. "Okay, and she does it!" the therapist
declares. "Forty-two points. I've really done it," agrees Sarah, who is
then cheerfully ready to move on to the next task.

The fundamentally social quality of the plot is underscored in such
subtle refinements. Occupational therapists, especially those who work
with children, emphasize that they cannot completely control therapy
but often must take the child's lead. A competent and effective therapist
must be a reader of unfolding stories not of her own making. An occupational therapy session, like many other healing practices across a
wide variety of cultures, is a "dialogic and improvisatory kind of event"
(Schieffelin 1996:64–65). Skill at reading the audience—including the
patient—and at shifting actions to suit the moment is integral to a
healer's very capacity to heal.

Experience itself also emerges as a clearly social matter, not the private ruminations or interior workings of a solo actor. Here is a social or
"cultural phenomenology" (Csordas 1994). Kapferer gives us a description of this socially lived experience:

Individuals experience themselves—they experience their experience and reflect on it—both from their own standpoint and from the standpoint of others within their culture. This is what gives to the practical activity of everyday life some of its movement and process. Further, I do not experience your
experience. Paradoxically, your experience is *made* mine; I experience my experience of you. The expressions revealed on your face, in the gestural organization of your body, through the meeting of our glances, are experienced
through my body and my situation. (1983:189)

Ellen and Sarah increasingly attune their bodies to one another as this
plot unfolds. This is not only a matter of making one another's experience their own, to follow Kapferer. They also actively shape the experience of the other. Ellen guides Sarah's experiences of her own body by,
for example, expressing enthusiasm over Sarah's successful jumps and
neglecting to support Sarah's anxiousness when she is not so agile.

EMPLOTMENT AND THE CREATION
OF SIGNIFICANT EXPERIENCE

Anthropologists generally emphasize a quality of vividness or heightened experience that sets the ritual moment apart from the merely routine. Like any other compelling ritual, this Olympic game creates "presence," in Schieffelin's and Desjarlais's sense (Schieffelin 1998, 1996;
Desjarlais 1996). It "make(s) present realities vivid enough to beguile,
amuse or terrify" (Schieffelin 1996:59). Meaning is defined, in contra-
distinction to the eternal text, as a lived moment, with all the vulnerability which that entails. There is a clear parallel between the depiction
of the charged ritual moment and the notion of experience as explicated
by Continental phenomenology and hermeneutics (Dilthey 1989; Gadamer 1975; Heidegger 1962). "Mere experience" (forgettable sequence,
dull routine) is sharply contrasted with "an experience," the extraordinary event, an occasion that becomes fixed in memory as a singular
time. In Gadamer's classic *Truth and Method,* he writes, "An experience
is as much distinguished from other experiences—in which other things
are experienced—as from the rest of life in which 'nothing' is experienced" (1975:60). While "an experience," taken in this sense, acquires
certain characteristics of a textual object, its meaning can never be reduced to a fixed text. Quoting Gadamer further, "The experience has
a definite immediacy which eludes every opinion about its meaning"
(1975:60). A dramatic experience has an evanescence that belongs to all
life in human time, the sort of quality that makes us feel, when recalling
memorable times, that however we try to recapture them, there is always

something lost, something we cannot bring to consciousness and certainly not to words. Even those moments most elegantly emplotted have a fleeting quality. But such moments also have the capacity to haunt us, to work their way into our lives in all sorts of unexpected ways; it "takes a long time to assimilate them, and this is their real being and significance" (Gadamer 1975:60).

For all their ephemeral qualities, emergent plots like the one I have described acquire a special significance precisely because they *seem* so real. It is clear that Sarah is not going to be a world-class athlete anytime soon, but in the adventure she sets in motion, she makes a world that carries its own authority. Just as a good story, no matter how fantastical, seduces listeners into dream time, suppressing the reality of the ordinary, so this imaginary world that Sarah and Ellen dream up temporarily overshadows the trivial reality of a treatment room. An emergent narrative such as this creates "verisimilitude" (Schieffelin 1996:60) even when the performers know perfectly well that nothing they are doing is literally true. It offers an especially authoritative vision of reality precisely because it heightens experience by calling upon the imagination. A sense of realness is further facilitated by the embodied character of this storymaking.

If Sarah and Ellen create a story, it is a story in motion. There are words, to be sure, and these are essential. But mostly there are Sarah's leaps through a hoop, the attentive gaze of her two admiring spectators, their cheers and applause, which gesture toward an imaginary world, a world dispersed as easily as it is conjured when Sarah and Ellen move on to the next exercise. The body plays a central part in helping to create a sense of vivid reality for Sarah. One of the most significant contributions of the performance literature in ritual is that the body is foregrounded as central in constituting reality, particularly the reality of the extraordinary moment. Schechner describes ritual as an encounter between imagination and memory translated into doable acts of the body (Schechner 1993:263, in Hughes-Freeland 1998:2).

By creating a healing drama through the body, key messages can be conveyed that draw upon a range of media. Anthropologists have often attended to the "multiplicity of communicative channels in curing rituals" (Briggs 1996:187), and this healing drama draws upon several. Exercise equipment is transformed into props, which Ellen and Sarah, doubling as stage hands, rearrange from time to time. A therapeutic song commonly heard in pediatric sessions ("Yeah! You did it!") is remade synecdochically into a chant offered by a throng of cheering spectators and enthusiastic sportscasters. (A subtle shift by Ellen from second to third person "*She* does it!" accomplishes this.) There is also, of course, the mask Sarah acquires by adopting a new name. She is herself but *not* herself, as she is quick to remind everyone when Ellen slips and uses Sarah's literal last name instead of the invented one. More central than song, set, or mask, messages are communicated through Sarah's body, her flying leaps and graceful bows as she acknowledges the crowd. All these media together produce a "fusion of experience" (Tambiah 1985; Leach 1976; Laderman and Roseman 1996; Briggs 1996) that is a hallmark of ritual action.

The body is implicated in another sense, not only as the medium through which imaginative meanings are created and communicated but also as that place in which meanings are registered as felt truths, as "existential immediacies" (Csordas 1990, 1996). Speaking of healing among charismatic Catholics, Csordas argues that touch and vividly imagined experiences of the body provide their own powerful healing effect and carry with them a persuasive message that participants have come into contact with something deeply real and true. "Efficacious healing," he writes, "is predicated not only on a cultural legitimacy that says healing is possible, but on an existential immediacy that constitutes healing as real. The immediacy of the imaginal world and of memory . . . have their common ground in embodiment. The moods and motivations evoked upon this ground in ritual performance are indeed uniquely realistic (1996:108).

Myerhoff notes that dramatic performances that catch the whole body up and fill the senses are very different from "just talk." "Our senses are naturally persuasive, convincing us of what the mind will not indulge. Presentational symbols have more rhetorical power than discursive ones (the latter require exceptional skill and some veracity); in ritual, doing is believing, and we become what we display" (1986:268). Myerhoff's comments go a long way to pointing out how acting out an Olympic game, being an Olympic star, can be so rhetorically powerful for Sarah. Symbolic dramas, Myerhoff argues, following Geertz (1973) here, are not "'mere reflections of a pre-existing sensibility, analogically represented'; they are 'positive agents' in the creation and maintenance of the subjectivity they organize into a proper, coherent tale" (1986: 268–69). Myerhoff also emphasizes the "visibility" that is an important part of a performance and central to the drama Sarah and Ellen create. Ellen makes Sarah visible. In this session, the camera adds a further element. A stage is set, and Sarah seizes the opportunity to make her debut.

Why might Ellen and Sarah seek out opportunities to create presence? Why are they so eager to shift from a familiar cultural scenario to a script that is far from their everyday lives, which, in fact, has nothing to do with the day to day? What is Sarah after, and Ellen, too, who joins her in this game with complete alacrity? I would say that they are after *desire*. What this session needs, Sarah has evidently determined, is a little excitement. Something to make life, clinical life, more worth living. A mundane cultural script is traded in for an exotic one, lending drama and significance to well-worn exercises. While routine cultural scripts might be narrative in some minimal sense, they are a far cry from a dramatic plot. And it is drama that Sarah is looking to create. Sarah and Ellen are also after *possibility*, the capacity to jump out of, to jump over the daily struggle by creating a persuasive image of another kind of self, one whose body gives pleasure, power, and a central place in a social world.

The difference between cultural script (taken as a routine and culturally appropriate sequence of events) and dramatic plot is beautifully illustrated by Renato Rosaldo, who reflects upon why the Ilongot choose to tell the hunting stories they do, and how different their stories are from the sort of accounts anthropologists are likely to give of such events when they explain them in terms of routine scenarios. Unlike accounts that link social life to such "programmed sequences as the daily round, the annual cycle or the life cycle," the Ilongot choose to tell stories about dramatic moments, about surprises and risky episodes. Furthermore, this is not only true of the stories the Ilongot tell but also what they seek out when they go hunting: "The significance Ilongot men seek in hunting derives more from cultural notions about what makes a story (and lived experience) compelling than from . . . routine subsistence techniques." Dramatic narratives "can provide a particularly rich source of knowledge about the significance people find in their workaday lives. Such narratives often reveal more about what can make life worth living than about how it is routinely lived" (Rosaldo 1986:98). Just as the Ilongot hunters seek out hunting experiences that make life worth living, so Ellen and Sarah seek out clinical experiences that make therapy exercises worth performing.

FROM EMERGENT PLOT TO NARRATIVE TEXT

There is a final act to the story I have been telling, the one in which an emergent and embodied narrative created one fall day in a private clinic outside Boston is converted into a narrative text written by an anthropologist. This transformation has its own history, which bears telling because it reveals another way in which narrative and action connect. It says something about how a narrative sketched in action is remade into a narrative text, one that lives on to shape the interpretations and future actions of the story's characters, as well as actors (like an anthropologist) who were never part of the original scene.

In this instance, the remaking of a more or less spontaneous emplotment to what Bauman and Briggs (1990) call an "extractable text" is certainly aided by the presence of a video camera. Though Sarah was accustomed to steering therapy sessions in creative directions, she may well have been inspired by the dramatic potential of a camera, choosing as her central plot a theatrical event that is routinely televised. Because of the tape, the session emerges as an increasingly public object. The tape allows for readings by a host of interpreters, including occupational therapy students at Tufts, where the video was shown in classes, Ellen herself, who watched the tape with students, and myself. I wrote an initial draft of this essay in 1997 to give to a national meeting of occupational therapists in Chicago. I forgot that Ellen might attend this meeting, and when I saw her in the audience I was surprised and more than a little disconcerted. Though I had received her permission to publish a paper based on her videotape, I had not bothered to inform her that I would present it to her colleagues. Somewhat nervously, I told the audience (and of course Ellen) a story of her storymaking. To my relief, when I went up to her afterward to see what she thought, she smiled and assured me I had gotten it "quite right."

We lost touch until a chance e-mail conversation just as I was doing a final rewrite of this essay. I asked if she had any other news about Sarah. Here is how she replied:

> I don't know if Sarah had a powerful impact on me or that hearing and reading some of your evolving interpretations of that session have influenced my thinking (perhaps both), but I do feel that I learned something from her that affects how I parent my own kids. It's hard to articulate, but it has something to do with letting them go explore that very wonderful imaginary place where they can enact something they are unable to do in reality. It gets played out when my kids are having a tantrum and they want me to fix it. I try to take them on a fantasy trip, to imagine what it would be like if I could indeed wave a magic wand and make the mean kid go away or give them what they want in the particular moment.

My writing of this chapter is one more act in a process that began with fleeting moments of therapy life with Sarah. From the evanescent time of lived experience, there is the creation of a videotape that is viewed by students and colleagues, and the creation of another object, a written transcript of the tape. Then there is more storytelling by a number of actors, including myself. There are oral stories and written ones hemmed in by much interpretation. Through all these storytelling efforts, narrative emerges not only as a public object that can be perused by others but also as a powerful guide for future action. Notably, Ellen's remembrances of experiences with Sarah, the child, and my storytelling of Sarah have become inextricable. The narrative that guides Ellen is a synthesis of all this; word and deed have inexorably intermingled. The reach of this guiding narrative is long, traveling into domains far from clinical life; Ellen feels its influence most strongly not in her clinical work but as a parent raising young children of her own.

CONCLUSION

A dominant contemporary view of the relationship between story (as something told) and experience (as something lived) is that there is a great disparity, even an unbridgeable divide, between the two. The most common contention among discontinuity theorists is that life as narrated is governed by a coherent, unifying plot in which time is marked by a beginning, middle, and end. Coherent plots are the creation of authoritative narrators, who—unlike the characters in the story—know how things turned out. By contrast, life as lived is characterized by flux, uncertainty, and the lack of a clear ending. If one wanted to challenge this discontinuity position, there are two obvious tacks one might take. One could argue that stories as told are not necessarily all that coherent or ordered, not so authoritatively rendered by a narrator confident of his facts and meanings as is sometimes supposed. This is the primary direction taken by Wikan (this volume) and a point cogently made by Kirmayer (this volume) as well, though this leads him to rather different conclusions than Wikan. Alternatively, one might argue that lived experience is not necessarily deficient in narrative form, that narratives may pervade our fundamental way of making sense, and further, that we may look to promote certain sorts of narrative dramas even if such emergent storymaking is never put into words. Wikan's paper hints at this, and it is the direction I have taken in this chapter.

My claim, made here and elsewhere, is that the opposition between lived experience and narrative discourse "registers sensibly only by positing a false notion of what prior events are and how they are structured.

Literary theorists . . . and others whose primary concerns are written and oral texts have not investigated the structure of lived experience and thus the distinctions between life and art rest on far too simple a view of how life in time is experienced" (Mattingly 1998a:44). Even anthropologists fascinated with the ethnographer's task of converting field experience into text have been too quick to dismiss the narrative structure of social action. Certainly, no life as lived has the congruence of the well-told tale. But there are strong narrative moments that arise in life and are even promoted and crafted by actors themselves. Further, congruence is not the primary quality that links stories to action and experience. If narrative offers an intimate relation to lived experience, the dominant formal feature that connects the two is not narrative coherence but narrative drama. We follow a narrative suspensefully, always reminded of the fragility of events, for things might have turned out differently.

In examining the narrative structure of social action, I have offered the notion of emergent narrative. Emergent narratives like the one I describe here are not the routine enactments of prior texts but are improvised as well as embodied. They are usually invented more or less on the spot, unrehearsed dramas that spring up in the course of everyday activity. Of course, an emergent narrative does not spring up from nothing. It is a cultural act, and its creation depends upon a complex repertoire of cultural resources. Actors draw upon familiar cultural stories and scenarios, though these provide mere starting points, skeletal plots at best. Improvisation is not merely decorative or incidental; it is the process by which a skeleton is transformed into a flesh-and-blood event. To read improvisations as reenactments of the canonical or the routine is to miss the whole point.

In describing a single healing drama, I also mean to challenge contemporary discussions that divide the world into the nonverbal, sensuous, felt, and immediate, on the one hand, and the verbalized, fictionalized, and reflected upon, on the other. I have presented an emergent and entangled view of narrative and experience, speaking of the emplotment of clinical actions. This picture of stories, as emergent, embodied, improvisational, fitted to context, is clearly allied to performative views of narrative and action. Linking narrative to the study of healing rituals makes it is possible to attend to the many nonlinguistic components of narrative events and even to see a largely nonlinguistic "performance" as the creation of a therapeutic narrative.

In speaking of a kind of story that is embodied, improvisational (though not outside or prior to culture), aesthetically compelling, and phenomenologically significant, I offer a view of human action and experience as a fundamentally narrative enterprise. And some moments, I have tried to claim, are more narrative than others. The healing drama I describe here is one such highly narrative moment, creating a significant experience for participants. It sketches a form—or, rather, the actors collectively create a form—out of what might otherwise proceed with the humdrum regularity of Forster's "clock time." A narrative form is sketched in action, one with beginning, middle, and end. This is a dramatic form, characterized by suspense, excitement, heightened desire, even a kind of foreshadowing, an elusive gaze into possible futures that live far from this small clinical encounter.

What has any of this to do with healing? What can we see about healing if we discover narrative moments, times when healing and recovery take on all the compelling power of the well-told story? It may bring us closer to the perspective of the sufferer. Oliver Sacks, recovering from a severe leg injury, was shocked to find his experience summed up in his medical chart as "uneventful recovery." "What damned utter nonsense!" he exclaims. "Recovery . . . was a 'pilgrimage,' a journey in which one moved, if one moved, stage by stage, or by stations. Every stage, every station, was a completely new advent, requiring a new start, a new birth or beginning. One had to begin, to be born, again and again. Recovery was an exercise in nothing short of birth . . . unexpected, unexpectable, incalculable and surprising. Recovery uneventful? It *consists* of events" (1984:132). Illness and recovery may be eventful to the sufferer when they are ordinary business for the healer. But even healers, across a wide range of cultures and practices, may concur with Sacks that recovery "consists of events." For patients like Sarah and some healers as well, there are powerful motives to transform therapy time into a domain of significance, one that acquires phenomenological weight because it creates a present which is threefold, which embodies connections to past and, especially, to future.

Coming to recognize narrative moments that arise in clinical practice may also illuminate some aspects of healing that are likely to be neglected. Even in Western medicine, not noted for its reliance on the aesthetic or dramatic (especially outside psychotherapeutic practices), the very possibility of healing may depend upon the capacity and desire of the actors to transform the merely ordinary into an extraordinary moment. Anthropologists have noted that the capacity of a healer and audience to create a dramatic moment, a "time out of time," is often culturally linked to the healer's perceived efficacy. While neither Ellen nor other therapists talk about therapy as an aesthetic form or connect therapeutic gains to their dramatic competencies, they are concerned that "something happen" in therapy time, and especially that patients come to see themselves in a new way through the therapeutic encounter. Effecting transformations of identity in patients is deeply rooted in a variety of healing practices in both Western and non-Western cultures (Danforth 1989; Kendall 1996; Csordas 1996; Mattingly 1994, 1998a). This evangelical bent, this need to act as transformative agents and not as mere technicians of the body, drives even some Western healers to engage in the creation of healing dramas in their efforts to assist clients in transforming their lives.

ACKNOWLEDGMENTS

An earlier version of this chapter was presented at the annual meetings of the American Anthropological Association, Washington, D.C., November 1995. A rather different version was presented at the annual meetings of the American Occupational Therapy Association, Chicago, April 1997. Later versions were presented to the Department of Philosophy at the University of Aarhus, Denmark, and the Department of Psychology at the University of Copenhagen. I wish to especially thank Paul Brodwin for some extremely insightful comments on earlier versions of this chapter. Discussions with Uffe Jensen, Mary Lawlor, Jerome Bruner, and three anonymous reviewers have also helped enormously in clarifying my arguments. Ellen Cohn graciously allowed me to write about her practice. Grant support was provided by grant MC5-060745 from the Maternal and Child Health Program (Title V, Social Security Act), Health Resources and Services Administration, Department of Health and Human Services.

REFERENCES

Abrahams, R. D. 1986. Ordinary and extraordinary experience. In *The anthropology of experience,* edited by Victor Turner and Edward Bruner, 45–72. Urbana: University of Illinois Press.

Aristotle. 1970. *Poetics.* Translated by G. Else. Ann Arbor: University of Michigan Press.

Barthes, Roland. 1975. An introduction to the structural analysis of narrative. *New Literary History* 6:237–72.

Bauman, Richard. 1986. *Story, performance, and event. Contextual studies of oral narrative.* Cambridge: Cambridge University Press.

Bauman, Richard, and Charles Briggs. 1990. Poetics and performance as criti-
    cal perspectives on language and social life. *Annual Review of Anthropology*
    19:59–88.
Briggs, Charles. 1996. The meaning of nonsense, the poetics of embodiment,
    and the production of power in Warao healing. In *The performance of heal-
    ing*, edited by C. Laderman and M. Roseman, 185–232. London: Routledge.
Bruner, Edward. 1984. Introduction: The opening up of anthropology. In *Text,
    play, and story*, edited by Edward Bruner, 1–16. Prospect, Ill.: Waveland
    Press.
———. 1986. Ethnography as narrative. In *The anthropology of experience*,
    edited by Victor Turner and Edward Bruner, 139–55. Urbana: University of
    Illinois Press.
———. 1997. Ethnography as narrative. In *Memory, identity, community*, ed-
    ited by Lewis P. Hinchman and Sandra K. Hinchman, 264–80. Albany: State
    University New York Press.
Bruner, Jerome. 1986. *Actual minds, possible worlds*. Cambridge, Mass.: Har-
    vard University Press.
———. 1990a. *Acts of meaning*. Cambridge, Mass.: Harvard University Press.
———. 1990b. Culture and human development: A new look. *Human Devel-
    opment* 33:344–55.
———. 1996. *The culture of education*. Cambridge, Mass.: Harvard University
    Press.
Carr, David. 1986. *Time, narrative, and history*. Bloomington: Indiana Univer-
    sity Press.
———. 1997. Narrative and the real world: An argument for continuity. In
    Memory, identity, community, edited by Lewis P. Hinchman and Sandra K.
    Hinchman, 7–25. Albany: State University of New York Press.
Carrithers, Michael. 1992. *Why humans have culture: Explaining anthropology
    and social diversity*. Oxford: Oxford University Press.
Chatman, Seymour. 1978. *Story and discourse: Narrative structure in fiction
    and film*. Ithaca, N.Y.: Cornell University Press.
Clifford, James. 1983. On ethnographic authority. *Representations* 1:118–46.
Crapanzano, Vincent. 1986. Hermes' dilemma: The masking of subversion in
    ethnographic description. In *Writing culture*, edited by James Clifford and
    George Marcus, 51–76. Berkeley and Los Angeles: University of California
    Press.
Crites, Stephen. 1997. The narrative quality of experience. In *Memory, identity,
    community*, edited by Lewis P. Hinchman and Sandra K. Hinchman, 26–50.
    Albany: State University of New York Press.
Csordas, Thomas J. 1990. Embodiment as a paradigm for anthropology. *Ethos*
    18:5–47.
———. 1994. Introduction: The body as representation and being-in-the-world.
    In *Embodiment and experience*, edited by Thomas J. Cordas, 1–24. Cam-
    bridge: Cambridge University Press.
———. 1996. Imaginal performance and memory in ritual healing. In *The per-
    formance of healing*, edited by C. Laderman and M. Roseman, 91–113. New
    York: Routledge.

Danforth, Loring. 1989. *Firewalking and religious healing: The Ana Stenari of Greece and the American firewalking movement.* Princeton, N.J.: Princeton University Press.

Desjarlais, Robert. 1996. Presence. In *The performance of healing,* edited by C. Laderman and M. Roseman, 143–64. New York: Routledge.

Dilthey, William. 1989. *Selected works.* Vol. 1. Edited by R. A. Makkreel and F. Rodi. Princeton, N.J.: Princeton University Press.

Fernandez, James W. 1986. The argument of images and the exchange of returning to the whole. In *The anthropology of experience,* edited by V. Turner and E. Bruner, 159–87. Urbana: University of Illinois Press.

Forster, E. M. 1927. *Aspects of the novel.* New York: Harcourt Brace Jovanovich.

Gadamer, Hans-Georg. 1975. *Truth and method.* New York: Seabury Press.

Geertz, Clifford. 1973. *The interpretation of cultures.* New York: Basic Books.

Good, B., and M. J. DelVecchio Good. 1994. In the subjunctive mode: Epilepsy narratives in Turkey. *Social Science and Medicine* 38:835–42.

Heidegger, Martin. 1962. *Being and time.* Translated by E. Robinson and J. Macquarrie. New York: Harper and Row.

Hoskins, Janet. 1998. *Biographical objects: How things tell the stories of people's lives.* New York: Routledge.

Hughes-Freeland, Felicia. 1998. Introduction. In *Ritual performance, media,* edited by Felicia Hughes-Freeland, 1–28. New York: Routledge.

Hymes, Dell. 1975. Breakthrough into performance. In *Folklore: Performance and communication,* edited by Dan Ben-Amos and K. S. Goldstein. The Hague: Mouton.

Jackson, Michael. 1989. *Paths toward a clearing: Radical empiricism and ethnographic inquiry.* Bloomington: Indiana University Press.

Kapferer, Bruce. 1983. *A celebration of demons: Exorcism and the aesthetics of healing in Sri Lanka.* Bloomington: Indiana University Press.

Kendall, Laurie. 1996. Initiating performance: The story of Chini, a Korean shaman. In *The performance of healing,* edited by C. Laderman and M. Roseman, 17–58. New York: Routledge.

Kermode, Frank. 1966. *The sense of an ending: Studies in the theory of fiction.* London: Oxford University Press.

Kleinman, Arthur. 1988. *The illness narratives.* New York: Basic Books.

Laderman, Carol. 1996. Poetics of healing in Malay shamanistic performances. In *The performance of healing,* edited by C. Laderman and M. Roseman, 115–41. New York: Routledge.

Laderman, Carol, and M. Roseman, eds. 1996. *The performance of healing.* New York: Routledge.

Lawlor, Mary, and Cheryl Mattingly. 1998. The complexities of family-centered care. *American Journal of Occupational Therapy* 52:259–67.

Leach, Edmund. 1976. *Culture and communication: The logic by which symbols are connected.* Cambridge: Cambridge University Press.

———. 1984. Conclusion: Further thoughts on the realm of folly. In *Text, play and story,* edited by E. Bruner, 356–64. Prospect Heights, Ill.: Waveland Press.

Lyotard, J. 1984. *The postmodern condition: A report on knowledge*. Minneapolis: University of Minnesota Press.

MacIntyre, Alisdair. 1981. *After virtue: A study in moral theory*. South Bend, Ind.: University of Notre Dame Press.

———. 1997. The virtues, the unity of a human life, and the concept of a tradition. In *Memory, identity, community*, edited by Lewis P. Hinchman and Sandra K. Hinchman, 241–63. Albany: State University of New York Press.

Marcus, George E. 1998. *Ethnography through thick and thin*. Princeton, N.J.: Princeton University Press.

Marcus, George E., and Dick Cushman. 1982. Ethnographies as texts. *Annual Review of Anthropology* 11:25–69.

Mattingly, Cheryl. 1991a. The narrative nature of clinical reasoning. *American Journal of Occupational Therapy* 45:998–1005.

———. 1991b. Narrative reflections on practical actions: Two learning experiments in reflective storytelling. In *The reflective turn: Case studies in and on educational practice*, edited by D. Schon, 235–57. New York: Teachers College Press.

———. 1994. The concept of therapeutic emplotment. *Social Science and Medicine* 38:811–22.

———. 1998a. *Healing dramas and clinical plots. The narrative structure of experience*. Cambridge: Cambridge University Press.

———. 1998b. In search of the good: Narrative reasoning in clinical practice. *Medical Anthropology Quarterly* 12:273–97.

Mattingly, Cheryl, and Maureen Fleming 1994. *Clinical reasoning: Forms of inquiry in a therapeutic practice*. Philadelphia: F. A. Davis.

Mattingly, Cheryl, and Mary Lawlor. 1997. The disability experience from a family perspective. In *Willard and Spackman's occupational therapy*, edited by E. Crepeau and M. Neistadt. Philadelphia: Lippincott.

Myerhoff, Barbara. 1986. Life not death in Venice: Its second life. In *The anthropology of experience*, edited by V. Turner and E. M. Bruner, 261–86. Urbana: University of Illinois Press.

Olafson, Fredrick. 1971. Narrative history and the concept of action. *History and Theory* 8:265–89.

———. 1979. *The dialectic of action: Philosophical interpretation of history and the humanities*. Chicago: University of Chicago Press.

Ricoeur, Paul. 1984. *Time and narrative*. Vol. 1. Chicago: University of Chicago Press.

———. 1985. *Time and narrative*. Vol. 2. Chicago: University of Chicago Press.

———. 1987. *Time and narrative*. Vol. 3. Chicago: University of Chicago Press.

Rosaldo, Renato. 1986. Ilongot hunting as story and experience. In *The anthropology of experience*, edited by Victor Turner and Edward Bruner, 97–138. Urbana: University of Illinois Press.

Roseman, Varina. 1996. "Pure Products Go Crazy": Rainforest healing in a nation-state. In *The performance of healing*, edited by C. Laderman and M. Roseman, 233–69. New York: Routledge.

Sacks, Oliver. 1984. *A leg to stand on*. New York: Summit Books.

Schechner, Richard. 1993. *The future of ritual: Writings on culture and performance*. New York: Routledge.

Schieffelin, Edward. 1996. On failure and performance: Throwing the medium out of the seance. In *The performance of healing*, edited by C. Landerman and M. Roseman, 59–89. New York: Routledge.

———. 1998. Problematizing performance. In *Ritual performance, media*, edited by Felicia Hughes-Freeland, 194–207. New York: Routledge.

Stoller, Paul. 1989. *The taste of ethnographic things: The senses of anthropology*. Philadelphia: University of Pennsylvania Press.

———. 1997. *Sensuous scholarship*. Philadelphia: University of Pennsylvania Press.

Tambiah, Stanley. 1985. *Culture, thought, and social action: An anthropological perspective*. Cambridge: Cambridge University Press.

Turner, Victor. 1969. *The ritual process: Structure and anti-structure*. Chicago: Aldine.

———. 1986a. *The anthropology of performance*. New York: PAJ Publications.

———. 1986b. Dewey, Dilthey, and drama: An essay in the anthropology of experience. In *The anthropology of experience*, edited by Victor Turner and Edward Bruner, 33–44. Urbana: University of Illinois Press.

White, Hayden. 1980. The value of narrativity in the representation of reality. In *On narrative*, edited by T. J. Mitchell, 1–23. Urbana: University of Illinois Press.

———. 1987. *The content of form: Narrative discourse and historical representation*. Baltimore: Johns Hopkins University Press.

Wikan, Unni. 1995. The self in a world of urgency and necessity. *Ethos* 23:259–85.

NINE

With Life in One's Lap

The Story of an Eye/I (or Two)

UNNI WIKAN

Suddenly one Sunday morning I awoke with black shadows dashing across one eye. I took it in stride. "Stress!" I thought to myself. No wonder my body had finally given in—the way I had been driving myself for far too long.

I had long marveled at my body's unfailing loyalty. It had supported me through thick and thin on my travels to some very rough places where I had gone, neglectful of ordinary health precautions. I had had just one health philosophy in life: don't think about illness and you'll stay well. So far it had worked: I had been spared even such ordinary ailments as headaches and backaches that compel many others to slow down. Now the black shadows reminded me that *my* limit had been reached. My body was in revolt.

So I proceeded as usual. I spent the whole day reading the page proofs of a book manuscript that was already overdue, but getting up from time to time to inspect my eye in the mirror. Was there no visible sign of the black shadows—a swollen eyelid or some other exterior mark? There was not. At night, I went to bed a bit early, hoping a good night's sleep might dispel the problem.

It did not. By morning the shadows had grown or multiplied, I no longer remember which, and seemed to be moving about with increasing speed. During the day, I had the feeling that people with whom I talked must *see* my shadows, or see *me* startling from something or other, and I felt like asking them if they did. But then I did not want to make an issue of things. First thing in the morning, I had a terribly important meeting at the city hall with myself in a key role. I did not function well. The shadows interfered not just with my optic but my cognitive vision. I had trouble finding my words. I had trouble focusing and thinking clearly. So I felt relieved when the chairperson suggested we cut the meeting short by half an hour (perhaps because she had noted my "indisposition"). On the way back to my office I thought of passing by my optician to ask what my problem might be. But it would take an extra ten to fifteen minutes, and I had a busy day ahead of me.

(More busy than I could have envisioned at that point in time.)

Back at the office I sat down to prepare a lecture for 3:00 P.M. But at 12:30 I could no longer contain myself. I grabbed the telephone book and searched in the yellow pages for an eye specialist whose office was close to mine. I phoned the man, describing my symptoms, which were rapidly getting worse. "Nothing to worry about," he said, giving me an appointment three days hence. Half an hour later I phoned him again: "I'm sorry to trouble you," I said, "but I *am* worried. I seem to be going blind on the eye!" He repeated what he had said earlier. "Don't worry. Come and see me in three days!"

With stoic calm, I gave my lecture. Then I drove home, had dinner with my son (my husband was away), and sat down to finish the proofreading of my manuscript. But it was no longer any fun. I was really very worried. At 7:30 P.M. I phoned a friend who is a doctor, no eye specialist, but a wise man. His voice was grave: "It sounds like you have a detached retina," he said. (I had never heard of such a thing.) "Let's hope it is not, but if you have, there's no time to lose! Go immediately to [a private clinic]. It will cost you a fortune, but it is worth it!"

(He also said that he had never heard a person in such a state being so calm—which made me slightly alarmed. Did he mean to compliment me or to tell me I was a fool? And what did he mean by "such a state"— *en slik tilstand?* I was soon to find out.)

At the fortune-costing place there was little they could do—no eye specialist in attendance at night—save refer me to a public hospital where by midnight the verdict was clear: A detached retina indeed: "You [that's me] have to stay here to be operated on tomorrow." I asked how long I would have to remain in the hospital. "A week," answered the doctor, who, seeing my shocked face, added, "But you'll be on sick leave for a month!" I looked at him aghast: "But please, let me go out tomorrow morning for just two hours," I said, (and so as to deter any protest) "I'm giving a lecture at the invitation of the health minister himself to all the staff at the ministry!" The doctor looked at me, incredulous. I assured him I would be speaking without notes, not even using my eyes, just standing up on my two legs. But he was unmerciful. I was ordered into bed and told to lie flat on my back until the operation could be performed.

HAVOC IN MY EYE/I

Thus began my sickness odyssey: with open admission of defeat—with the cancellation, at the last moment, of a lecture that it would have been my pride to give. And when I did give it a month later, I did not feel it was me who did. Unni was there, and the lecture went well, but I was someone observing myself giving the lecture. The whole thing was unreal, as unreal as my whole being-in-the-world at that time. Thus, on that memorable day when I spoke to that large, impressive audience, headed by the health minister, I wore a pink sweater, pink as pink can be. Under normal conditions I would have considered it crazy. I would have dressed in formal attire. But on this occasion I had just one thought in mind: to keep in touch with myself, and bright pink was the only color I could barely discern with my Eye. Thus, when I would move my arms, as I do when I talk, I would know that they were *my* arms, that it was indeed me.

I needed the color as a crutch to steady me, for it was not just that I did not see much with the Eye. Worse, the Eye was in chaos—utter, complete chaos. I had two simultaneous visions on the world: one orderly, normal (if nearsighted), letting me view the world as the world had always seemed; the other made a mockery of all this seeming naturalness and created havoc: there were huge black gas bubbles dashing about frantically, constantly shedding off smaller "bombs" and then regrouping, recombining into new forms and monsters. (The gas stemmed from the operation and was intended to put my retina back in place.) I later learned that these "gas bombs" were in fact minuscule, so tiny they could just be discerned with the eye surgeon's special equipment. But to me they loomed huge, a dreadful intrusion into my world. Try thinking clearly when your world is in chaos, try keeping calm and follow a steady line of thought when your vision—or one half of it—projects thunder and lightning, a world overturned. Thus, the pink sweater to steady me. In retrospect I realize I must also have had a craving for color to counteract the gloomy blackness of the Eye/I.

WITH LIFE IN ONE'S LAP

To make a long story short, the operation did not go well. On the fourth night I awoke with a terrible pain, and in the morning my Eye was completely blind: it had exploded in infections and bleedings. What was worse, the surgeon (one of Norway's leading retina specialists) had no explanation and no hope to give me. He had never come across such a case. My Eye was a mystery to him and everyone else around. So this is where it began the second time: with the blindness and the loss of hope; the black shadows marked the first-time beginning. These are moments in time that stand out and mark my illness story—not so much because of the medical developments involved as because of their impact on me, on the I.

Both threw me out of life, landing me with life in the lap (*livet i fanget*), as the Norwegian saying goes. At the first beginning, I was jolted into a hospital or sick-house (*sykehus*), as the Norwegian concept graphically renders the place, and I soon learned that a sick-house was a place to be sick, not well. So my one thought in life was to get out, get home—which I was to have done (at my own insistence) on the morning that marked the second beginning. It was then that I had to admit defeat. I was ill, I was sick. Until then, I had denied even my son to come and see me; my stay in the sick-house, I told myself, was a parenthesis in my life, it did not count. Now I had to face up to my utter vulnerability: I was not just sick but inexplicably sick. And so I was thrown out of life the second time: ordered (and this time I did not object) to lie still *on my left side only* for the next few weeks and abstain from all reading. It was like being told "you're lame *and* blind." This, then, is my story.

THE BEGINNING, NOT THE END,
MARKS MY NARRATIVE

It is a story with a definite beginning (or two), a moderately clear middle, and a muddled, unfinished end. Who says that narrative begins with an end, with knowing how it all went? I shall argue the contrary. What marks my illness narrative, as well as the narratives of many people I know, is the absolute certainty of the beginning. The reason is evident: the beginning is the turning point—the end is simply what then happened or how it all went. Life goes on, and so I do not know how it all went; the ending is not yet clear. I wish I knew, wish I could say, this is where it ended, here is a new beginning. But I can't. Life goes on, and my illness story is caught up in life. So I give you the beginning(s).

Thus I support (and lean on) Cheryl Mattingly's lucid critique of literary theorists, set forth in this volume and elsewhere. She invokes Frank Kermode to the effect that (to quote Kermode) "we have a need for endings" (1966: 37) and goes on to describe the literary theorists' position thus:

> The narrator knows the ending. From his retrospective perspective, he is able to select the relevant events and reveal their causal relations because he knows how events unfolded to bring about the particular ending which, narratively speaking, gives meaning to those events. Stories are read backwards. Narratives are . . . ordered around an ending, and it is the ending which has a fundamental role in shaping the meaning of the narrated events (Olafson 1979; Ricoeur 1984). . . . the story's structure exists because the narrator knows where to start, knows what to include and exclude, knows how to weight and evaluate and connect the events he recounts, all because he knows where he will stop (1998:38).

This is absurd, in my view. It presumes a narrator in full control of his material; and I deliberately say "his," for I think there is a gender aspect here. Moreover, it presumes that narratives are always ex post facto, that the story "has come to an end," or the narrative could not proceed. And third (and linked to the first point), it presumes that the narrative is textual, written or talked-as-written, undisturbed by reactions from the audience. I have met such people sometimes: people who seem to proceed as if the audience were not there, or were there only for their own satisfaction. But to claim that this is the essence of narrative, that the end is the central linking piece to which all else is related, seems to me absurd, and remote from lived experience.

I certainly did *not* know where to stop, as I began telling you my story. And I could have given you many different endings, depending on what direction I had let my story take. Nor did I know, as I began telling you my story, where it would take me. For it (my life, my illness) branches off in all kinds of directions, some of which I have not even thought through at this point in time, though telling you my story here might have been an occasion to do so. What was absolutely certain to me from the beginning, however, was the beginning of my story, as of my illness, or the two beginnings, as I have called them. Both caught me unaware; both marked that terrible divide between "before" and "after." Seymour Chatman argues that "the notion of 'beginning,' 'middle,' and 'end' apply only to story-events as imitated rather than to real actions themselves, simply because such terms are meaningless in the real world" (quoted in Mattingly, 1998:37). I contest this view. There *are* beginnings, middles, and ends in life as in stories. And while we may have a need for endings to make a good story, stories can just as well be made out of beginnings, a good beginning. It may not satisfy the literary theorist, but yet it may be entirely in tune with how people experience their own world, and therefore true to life.

STORY, NOT NARRATIVE

"The sick bleed stories," notes Broyard (1992). Try rephrasing the sentence: "The sick bleed narratives." No, we don't. People bleed stories, but academics gather narratives. What is the difference?

"Story" is experience-near, probably a universal concept that taps a universal aspect of living: everyone can tell stories, whereas only academics can find narrative. Because my native language (Norwegian) does not have a word for "narrative," only for "story"[1]—nor do the other languages I know (Arabic, German, Indonesian)—I find it difficult to believe that I need "narrative" to comprehend people or their world (see my critique in Wikan 1995). To be frank, I am always suspicious when I encounter the concept. I wonder what it is going to deliver that "story" could not. And I am often supported in my conviction that the emperor has no clothes.

Mattingly's chapter in this volume made me momentarily revise my position. I felt I finally understood what narrative meant, only to have the concept dismantled again when I realized that all the presuppositions she spells out from literary theorists did not fit my illness story (or narrative, if you will). Indeed, Mattingly herself presents a lucid critique of these same presuppositions, arguing that their relevance to real life is questionable:

> The opposition between lived experience and narrative as discourse "registers sensibly only by positing a false notion of what prior events are and how they are structured. Literary theorists, historians, sociolinguists, folklorists, and others whose primary concerns are written and oral texts have not investigated the structure of lived experience and thus the distinctions between life and art rest on far too simple a view of how life in time is experienced" (Mattingly 1998:44). Even anthropologists fascinated with the ethnographer's task of converting field experience into text have been too quick to dismiss the narrative structures of social action. (Mattingly this volume)

In telling you my story, I am not just giving you a coherent account of events. I also claim that this is what truly happened (from my point of view). Story (*historie*) also means history in my language. The coherence I depict is not an artifact of my story; it is the essence of my life. Things cohere, even when they maddeningly jar. I experience my life through my efforts to make sense of events. It is not that experience is formless, languageless. From my first experience of the black dashing shadows, when I didn't have a clue other than "stress" to what they meant, I put words to my experience, I told myself stories to account for them. And yet the literary theorists tell us life does not cohere, only narratives do. Where is the raw material that is the evidence of their claims? Again, I follow Mattingly:

> A narrative portrayal of experience is artifice in the sense that no life has the congruence of the well-told tale. . . . [However,] the intimate connection between story and experience results from the structure of action itself. . . . If narrative offers an intimate relation to lived experience, the dominant formal feature that connects the two is not narrative coherence but narrative drama. . . . We follow a narrative suspensefully, always reminded of the fragility of events, for things might have turned out differently. (Mattingly 1998:154)

ILLNESS VERSUS MULTIPLE COMPELLING CONCERNS

In telling you my illness story, I am making a series of choices. First and foremost, I am giving you what you are asking for: an account of my illness. But this is a skewed perspective on my life, and even on my illness. Indeed, I have been surprised that illness narratives, as presented in the academic literature, are so often about "my illness and me"—whereas the illness stories I hear from people in the field, as well as from friends at home, usually take a different form: they deal much more with the person's relationships to significant others and to her world. The stories I hear people tell of their illnesses are more inseparable from the ongoing stories of their lives (in line with the stories presented by the other contributors to this volume). One question that concerns me, then, is: How can we know that the illness narratives we elicit as researchers tap the experience of suffering? People's compelling concerns could be different; they need not be the illness, even when illness looms large in a person's life.

Take as an example my friend Umm Ali in Cairo, a poor woman of immense personal resources whom I have known intimately for twenty-seven years (Wikan 1996b). Now she is sick with diabetes and also blind. Back in 1975—the year the following story is drawn from—she had only the diabetes. A typical excerpt of my field notes from that time reads as follows:

> Umm Ali goes to make herself a glass of tea while spewing forth a stream of complaints. Mustafa (husband) left only [a few pennies] for food this morning, and nothing for medicines. It is ten days already since she was at the doctor's who wrote out a prescription for insulin. Now she feels so poorly, she gets dizzy every time she tries to stand up. But Mustafa doesn't give a damn. The doctor has said she *must* try to live a regular life, get up early in the morning and eat properly and take her pills. But it is impossible because she gets too little sleep. If she goes to bed early, the children wake her up with cries of "Mama, where's my this? Mama, I want my that!" In the morning when she wakes up, she asks for a glass of tea so she can take the medicines. But she must ask a dozen times before anyone cares to listen. So she gets tired and lies down to sleep again. "You have seen it yourself, when I ask for tea, it takes two hours before anyone brings it!" Mustafa is mad because she can't get up in the morning. She asks him to wake her up before he leaves, but he mocks her and says that if she can't wake up on her own, she can go to hell and sleep there! The doctor has said she needs a lot of nutritious food. But that is impossible in a house like this. For the children beg and she does not have the heart to refuse. (Goes on to tell how yesterday, when she had two eggs for dinner—a rare luxury—she split her own eggs with her children: "And there went those nutrients!"). (Wikan 1996b:134)

On another occasion, Umm Ali told this story:

> If only Mustafa would help me and cooperate, my health would be good as gold. For they have said it on the radio in a program on psychology: "The husband is the wife's best doctor."
> . . . But Mustafa is never willing to help me. When he was sick with a pain in his knee, he used to ask me to massage his leg, though my arms and back were aching. But he will never massage me. . . .
> When I was pregnant with Nosa, I was so huge because of the water in my body that people believed I was going to have twins. I could hardly get out of bed. I asked Mustafa to let me lie on the outside of the bed in case I needed to get up and pee. "What d'you think you are, that you can bully me about as you please," he thundered. One night as I woke, I couldn't manage to step across him, and I let out a terrible cry for I was so afraid to pee in the bed. (Wikan 1996b:98)

Thus Umm Ali's illness narratives are shaped in the same form as her litany of complaints: they deal with her relationships to her nearest and dearest: the constant enervating struggle between her and her husband, his power abuse and lack of care, her constant yearning for affection and reciprocity, the children's painful neglect of her, and her never-to-be-fulfilled desire to give them what they need. Money, or its lack, is a constant, all-encompassing cause of all problems. Diabetes enters, of course, as a significant source of suffering, but in every story I have heard her tell through all these years, even when she has been at her most self-absorbed, diabetes has never taken center stage. Her illness is inextricably bound up with her relationship to her nearest and dearest—which she never tires of telling about.[2]

This may be partly linked with the fact that she lives in a society where *getting one's bad feelings out* is considered a precondition for health. Thus telling one's sorrow is a health-sustaining activity, and sorrow is always linked with one's nearest and dearest, in Cairo as in most other places in the world. Egyptians are lucky, though, to live in a society where exposing one's private life sorrows is supposed to be natural to humans; it does not brand the person.

NARRATIVE AND OBSERVATION

It is different with me. I live in a society where it is not normal or natural to expose one's private life. So I am giving you just the story of my Eye, and in so doing I make sure you sympathize with me, for it was a trauma. But I am *not* telling you numerous things—experiences, sensations, events—that concern my relationships to persons dear to me and how these were affected by, and in turn affected, my Eye/I. Thus I partly misconstrue the source of my suffering and its consequences. I make sure you get what you asked for, and not more. My story, then, like so many illness narratives presented by academics, is about "my illness and me"—not about my multiple compelling concerns and the way they impinged on my experience of illness and healing. Husband, son, mother, friends, and colleagues have been wiped out of the picture—which is why you will never comprehend what my illness truly meant to me. I do not want to expose myself unnecessarily.

Had you been there with me when it happened, or in the first few months after it happened, you would have had another basis on which to judge my illness story. You would have seen and sensed and known things about how I reacted, how my illness affected me, that would fill in, support, or undermine the snippets of story that *I* am giving you. You would have been able to make your own observations. I have elsewhere contested the place of narrative in much current anthropology, arguing that it has been given a place out of all proportion to the role of stories in real life for many people (Wikan 1995). I have deplored the downplayed role of *observation* in making sense of a person's experiences, ar-

guing that we need observations of real-life events to anchor and also offer *resistance* to a person's telling-it-as-it-was (Wikan 1996b). If you had
seen me and talked with me at the time when I was sick, and for some
time afterward, you would have had a reference point, a context, for my
story. Better still, if you had met and talked with persons close to me
who would be willing to tell *their* stories. My point here is to contest the
preponderant place of self-narrative in anthropological analysis currently, and to argue that the balance should be redressed.

While no anthropologist (that I know of) seems to argue explicitly
that self-narrative renders experience as it is, yet the underlying message
often seems to be that this is as close as we can get. Truly, sometimes it
is. There *are* situations in which other kinds of data are simply not available. But these are exceptions—for an anthropologist. I argue that observation of real-life behavior—what Ingold (1993) calls *attending* to a
person's world—is necessary to fill in the picture and understand what
a narrative is all about, and that we can indeed get closer to a person's
experience that way (Wikan 1996a, 1996b). Since you were not there to
see me through my eye illness, you get only my story with myself in the
role of hero, and I can tell you anything I want; you have no other evidence with which to contest my story.

Let me elaborate on these points. Among the many things that I find no
place for in my illness story, but tell you here to let you know some of
what you were missing by not being there and attending to my world,
are the following:

Had you been there, you would have noticed that my body language,
quite different from how I normally behave, indicated a loss of self-
confidence or balance. You might have noticed that I strained to talk,
that my words did not come as easily, that my mind did not seem to be
working as well as before, and that I was severely troubled by this fact.
You would have noted that I fumbled more, that my sense of orientation
suffered, and that I was therefore also more forgetful. You might also
have noticed that I looked more untidy, in part for sheer physical reasons (I did not see the loose hair straws hanging down over my right
eye), but also because I had ceased to look at myself in the mirror: I resented what I saw—a face not mine, a face with two entirely different
eyes, one blue, normal, the other greenish and with a huge pupil (caused
by medication) that, to make matters worse, was entirely out of focus; I
was entirely cross-eyed, since I had no control over my Eye. You would
have noted that people treated me with some awe and with great con-

cern: having an Eye, I learned, is no ordinary disease. Many of us feel that the soul sits in the eye; thus having a mysterious and sudden eye illness with a fearsome outcome (that could potentially strike anyone) elicits great sympathy and interest. This again affected how I viewed my Eye/I. You would have noted that I would not let you meet me without going by way of my Eye, that is, by telling you some of my story. It was as if my I had been displaced and now reached out to you from the vantage point of my Eye—*one* particular part of my body.

But if you had been there with me at the time and made your own observations, you would also have done well by attending not just to me but also to *others* who were significant in my world. There is an indisputable advantage not just to hearing (or eliciting) a person's story, but also to talking with persons close to her or him who might be able to give *their* versions of relevant events. Let me invoke Mintz's succinct observation from long ago:

> Even if fieldwork is confined at some point to dealing with a single informant, there is great benefit in being able at least to observe that informant interacting with other members of the group. Though there is no way of proving it, I suspect that a good deal of the confidence an anthropologist may feel in a particular informant arises from his or her judgments of how *others* regard that informant, as manifested in their interactive behavior. Even in confining my interest in interviewing for the life history, I would certainly not argue that communication between biographer and informant can or should be the sole source of relevant information. (1979:20)

His words apply to all sorts of narrative, including illness narratives, and have perhaps greater relevance today than ever. Because in my case, you were not able to do what Mintz suggests, you are almost totally in my power. I can tell you almost anything I want, and you have little or no other evidence with which to contest my story.

WHAT PERSON THE DISEASE HAS

"Ask not what disease the person has, but rather what person the disease has" goes a saying.[3] Among the "safe" things I can tell you about how my Eye affected my I, and vice versa, are the following:

My disease had a person who did not know how to be sick. I had grown up in a family where sickness did not exist. I cannot remember my parents or grandparents ever being sick. I then married a man who also was "above" illness. Thus, apart from having to deal with the normal child ailments in my son, I had no personal experience and no *com-*

petence in being sick. This had to be learned, and I learned it the hard way, by making numerous mistakes.

My analytic point is the following: the fact of growing up in a society where there is a certain fund of knowledge regarding illness and healing does not mean that people, ordinary people, necessarily acquire such knowledge. Cultural knowledge is accumulated only as it becomes relevant to one's life, and it is surprising to what extent taken-for-granted knowledge can be irrelevant.[4] Thus in my case, I simply could not comprehend what one does when one is sick. The role and its attributes had never registered with me. So I did most things wrong. And when my Eye is as bad as it is, it is probably in part because I am paying the price of my ignorance or folly.

The term *sick role,* coined by Parsons, is often used to refer to a new set of social roles associated with the illness that the person enters into because her usual social roles have been seriously undermined, both by the physical limitations encountered in the disease and by the social identity associated with patienthood (Hunt this volume). I want to underscore another aspect: the pragmatics of the case. "Being sick" requires a certain competence, I learned. For instance, it entails eating and drinking properly; resting; taking time for recovery; doing as the doctor says. I, on my part, had always lived by the counterformula of a Balinese friend-physician's saying: "If a person *feels* sick, who can make him well?" (Wikan 1990). My motto read: "If a person *feels* well, who can make her sick?" Thus I had deliberately avoided thinking about sickness or taking ordinary health precautions. I had never cared much about what I ate (quite functional in my case, with all the fieldwork I do), never taken vitamins, never rested much, and always considered working the best way to stay happy. It follows that when I now had to learn "being sick," some parts of the sick role would register better with me than others: I could easily understand the injunctions "lie on your left side only, don't lift anything heavy, don't bend," whereas when it came to "don't go out in the cold, protect your eye against strong light (but don't cover it), rest, take months for recovery and you might get your sight back in some months (or a year or three)," I was uncomprehending. How could I avoid going out in the cold when this was Norway in winter? How could I stay home a single day more than needed when getting well meant feeling well? How could I take it easy for several months in the hope that this would give me back my sight when the one thing I had learned from my experience was that you don't know if you even have the next day. *Ingen kjenner dagen før solen går ned,* as the Norwegian saying goes: No one knows the day before the sun has set. I needed to get working as soon as possible to use whatever little time I have left in life, not to postpone things for a morrow that might not ever come.

So I chiseled out my own version of the "sick role"—a compromise of sorts between medical injunctions, bodily needs, and the me, the I, and my mental needs. As part of this, I moved home from hospital on the eighth day—against strong medical advice—but by then my Eye counted less to me than my I: it was a matter of survival, of escaping the dreadful sick-house routines, there among being shuffled about like a parcel, as I was to be laid in the fifth consecutive room in eight days (due to room constraints), with ever new roommates and their often noisy visitors.

Also, I was desperate to be able to *see* the beautiful flowers that family and friends had sent to me, and that would have graced my bleak days, were it not for the sick-house setup: *I* had to be on my left side only, whereas the flowers were placed on my right side only, behind my back, in the only available space. I could stand it no longer; I was getting sicker by the day in my heart. So I moved home.

It is often taken for granted that people know how to be sick, that the "sick role" is simply part of any sensible person's role repertoire, apart from the modification of her social roles that may be necessitated. I have wanted to focus on another, underestimated aspect: the pragmatics— how to be, how to do, and how to find a compromise one can live with.

Second, my disease had a person who considered it a defeat to be sick. Thus I felt terrible when I had to go public about my "condition," as I must, for the disease struck me at a time when I was giving several public lectures a week and appearing frequently on radio and TV. I had to let down one audience after the other. I tried to make sure everyone was told that it was because of an eye, no other bodily ailment. Having an "eye" seemed more physical, less personal. Broadcasting my physical "speciality" removed the disease from personhood; though it is ironic that I should choose such a strategy when what I deplored in the hospital was precisely that I-my-body did not exist, just my Eye. I did it to try to counter my experience of defeat.

Third, I feel as if I have attended my own funeral. On visiting me (at home) one day, a friend burst out: "This does not look like a sick bed, it looks like a funeral parlor!" and she was right. The room was packed with flowers and very beautiful to behold. Necrologues have always intrigued me. I have been struck by the fact that every dead person was the best and most wonderful there ever was—to judge from the necrologues. And I have resented this discrepancy between how we people talk about each other in ordinary life versus the praise we lavish on others after they are dead. I have wanted to be different: to tell people the good things while they are still alive.

The flowers warmed my heart and told me people cared — even people whom I would otherwise never have known did so. I will hopefully never in life again receive so many flowers.

Fourth, my disease had a person who thought she would remain forever in strong health, a person who felt her energy to be quite limitless. That person is gone. I am acutely aware of my own vulnerability and of the fact of living on borrowed time: at any point it could be over, just as my Eye failed me without warning. And though the surgeon insists that there is no medical evidence that stress can produce a detached retina, I am sure that it does. He says that this disease is only the result of strong myopia or (in some cases) to being knocked hard in the head. But I don't believe him. I am convinced that my Eye illness was my body's revenge. It is the only sensible response to the "Why me?" question. Moreover, I am convinced that I know when it started, how it all began. For it was not just stress that attacked my weakest point, but clear, identifiable stress stemming from a particular life experience.

But that is a story I will not tell you — the true beginning to all my ailments (for others followed in the wake of the Eye as a result of complications and medication). However, I repeat my point about story: what it needs for a plot is a good beginning, the rest takes care of itself, more or less. True, we have to produce endings to finish the story, but stories can also be unfinished like this one. What stands and gives the narrative power is the beginning — what marked the true turning point. So it is with me; so it is with Umm Ali; and perhaps so it also is with you, my reader, who may have your own experience of beginnings that changed the course of your life.

SUMMING UP

More than two years have passed since the preceding was written. I approach it again with extreme reluctance. Were it not for the editors' advice that I write a conclusion, I might never have done so — read the story again. "The critique of narrative was difficult to get a handle on, perhaps because it was so well integrated into the narrative. The concluding remarks seem to warrant some expansion," wrote a reviewer for the press. So here I am, having just forced myself to overcome my resistance to meet myself at that dismal point in time. Or, to tell you the truth, this is how it happened: I brought forth the paper and started reading, then put it aside for a long time before I could proceed. I felt like a furtive viewer peeping in on some very personal, very private matter. So I proceeded slowly, uneasily, afraid of what I would find, and of having to relive a pain that is best forgotten.

Two features of the story line cry out to me as I read: the minimalist, staccato language and—the silences. I am struck that my story is a story of events, of happenings, rather than of digested emotional experiences; there is little florid language; the text is bare to the bone, *thin*. After rereading, I start revising. Fill in some context here, an explanation there. Contextualize! is the mantra of the anthropologist. And I contextualize, until I realize that I am changing the tone and nerve of the text. The story of my Eye/I, as written in August 1996, becomes the story of my Eye and my illness, as viewed from the vantage point of January 1999. Thick description, yes. But thick of what?

I realize that the story as written is authentic in a way that can only be undone by thick description from the present. My "context" now is not what it was then. True, I realize that I have omitted telling you things that might change your ideas of me and my illness. For example, there are few references to my nearest and dearest: my husband is unmentioned, except for his being away; my mother, likewise, no mention; only my son features, in a couple of brief references—when the truth is that my husband was quite beside himself and eventually broke off his engagement in the States to be with me; my mother was desperate to come and look after me; and my son did all in his power to help me.

But my *experience* was of being utterly alone in a trauma that shook me out of my life. The structure of my story, as originally told, captures this. So I go back and undo all the changes I had made. Back to basics. Let the events stand, unembellished, unexplained; the problem with "context," I realize, as I heap explanation on explanation, is that it easily points in many directions at once. Yes, I would like you to know the terrible state of the Norwegian general hospital in which I lay; I don't think you can imagine what one of the world's richest welfare states offers its citizens in the way of hospital care, and why it was therefore urgent for me to move home, against medical advice, unless I spell it out to you. But, then, why should I tell you? When my story is about me and my Eye.

There are stories within my stories. One is about the Norwegian welfare state. As I told the audience when I finally gave my lecture to the staff at the Health Ministry: next time I would like to speak on "How to get well in a sick-house" (*sykehus*). But at the time when I was living the trauma of my Eye/I, and writing it to you, it did not strike me that a critique of the Norwegian welfare state should be embedded. I had far more crucial things to think about; my compelling concerns were other. And the omissions I made, the silences that now cry out to me with deep-felt sorrow and pain, will remain covered. Only to me they talk—which is why I could hardly bring myself to reread my story.

Now here are the key points of my critique.

Against Narrative—Let Story Remain

I have written *against* narrative, arguing that "story" serves us quite as well—or indeed better. It is better in that story is experience-near, probably in every language, whereas "narrative" may be so only among (middle-class?) educated Americans and European intellectuals. By being experience-near, story forces us to stay close to the ground, whereas narrative entices us to take flight into some superior realm where the connection to lived experience is easily missed. As I have written elsewhere, personally, I have been perplexed at the cavalier attitude that many anthropologists have displayed towards a term—narrative—that has been made to carry a heavy analytical load. It is rare for people to define it, and it is common for the author to lapse between story and narrative without explanation (1995:264).

I think these lapses may reveal a gut feeling that many have: the emperor has no clothes. Indeed, an early edition of *Webster's* dictionary (1909), when the concept was more experience-near than now, defines *narrative* as a "recital of a story, or continued account of the particulars of an event or transaction." Jerome Bruner, nearly a century later, identifies narrative by the following three constituents: it conveys a sense of *plight* into which *characters* have fallen on account of *intentions* gone awry, and thus it says something of the protagonists' consciousness. The question of truth value of the narrative is irrelevant; what is critical is that it could be true, that it has a quality of verisimilitude (1986:21). But so it is with story.

Mattingly makes the point that "the opposition between story and narrative registers sensibly only by positioning a false notion of what prior events are." She is referring to the literary theorist position that narratives are ordered around an ending, and that it is the ending which gives meaning to those events (1998a:44). Those who make that claim,

Mattingly argues, "have not investigated the structure of lived experience" and presume a "far too simple view of how life in time is experienced" (1998a:44). I am wholly in line with her, as my story of my Eye/I shows. From the beginning to an end that is yet not clear, I told myself (and others) stories, all along the way, to account for what was happening, or to try to make sense of a life in turmoil. Such is the structure of lived experience and life in time. I have no need for "narrative" to tell you my story. All it does for me is create an impression of something fancy—narrative analysis sounds better than story analysis. But I have yet to see what it can deliver that story cannot.

Toward a Pragmatic View of Experience and Self

Second, I have argued against narrative—or story—as offering privileged access to lived experience. By privileged I mean authentic. And to the counterargument that anthropologists were never so naive as to harbor such a view, permit me to express my skepticism.

I think it is in the essence of the anthropologist's trade that we should tend to be taken in by what people tell us. *Rapport* is the trick of the trade, and rapport presumes trust and good relations. Because so much hinges on rapport, because we are so wholly dependent on the trust and confidence that others will show in us, in the field, we will easily be duped. It does not work to take a laid-back, skeptical attitude. Humans are extremely alert to the signs given off of trust or confidence by others. Truthfulness is further a sign of respect, and who would not like to be respected? So the reward system of our discipline, with its emphasis on good fieldwork, also nurtures the values of rapport, respect, confidence, and trust.

Perhaps it is human to tend to be taken in: we feel good when others open their hearts to us and tell us their stories. In a police office in Oslo, a note with the following words is pinned to the wall: "We lie and lie— and you write and write!" They were spoken in exasperation by a Pakistani who finally could hold his tongue no longer against the gullibility of the Norwegian police. Some are better than others at telling untrue stories that have the quality of verisimilitude, and some are more easily taken in. Norwegians are held to be pitifully naive by Pakistanis in Norway (Lien 1997).[5] Perhaps anthropologists also tend in that direction— simply by virtue of our subject matter, our methods, and our training.

How to offset the drawbacks of such a career syndrome? I shall offer two views, dealing with method.

Acts and Observation, Not Just Narrative

In telling you the story of my Eye/I, I cautioned that you were in my power because you do not have (or are not likely to have) subsidiary sources of information with which to contest my story. As long as my story displayed a certain coherence, it would appear truthful. Now, there is no reason why I should mislead you. So I think you were wise in taking my story in. But you would clearly know so much more if you had *other* sources of information to help put my story in relief.

Observation of acts and behavior is an inestimable source of insight. Talking with other spectators, protagonists, or actors enhances one's point of view while also offering contesting material at times. As I have written elsewhere:

> A feature of narrative is the narrator's freedom to construct a plot, to control fully in what order [things happen] (Bruner 1986:19). Action in and on the world, on the other hand, is constrained by causality and less manipulable with regard to making information available to others. A person's work in crafting a self must take place on many fronts, only one of which is that of presenting the self, or repairing the public image, by narrative. The person must also respond to the flow of events, create and consume resources, and influence the events and course of social interaction. And surely for the anthropologist to use people's own narratives as their source for data on these latter processes is a very poor method. The context of other actions, options, and circumstances, ascertained from other sources than the partisans' own accounts of them, provides the necessary background for our understanding of the purposes, indeed the meaning, of narrative. (Wikan 1995:265)

Attending to the person's world is Tim Ingold's captivating phrase for what I have in mind. I argue that it is more necessary for anthropologists to practice this at a time when narrative analysis has long worked to pull us in the opposite direction.

On Pragmatics and Multiple Compelling Concerns

Is an illness narrative necessarily about illness? How to gauge the meaning? What warning lights could we use?

I argue for a *pragmatic* view of meaning (Wikan 1992). *How to Do Things with Words* is the title of a well-known book by the philosopher Austin ([1962] 1975). To take my Eye/I as an example, I told you the story as it was at a particular point in time. I gave it to you as truthfully as I could. But I was acutely aware that there were things I could not say—in part because I am writing under full name to an audience of co-professionals. Hence there are constraints on my telling-it-as-it-is that would not be there if I were anonymous.

"If my husband would cooperate with me and help me, my health would be good as gold," Umm Ali said. I could not say the same, even if it were true. What would it not convey about my private life to a public of significant others? So my story is pragmatic, embedded in time, written for a particular audience with particular goals in mind. It was the best I could do, and it tells you a lot without being in any way a "full story."

I have further argued that it is easy to be taken in by the stories people tell, especially when they are personal and private, and thus apparently told in trust. To take this argument a step further, I would warn that the sheer pragmatics of storytelling stand in danger of getting lost on an empathetic anthropologist trained to be attuned to illness and suffering. To make this less cryptic, more concrete: an illness story need not be about illness at all, or illness may be only a part, and not the most salient part, of what the teller (or narrator) seeks to convey. Let me give you an example from personal experience.

On a recent visit to Indonesia, I spent time with longtime friends in Bali. On the last evening, a very close friend who had been sick for several days with acute stomach problems and headache rested on my bed, trying to sleep off the pain before she must go home. Sleep did not come, and we spoke instead. She confided in me more of her severe marital problems. I knew a lot already. Now I got her illness stories placed in relation to her husband's neglect and oppression, her financial problems, her in-laws' arrogance and corruption, and her own despair at keeping a mask: "I have told my husband, I will not wear a mask anymore to cover him!" All the while my friend battled with her stomach pain and headache; her illness story was in the forefront, but it was set against a life full of turmoil and despair.

I listened carefully and sympathetically, taking in her every word. After some three hours she laboriously got on her feet, and I put her in a taxi to go home. (I wanted her to stay, but her family did not have a phone, and would worry about her.) Early the next morning she came back, unannounced. We had already taken farewell. She was desperately in need of some money that I owed her and had promised to send her, but she needed it now. I was surprised. Why hadn't she told me last night when it was so urgent? It would have spared her a strenuous three-hour journey that morning. Well, she felt shy, and she thought I would have understood from her story.

In short, whereas I had been overwhelmed by her story of suffering and illness, thickly described, she had been at pains to tell me a much less exotic tale. But in characteristic Balinese fashion, she must do it implicitly, or be impolite. And I missed the point.

A feature of narrative is the narrator's freedom to construct a plot, to control fully in what order the reader or listener becomes aware of what happens, notes Jerome Bruner (1986:19). My encounter with my Balinese friend shows him to be incorrect. She was *not* in control as she told me story upon story, each one coherent, all of them beautifully interlinked. And yet she failed to cause the awareness in me that was necessary for me to get a main message, and this though I knew her intimately.

Let me expand on this point: control with one's own narrative is constrained by several factors. Few people, in my experience, are so tenacious that they can ignore, or choose to be fully insensitive to, the clues and responses from an audience. Hence it makes a difference if a story is told in person, face-to-face, or written. To take my Eye/I again: had I told you my story in person, even as a monologue, you would have known and sensed things I do not convey on paper. Had I told it in dialogue, my story would undoubtedly have taken a different form, perhaps a different direction even. It would depend on what clues I got from you. And under no circumstance could I control fully in what order you became aware of "what happened." My multiple compelling concerns would interweave and intersect, as did my Balinese friend's. And you might miss out on "my story," as I did on hers.

Text and Gender

Could it be that the literary theorists' view of narrative analysis rests on a male-centered, textual basis? Writing a narrative, you are in control; telling a story, much less so. Indeed, one of the advantages of using the experience-near "story" rather than the experience-distant "narrative" is that "story" rings with the connotations "told to." One usually tells a story *to* someone, whereas with narrative . . . ? Since I don't even have the word in my language, I really don't know. But I suspect that narrative has a more textual bent.

In real life there are different constraints on male and female storytelling. Males, in most societies, have more free time, are less burdened with children and household chores; their time and social relations are structured differently. At least, this goes for the societies where I have worked: Egypt, Oman, Bali, Bhutan, and Norway. Age intervenes to nuance the picture, as do class and forms of sustenance. But, generally speaking, there is a gender difference that comes clearly to the fore in storytelling.

Women's storytelling is haphazard, often interrupted, disturbed, distorted by children, visitors, and other family members making their claims felt. There are false starts, unfinished endings, musings, hesitations, interruptions, and so on. In consequence, you often get only the beginning, or only the middle, and so it's back to the beginning again, since we have lost track. Storytelling in natural settings has this contingent quality: it is part of life, it takes place in a world of urgency and necessity, a world of multiple compelling concerns. Telling a neat narrative, nicely structured around an ending that gives meaning to the whole thing, is a luxury life does not afford to many of the world's inhabitants. So should we define them out of narrative analysis? If narrative theory is to carry us *toward* lived experience, rather than away from it, there is a need for serious reconsideration here. Rehabilitating "story" will be a good starting point, for reasons I have explicated before.

Silence

Finally, a word on silence. Narrative analysis deals with the spoken word. As if all could be said. In my own life and work, I am struck by the power of silence. The untellable and untold cry out to me and instill me with deep sorrow and pain: Why is it that when humans need each other most, we are so often constrained to bear the burden all alone? Why—if narrative is such a darling in academe—does silence, its counterpart, derive short shrift?

There are reasons, of course, and we know some of them. Notions of honor and shame seem to me to be deeply embedded among people in all cultures where I have lived and worked, even if the conventions and categories of what is shameful and honorable differ. "The personal is political" is how some feminists framed the issue in an effort to start speaking and make the untellable told. But it is not just women who labor under the issue of what "is" tellable and what not. Narrative is simply not an option for many people in their most trying life circumstances. Everyday ordinary life, with its ordinary pot of trials and tribulations, often does not offer the consolation of letting words take flight thus to share one's burden with another.

I have written on these issues elsewhere (Wikan 1992, 1995) and here shall confine myself to a simple observation: the story of my Eye/I reverberates with pain and silence. The connection is twofold: silence breeds pain, and pain nurtures silence. As with my friend in Bali, so with me: we keep a mask. And that mask is the refractory through which our illness stories take on public light. "Let them keep their secrets," I wrote of people in Oman who treasure silence and privacy (Wikan [1982] 1991). What I advocate here is not imposition/intrusion but a better and sharper exploration—in anthropology—of the counterplay between silence and narrative, not as an academic exercise but as a way to enhance our understanding of lived predicaments.

AFTERWORD

The story of my Eye/I was written in August 1996, when the experience was still very raw; my illness had struck me seven months earlier. The outcome—or end—was still unclear. But the prospects were positive: I would regain my sight in due course, because the retina *was* back in place. This had been diagnosed in June, when the infections and bleedings had subsided enough to permit the eye specialist to discern the retina. So the operation had in fact been successful. What was needed was for the eye to absorb all the particles floating about in the glass fluid. The eye specialist did not promise anything, but I was optimistic.

My hopes started to go when, in March 1997, I consulted a star specialist in the States, and he discovered a membrane growing over the retina. And when in April of the next year I took a second opinion from another star specialist, whose verdict was the same, I gave up. Almost. Then a third specialist said the same. No one knows why a membrane starts growing over the retina at times, but it does so in 4 percent of operation cases; and I was among the four.

Nothing to do. The risks of a new operation outweigh the possible gains. My body's erratic behavior last time, when the Eye exploded in infections and bleedings, does not promise well. So I have accommodated myself to my fate. Not that I have given up all hope. One can't. I still have hope (though it is dwindling) that some miracle might happen someday, somehow. It is silly. The nerve cells are dead, say the specialist. No hope of recovery. But I hope at least that the "noise" in my Eye, the floaters that create disorder, will go away.

So the Eye/I is still with me: a constant, daily reminder of a view from the margins. The black shadows are gone. But there is a flurry of movement, a constant activation of particles (don't ask me what they are), that maintains this in-tandem vision of order/disorder. I would not call it chaos today. The situation is better. But it is like having simultaneously two quite different visions of the world, with one so blurred it can hardly be called a vision; rather, it is some kind of reflection that throws the world in peculiar relief.

And all the time I struggle to try to look normal.

"How is it with your Eye?" people still ask. I brush the question aside. "Oh that . . . , it is gone," I reply, not quite truthfully. For I am not blind, the Eye still serves me to take in some information, for example, when I am driving, I can see/sense the lights of a car coming from the right. And yet it is true what I say, for this is how I feel: the Eye is gone, and so is the I that depended upon a "normal" vision of the world.

I try to look ahead. "I'm lucky," I say, "in that I still have the other. That's what makes all the difference." Whereas only one in ten thousand suffers a detached retina, the chances of it happening to the second eye is one in ten. And the risk is highest for the first two years. (As I know full well; I had constant problems for almost two years.) So I am lucky. And this is what I want to convey: lucky in having an eye, and lucky in having an I that weathered the crisis that my Eye brought to the fore. But that is another story, the story that is too private to tell you. In the end, this is what my story is all about—to me, just as Umm Ali's illness stories deal with her relationship to her nearest and dearest.

So I have done the best I could: given you my illness story bared to the bone, written in a staccato language conspicuously void, so it seems to me today, of emotional expressions and overtones. It is true all I have said, each and every word of it. And yet I could not have repeated the story today. I am another human being now, in many ways. The hindsight, the fact of having come to an "end," *changes my narrative* of my Eye/I.

This bespeaks the fallacy of the literary theorist position. To understand lived experience, we need narratives, stories of unfinished, muddled, in-the-midst-of experiences whose only certainties are the beginnings or turning points—as with my Eye. And we need stories/narratives of experiences groping for meaning, whose onset as well as ending line are in the blue. So it is with life. There is a continuous groping for meaning that, as Mattingly notes (1998, this volume), determines the structure of lived experience.

The story of my Eye/I, that I told you before, is a time slice, a view from a particular vantage point. The tenseness of the telling, the narrative nerve, was occasioned by my being in the midst of it all, still shocked, with an all-too-vivid memory of the beginnings, and not a clue to how it would end. I know it now, and it does not make my story any better. It is, as Mattingly says, the sense of drama that links narrative and life. "We follow a narrative suspensefully, always reminded of the fragility of events, for things might have turned out differently." They might indeed. But that is a different story.

NOTES

1. Though Norwegian does not have the word *narrative*, the Anglicized *narrativ* is making headway among some academics.

2. Indeed the *beginning* of her eye illness story is also bound up with her nearest and dearest. It dates back to a time before the onset of her diabetes (in 1972), which occasioned her blindness (fifteen to twenty years later). Her diabetes, she is sure, was brought on by two tragedies that struck her in the summer of 1972. First her dearest sister, only twenty-five years old, died from a tonsils operation. Then her son, Amin, only nineteen years old, died by setting fire to himself. Any account of Umm Ali's blindness or diabetes, whether by herself or others, will inevitably take you back to Amin's tragic suicide—the real beginning of an end that, as Umm Ali is growing old, is slowly coming to sight.

3. Attributed to William Osler, quoted in Sacks (1995).

4. In retrospect, I would rephrase this. Cultural knowledge is *not* necessarily accumulated as it becomes relevant to one's life, simply because it is not available, or one does not know where to look. Life catches us unaware, time and again. Notions of privacy, secrecy, shame, honor, dignity, and respect work in conjunction with (often limited) networks of social relations to make cultural knowledge simply unavailable at times when it is most needed. Indeed, there are a number of basic assumptions about cultural knowledge that I would now question, on the basis of my experience of my Eye/I that threw life (and not just my own) into new relief for me.

5. As several Pakistanis say, "We are so clever/shrewd and they (the Norwegians) are so naive/stupid; we should stop being so clever" (Lien 1997).

REFERENCES

Austin, J. L. [1962] 1975. *How to do things with words.* Cambridge, Mass.: Harvard University Press.

Broyard, Anatole. 1992. *Intoxicated by my illness.* New York: Potter.

Bruner, Jerome. 1986. *Actual minds, possible worlds.* Cambridge, Mass.: Harvard University Press.

Chatman, Seymour. 1978. *Story and discourse: Narrative structure in fiction and film*. Ithaca, N.Y.: Cornell University Press.

Ingold, Tim. 1993. The art of translation in a continuous world. In *Beyond boundaries: Understanding, translation and anthropological discourse*, edited by Gisli Pálsson, 210–30. Oxford: Brown.

Kermode, Frank. 1966. *The sense of an ending: Studies in the theory of fiction*. London: Oxford University Press.

Lien, Inger-Lise. 1997. *Ordet som stempler djevlene*. Oslo: Aventura.

Mattingly, Cheryl. 1998. *Healing dramas and clinical plots: The narrative structure of experience*. Cambridge: Cambridge University Press.

Mintz, Sidney W. 1979. The anthropological interview and life history. *Oral History Review*, 18–26.

Olafson, Frederick. 1979. *The dialectics of action: Philosophical interpretation of history and the humanities*. Chicago: University of Chicago Press.

Ricoeur, Paul. 1984. *Time and narrative*. Vol. 1. Chicago: University of Chicago Press.

Sacks, Oliver. 1995. *An anthropologist on Mars*. New York: Knopf.

Wikan, Unni. 1990. *Managing turbulent hearts: A Balinese formula for living*. Chicago: University of Chicago Press.

———. [1982] 1991. *Behind the veil in Arabia: Women in Oman*. Chicago: University of Chicago Press.

———. 1992. Beyond the words: The power of resonance. *American Ethnologist* 19:460–82.

———. 1995. The self in a world of urgency and necessity. *Ethos* 23:259–85.

———. 1996a. The nun's story: Reflections on an age-old, postmodern dilemma. *American Anthropologist* 98:279–89.

———. 1996b. *Tomorrow, God willing: Self-made destinies in Cairo*. Chicago: University of Chicago Press.

TEN

Psychotherapy in Clients' Trajectories across Contexts

OLE DREIER

The work I shall present is based on my previous attempts at a comprehensive theorizing of people's lives as participation in social practice (Dreier 1993, 1994, 1996). Though I cannot go into the theory in any detail in this chapter, I hope that the links to the materials I shall include come across as I unfold my argument. First I shall sketch some central contentions on how to theorize about subjects in social practice, emphasizing that people live their lives participating in multiple social contexts and moving across them. Then I present a study of psychotherapy that illustrates the place of sessions in clients' practice across social contexts. In the next section I elaborate some general points about my understanding of psychotherapy and of personal life trajectories in subjects' social practice. And in the final section I relate my analysis to some general features of a narrative understanding which many find fruitful in the study of psychotherapy and which has much in common with my approach. My analysis in particular raises questions concerning the place of narrative in personal action and experience when one takes into account that persons configure their actions and experiences as they participate in diverse social contexts and move across them. I shall be warning against limitations and distortions if one focuses too closely on narrative and loses sight of its performative significance and place in people's ongoing personal practice across social contexts.

SUBJECTS IN SOCIAL PRACTICE

My work is inspired primarily by the theoretical tradition of critical psychology (e.g., Holzkamp 1983; Tolman 1994; Tolman and Maiers 1991). This cultural-historical, Marxist approach reconceptualizes psychological theory from the point of view of the individual subject in her immediate local situation in the social world. To the individual subject, *the meaning of any local situation is the concrete scope of possibilities for action which it affords and which is mediated by the overall social structure.* The personal potentiality for action that enables the subject to live by means of such possibilities for action is, therefore, the widest and most crucial characteristic of individual subjectivity. The development and restriction of personal action potentiality plays the key role in the study of individual subjectivity. The theoretical analysis of particular situations and episodes focuses on understanding how the individual subject arrives at grounds for a particular course of action and attempts to realize it. Individual action, it is argued, is not caused, but subjectively grounded. The subject grounds her actions by relating her perceived needs and interests to the concrete possibilities for action in the situation at hand. Her immediate mental state reflects the degree to which she anticipates being able to have relevant possibilities at her disposal or to be dependent and exposed. Subjective experiences are, thus, not seen as free-floating views from anywhere and nowhere in particular but as located experiential perspectives from a particular situation. In general terms the subject may adopt one or the other of two basic modes of action. She may either (1) attempt to expand her present scope and increase her disposal over relevant possibilities or (2) act within the existing limits of the situation. A matching distinction is made between two basic forms of action potentiality. The subject may adopt (1) an expanding action potentiality by developing new possibilities and potentialities and increasing her disposal over these possibilities or (2) a restricted action potentiality of keeping within pregiven limits. The choice of one or the other basic mode of action is not a characteristic of a particular individual "personality" but of what a subject may find grounds to do in relation to the present scope of possibilities and her perceived needs and interests. For instance, she may turn her back on the alternative of expanding the present scope because she anticipates that this would lead to conflicts that might make matters worse and threaten her present degree of disposal.

Lave's work on situated learning through participation in communities of practice (e.g., Lave and Wenger 1991) encouraged me to place greater emphasis on the contextual and participatory nature of individual subjectivity in the development of my framework. It led me to highlight the notion in critical psychology that any local individual situation really is part of a local social *context of action* in which individual subjects participate. These social contexts of action have particular structures of social positions that offer individual participants different scopes of possibilities, and individual participants' degrees of dependency or disposal vary accordingly. But as soon as one starts to conceptualize individual subjects through their participation in relation to other participants and their context as a whole, some further characteristics of individual subjectivity come to the fore. Any individual participant realizes a selective, partial, and particular set of possibilities compared with the possibilities other participants realize and with the possibilities for action which the context affords. Consequently, individual subjectivity assumes a partial and particular configuration. This is equally true of participants' action potentialities, their grounds for action, the significance of their actions for everybody involved, their dependency and disposal, their experiences, thoughts, and emotions. The partiality and diversity of individual subjectivity must also be taken into account in understanding the dynamics of the relationships among participants.

Moving situated participation to the center of my theorizing about subjects in social practice, however, only made the next necessary conceptual expansion more obvious. Once we stop considering subjects as free-floating agents and study their local participation, we must also recognize that subjects do not stay in one place and participate in only one context of action. On the contrary, subjects move across social contexts and participate in several contexts at different locations. This has consequences for our understanding both of social practice and of individual subjectivity. As for our understanding of social practice, it leads us to recognize that social practice is structured in a multitude of social contexts. These contexts are connected and disconnected in a variety of ways. They are accessible and inaccessible in particular ways for a variety of groups and persons. And many social contexts are arranged as settings for particular kinds of social purposes and tasks and for people to pursue particular kinds of personal activities, concerns, and obligations in them and through them.

And as for our understanding of individual subjectivity, it means that in a social practice with such a complex structure, each subject must conduct his life by participating in multiple social contexts and moving across them in pursuit of his concerns and obligations. In so doing, the subject's personal mode of participation varies from one context to another and is, at the same time, affected by the contextual complexity of his conduct of life. Let me briefly point out some important features of this variability and complexity of individual subjectivity. First of all, subjects' modes of participation vary from one context to another because different contexts offer different scopes of possibilities for action and because subjects have different personal concerns at stake in these different contexts. Each subject, then, has good reasons to participate in different ways in different contexts, and the subject's personal action potentialities and psychological processes assume a contextual multifacity. Still, the subject's grounds for a particular mode of participation do not stem only from the context he is presently located in. Since the subject also participates in other contexts, the interrelationships between these contexts matter to him. So a person's participation in a context is also influenced by its significance in relation to that person's participation in other contexts. As a consequence, a subject's local mode of participation assumes a particular, mediated, cross-contextual complexity. This cross-contextual complexity is further strengthened by the fact that subjects often pursue particular concerns across several contexts, varying the way they do so as they move from one context into another, depending upon the nature and significance of the context they are presently located in. Just as a subject's local modes of participation are complexly grounded and motivated, the same, of course, holds for his experiences. The subject's experiential perspective is grounded in his immediate location and follows the embodied subject as he moves around in his complex social practice. The subject's experiences are located in his diverse participations in disparate contexts and, at the same time, involved in directing his pursuits across them. The subject configures his experiences as part of his trajectory across times and places.

In order to manage to live a life in and across diverse contexts of social practice, the subject must create and sustain an everyday personal conduct of life (Holzkamp 1995). The subject must contrast and balance the demands and concerns associated with her diverse social contexts and integrate them into a particular ordering and configuring of her everyday activities. By establishing an everyday conduct of life, this complexity becomes manageable in practical terms. However, the contextual complexity is not only a matter of everyday life. It is characteristic of the whole life course. At any given time during the life course, the individual subject lives her life by taking part in a particular configuration of several, diverse social contexts. Which social contexts the individual subject participates in may, of course, change during the life course, as may their personal significance. Still, throughout her life, the subject lives by directing herself not only ahead but also across. I suggest to use the term *life trajectory* to capture this complexity of the life course (Dreier 1994). I shall illustrate this notion later and conclude the introduction to my general framework of analysis at this point.

The development of the framework I have introduced was in fact heavily influenced by challenges raised in my study of psychotherapeutic practice. Some unresolved problems in our usual understanding of psychotherapy pushed me in the direction of this kind of theorizing. The framework is geared to allow us to reconceptualize subjects in social practices such as psychotherapy. When clients attend psychotherapy, this adds, for a period of time, another context, the therapy session, to the structure of their everyday practice. Therapy works precisely because clients pursue their concerns across as well as in the contexts of the session, their home, school, workplace, and so on. Treatment does not progress as an effect therapists make on their clients. It progresses primarily because of the clients' changing pattern of interrelating different modes of experiencing and dealing with their problems in their diverse social contexts. It is not the therapists but the clients who are the primary agents of therapy, those whose practice will hopefully change and for whose sake the practice of therapy takes place. Contrary to widespread notions, treatment is promoted not by the transfer of an identical mode of experiencing and dealing with problems but by particular, significant differences in the ways clients experience and deal with their problems in their different social contexts. In fact, since treatment is carried out for the sake of resolving problems that occur in clients' everyday lives, clients' everyday concerns and perspectives do and should play the main role compared with those of the therapy session.

These propositions lead to a different understanding of therapeutic practice. This understanding emphasizes that participants are involved in different activities and experiences in therapy sessions than, say, at home and that they experience and deal with their problems in different ways in these places. Talk has a different role, and different aspects of talking matter in the two places. The practice and experience of therapeutic change is deeply conflictual and not based on a consensus, which many assume that "good understanding" should all be about. Clients' circumstances and possibilities outside of sessions are more important for the realization, range, and direction of changes than is the practice within sessions. As therapy gets under way, participants forge stakes and stances to pursue across the different times and places of their everyday practice. In this way they come to pursue dealing with conflicts in particular ways within sessions and by means of them.

This new understanding of psychotherapy requires a different way of conducting research. Accounts of therapy in the research literature and among practitioners normally focus only on what happens within sessions or even on what the therapist does to the clients in sessions. But this gives us no good understanding of why and how therapy works. We need a kind of research that fits the complexity of the social practice we study. In short, we need to study it from the perspective of its multiple participants and as a particular part of their life trajectories across multiple social contexts. This insight was substantiated further by discovering that in this respect the practice of psychotherapy is no different from a range of other social practices that show similar complexities and would need similar frames of analysis and modes of conducting research to advance our understanding of them (Dreier 1996; Lave 1997).

A STUDY OF PSYCHOTHERAPY

To illustrate my framework, I shall draw upon materials from my study of change processes during family therapy. My materials consist of transcripts of the therapy sessions and of interviews with a small number of families about their everyday lives especially in relation to their ongoing therapy. I was a co-therapist in these cases. The interviews took place in the clients' homes. They were conducted by an interviewer hired especially for that purpose, with all family members present and at regular intervals throughout their $1\frac{1}{2}$ to 2 years of therapy until about half a year after treatment termination. It was such a dual set of materials that allowed me to develop a new analysis of therapeutic practice that focuses on relations between therapy sessions and everyday family life from the clients' point of view. I cannot cover the range of topics from these materials here, but I am in the midst of writing a fuller account in book form (Dreier in prep.), and other aspects of the design and materials are presented in Dreier (1998). I also must omit the therapists' participation in multiple contexts altogether.

In this chapter I shall focus on aspects of interview materials gathered outside and in between the therapy sessions to illustrate how clients reflect on the meaning of sessions as part of their ongoing everyday life. When talking about the therapy sessions, clients show how the sessions become a part in their everyday pursuit of concerns across contexts. I shall illustrate some of these key points with materials from the first two interviews, carried out approximately 1½ months apart in the beginning of one case as family conflicts gradually came to the fore. It is a working-class family of four: a mother and father, a fifteen-year-old daughter, and a thirteen-year-old daughter. The family was referred to an outpatient child psychiatry unit in Copenhagen because of the younger daughter's anxiety symptoms, which heavily constricted her life.

I shall focus on what is conventionally assumed to be three main features of therapeutic practice as seen from the clients' points of view: the role of talk, the therapist, and client conflicts. To this I add a fourth feature, the reinterpretation of sessions in other times and places. I hope to show how clients' multiple relations with talk, therapists, and conflict in multiple settings create different processes of participation and different meaning especially to participating in therapy.

SESSIONS AS PART OF CLIENTS' SOCIAL PRACTICE

Session Talk

A main feature of the practice of sessions is talk. But in the first of the two interviews, the family states they "cannot quite understand how talk may work on anxiety symptoms," as the mother puts it. In other words, they have no clear notion about the relation between the nature of their daughter's symptoms (anxiety), and the main activity of sessions (talk). In fact, they state that at home they don't talk much about these problems. The diverse ways of dealing with problems is further highlighted when the family tells the interviewer that two years ago, when the older daughter was in individual therapy for about a year, they never talked about her therapy at home. They state that a main reason they do not talk about the present problems at home is that if they do try to talk about them, they cannot resolve them. Instead, the situation soon explodes into open conflicts they cannot handle. Everybody starts to yell, slam doors, leave, and so on. Another important reason, they say, is that they virtually never set aside a time slot for everybody to talk something over. They aren't even all gathered at many other times than during meals. Most talk is therefore done more in passing and with different constellations of mostly two members, the mother being the most common figure. Let us for a moment compare with interview materials from the whole course of their therapy. We then find that the "concerted problem talk," which is typical of sessions and which takes place here regularly over a period of time, remains a peculiarity of sessions and makes them stand out as a special experience in contrast to other kinds of talk and other activities at home and in other places. Session talk plays a significant role by being different in particular ways. To them it is a significant experience that has an impact on their everyday practice at home not by being transferred into it but by virtue of being different and being transformed in their everyday practices.

Intimate Strangers

The second topic concerns therapists: Clients give meaning to their therapists as a part of their everyday lives by emphasizing that taking part in therapy sessions in many ways differs from taking part in their family life. In therapy sessions "there are strangers present," everybody says. Their therapists remain "strangers" to them in the sense that they "never really come to know them," even though "they [come to] know all about us," says the father. In addition to this asymmetry, the clients emphasize a difficulty: "It must be difficult for them to understand our problems," the mother holds, and "to place themselves in our situation," the father adds. They state two reasons for this difficulty. One is that they find it hard to explain what goes on in problem situations at home. The other is that the therapists do not know their everyday situation at home. Both these reasons arise because of the gaps between practices in different places: the session where clients and therapists meet and other contexts of the clients' lives in which their therapists do not take part. On the other hand, the gaps between the contexts and their different constellations of participants are also a relief. "It would be difficult if they weren't strangers," the mother contends. If they talk to people they know about their problems, "they would use it against us," the older daughter says, "tell it to others," the younger daughter adds, "believe we were crazy," the mother says. Therapists are strangers whom the clients believe have not already taken sides in their conflicts, or at least the clients do not yet know where the therapists stand. So first the clients must find out "what sort of baboons they are," as the father in another case puts it, "what they might be up to," as the father in this case says, and whether the therapists might come to side more with one member of the family than with others—or even in some respects against others. But the clients also say that they can—and in a sense must—all join in the hope for some sort of more balanced mediation in the session with their therapists, which will allow them to enter a new dialogue with each other. What is more, being "strangers" means that therapists may introduce "new angles" on their problems, which they themselves or the people they know have not already brought up and thought about, as first the mother, then everybody else, emphasizes. They all repeatedly stress that the introduction of these new angles sets them reconsidering and reevaluating their problems, their relations, and their ways of dealing with them in many situations during their everyday lives. In fact, this is a major feature of the transformation—rather than the transfer—involved in the impact of sessions.

Client Conflicts in Sessions and Elsewhere

I now turn to the third topic: How do the clients see the ways they deal with conflicts in therapy sessions as part of their ongoing everyday lives? The mother says about the older daughter's earlier therapy: "There it is again. It was a stranger who told her. And the psychologist sort of turned her thoughts in the direction that the solution for her simply was to move to another school. And then she told herself that now she wanted to move to another school. We had talked about it for years. But the psychologist could turn it so that now she decided that she had had enough." So therapists may introduce "new angles," and they may even bring up old ones. But since they are strangers, clients will "listen" to them, which they would not do if a family member said the same. They "listen more to strangers," and they "listen more to each other when strangers are there," they all say. The father in another case says about his wife: "She listens more to me." And his wife continues: "He doesn't just shout at me." They are better able to unfold a conversation about problems without it ending in explosions or some other sort of communication breakdown. They emphasize that "we sort of pull ourselves together a little," as the older daughter puts it. She adds: "In sessions we sort of turn things in our heads before we say something. At home we say it point blank." The others confirm this. She continues: "I believe we have never talked so nicely to our mother and father as when the therapists are present." Her mother confirms and contradicts her at one and the same time: "You never become agitated, furious, and crazy [in sessions]." They all work to make talks in therapy sessions proceed more calmly. The younger daughter says: ". . . then we all talk, and then it goes better." While, "when the therapists aren't there, they keep interrupting me." In this way conflicts may gradually become articulated, and other members' perspectives on them and grounds to do what they do may become more apparent. The older daughter adds: "We are more daring about saying something." The therapists "may defend us a little when the others say something." Here the family gives us their perspective on how they pursue their everyday conflicts with each other in and through therapy sessions. Conflicts they have at home are gradually introduced and pursued in other ways in the therapy setting. The older daughter says about the younger daughter's ways of being within sessions compared with at home: "She is totally different when others are present." And the mother adds that the difference is that "the children stay quite calm and relaxed." Note that in both these instances differences are emphasized—or maybe noticed—only in others: the older daughter sees them in the younger, the mother in the children, the children in the parents, and so on. This fits with everybody's belief that in order to resolve their problems in the way they each see them and imagine their resolution, it is the others who will have to change. Thus the mother states that she hopes the therapists "can make the children do things which they wouldn't do if I corrected them."

Reinterpretations of Sessions Elsewhere

So conflicts do arise in sessions and are pursued in a variety of ways. For instance, in sessions clients attempt to turn the therapists as persons and their interventions into instruments of their family struggles. But conflicts over sessions, therapists, and interventions are also pursued in between sessions and afterward, at home and in other places where the therapists are not present. Clients do not stop processing session topics when the therapy session is over. A therapy session is no well-bounded thing that a therapist can know all about. At other times and places, clients reinterpret session topics and put them to other kinds of uses than the therapists imagine or ever come to know. Since part of this is conflictual and may end up utilizing therapist suggestions to serve quite opposite ends from those the therapists stand for, clients deal with these differences discreetly and even secretly. Instances of this slip through in glimpses in the interview materials, as we shall see later. There are also many instances of other kinds of continued processes and reinterpretations of therapy session topics in other settings afterward. In fact, our analysis has led us to a fourth topic besides the role of talk, the therapists, and client conflicts—namely, the reinterpretations of, struggles over, and diverse uses of sessions in other times and places outside of sessions. One instance of the reinterpretation and struggle over therapy sessions is closely related to the episode just described. In the therapy session prior to the latter of the two interviews I quoted from, therapists and clients worked with the younger daughter's passivity in dealing with her own affairs. The therapists were trying to make it clear that there is a striking pattern by which her mother takes over on her behalf out of care and consideration for her sensitive child and the risks of her daughter's various impending states of anxiety. In this way the daughter is relieved of any responsibility, and, especially if things do not turn out the way she wants, she sullenly reproaches her mother. In addition, her parents disagree about what would be a suitable degree of coresponsibility for the daughter. At the end of the session, one of the therapists remarks in passing that the daughter seems to be quite sullen.

How did the clients reinterpret this session issue of "responsibility" afterward? That is documented in the interview that took place only a few days later. At this time the family members' participation in therapy sessions has itself turned into a matter of mutual conflict among them, so that they do not consider the same topic to be the most important one. In the interview the older daughter states what she considers to be the most important topic in the prior therapy session: "I know. It was being cross. . . . We couldn't stand any more that mum and dad were cross. Especially dad." The mother responds: "It is not funny to be accused of something one is not." Then she fires back at the children: "If the therapists were not there, the children would get cross if we talked about something problematic. . . . As soon as you say a word they do not like, then we are cross." The older daughter wavers: "What else should one call it?" And the mother continues: "We have to put up with whatever you say and do with a smile. We are not allowed to make any demands on you." Now the very same person who out of consideration and care would do on her daughter's behalf what she feared her daughter might not like to do herself starts marking out a polarity: the parents as a "we" against the children as a "you." She continues to criticize the children for "turning around everything we say." The older daughter retaliates by critiquing her for shouting and being cross. The mother shouts back: "I am not cross!" Asked whether she has taken any ideas from the session for her future behavior, the mother responds: ". . . that I too am to intervene more: 'I won't talk to you like this any more. Come back when you have calmed down.' We have always paid too much at-

tention to the children. So maybe it's time to pay attention to ourselves."
The father sides with her. Here we see that after the session both parents
have turned 180 degrees compared with their prior attitude of being
considerate and so forth. The older daughter then says that she learned
from the previous therapy session "that one should never say that mum
is cross." The younger daughter retreats into saying, "I don't think we
got anything out of the session about being cross. I think we should talk
about it once more so that we could get more out of it." Here it is clear
that what each member pays attention to as "getting something out of
it" and what they all focus on in their experience of therapy sessions differ according to the stakes they each believe they have and pursue in and
through therapy sessions. And, of course, these are in part relations between stakes here and in other settings of their lives.

Now all members of the family in a way agree on a common problem—which, by the way, is not the "anxiety symptoms" for which the
daughter was referred to the therapy in the first place—namely, "being
cross" as a widespread burden of family life. But they all locate it differently, attributing it to others while holding themselves to be innocent
victims of these others. And they do not agree on which means to use to
resolve the problem, nor does their therapy have the same meaning for
them. On the contrary, now there is open conflict over the therapy, too.
Or, to be more precise, sessions have become a peculiar part in the unfolding of their everyday conflicts. Therapy is a conflictual matter also
in the ways in which its meanings and impacts are negotiated and change.
Furthermore, they share views that are only a small step away from the
mother's notion about what therapy should be used for: "to teach the others that one can talk about things," which she considers to be the most
important topic in the previous therapy session because "the others
could really need that a lot." She draws the connection between talking
about things and the omnipresent "being cross": "But that is because
you won't discuss." Now the conflict has been taken to the very level of
talk, the main vehicle by which therapy sessions are carried out. The
older daughter says sarcastically: "You say all problems can be solved
just because the therapists are here, or . . ." The mother interrupts:
"Problems are there to be solved. And I think one does that best by talking about them." The older daughter responds defensively: "Everything
cannot be sheer delight. . . . One doesn't always feel like discussing it,
does one." Her mother retaliates: "I know, but I do." The daughter again:
"Yes, you do. But I won't." "No" is the mother's only response; her assured tone of voice implies that she sticks to her commitment to pressure

her daughter into participating in talks about their problems. Insisting on talk can certainly be a means of power in mutual conflicts.

THERAPY IN SUBJECTS' SOCIAL PRACTICE

Let us step back from the details of ongoing interviews and sessions. In this chapter I have focused on the ways in which clients deal with therapy sessions. By doing so, I wanted to show that we need a new understanding of therapy that emphasizes the relationship between sessions and clients' everyday lives in other places. I argued that clients compose their participation in sessions as a part of their complex social practice in and across contexts. Their experience of therapy, its meaning for them, and the reasons and motives for their participation in it are also a composed part of their complex social practice. In fact, their therapy evolves in a complexly composed way, and it works precisely because it becomes a particular and changing part in clients' complex social practice across times and places. Put in more general terms, in developing a new understanding of therapy, we need to focus on the following.

First, it is the changes which family members realize outside therapy sessions that really matter. Here are the primary locations of their problems and their change. These changes which family members realize outside of therapy sessions in the various contexts of their everyday lives are not brought about primarily by means of talk. They primarily rest upon their attending to other aspects of their everyday situations than before, discovering opportunities they had not realized were there, evaluating and utilizing existing opportunities in different ways, bringing about new possibilities and arrangements, and in so doing forging new relations with each other, supporting each other in new ways, launching new activities, some of them in new contexts, and so on. For some time they may be preoccupied with issues addressed in sessions, but so they are because they consider them relevant for the concerns and problems of the conduct of their lives outside of sessions. In interviews the clients emphasize that new angles introduced in sessions make them reconsider and reevaluate important parts of their everyday lives, but these reconsiderations are occasioned by situations and events of their everyday lives in other contexts. And it does precisely take some reconsiderations to become able to put the new angles to use in the contexts of their everyday lives. In order to make use of them, they first have to find out which other place and meaning the new angles may have in the particular constellation of their present context, and they need to find out how to approach and exert influence upon the occurring everyday situations in re-considered ways. In so doing, they modify and further transform these new angles. Therefore, the range of changes that are brought about during the course of therapy primarily depends on the nature of their social situations outside of the therapy sessions and on their changing the ways they deal with them. Here new events and opportunities of everyday practice, new scopes of possibilities, new qualities to their mutual relations, new arrangements, and new things to talk about may be brought about. In other words, the workings of therapy primarily depend on circumstances and client activities that lie beyond the immediate reach of sessions and therapists.

Second, therapy does not eliminate conflicts among clients and over the ongoing changes. Some conflicts are resolved, some are transformed, while other new conflicts arise. Indeed, the changing constellation of conflicts alters the agendas and dynamics of therapeutic change. In the case described earlier, the loosening of symptoms and the gradual resolution of some conflicts increasingly make the two daughters engage more and differently outside of the family. They become involved in new activities with new friends, jobs, and new relationships with each other in these contexts. This creates a new conflict for the parents, who are left behind to reevaluate and redirect their future perspectives and their life as a couple. It interacts with the parents' preoccupation with the issue of the reasons they came to pursue a form of care for their children in which they, as they now realize, tied each other down out of love. Both parents call this discovery "terrible." They are deeply shaken by it, and it sets them reevaluating major dimensions of their past, present, and future family life as parents, husband and wife, and individual subjects.

Third, it would be a mistake to consider only the clients' practice at home and in sessions. Outside of sessions their practice is also composed of diverse participations in diverse contexts. In fact, their family life has a different weight and meaning in the different complex practices of its individual members. As briefly indicated, the meaning and weight of their family life change for the mother in this case. At first she unquestionably considers it to be the main context in her life and herself to be the person who holds the main responsibility for the qualities of well-being and care in the family; if the family members disagree among themselves over these matters, she is the one to decide what is right. Later she realizes that this practice ties her and her children down at home. She begins to search for ways to better combine activities and involvements within and outside home, for herself and others, together and separately, and she thrives on the possibilities this new approach opens for her. Her changing modes of participation at work and in the new contexts of her leisure time change the composition of her personal social practice and the subjective meaning of its parts for her. By contrast, the younger daughter triggers their referral to family therapy, but it does not mean much to her, and she cannot really see why. She spends most of her time after school at home in a sullenly passive manner, but it is emerging relations and activities outside of the family (new hobbies and relations in her leisure time and an upcoming one-week trip with her school class) that urge her to change her symptom-ridden life. For her the primary meaning of engaging in these changes is to be able to participate in these other activities with friends of her age, and not to be excluded or ridiculed by them. The family therapy is first of all a means of support to that end. Against this background, it should come as no surprise that not only their family life but also their family therapy has a different meaning and weight to the individual members of the family.

Fourth, their family life plays a different part in their different individual life trajectories. This may already have become clear from what was just mentioned about the mother and the younger daughter. In general terms, the subjects' individual life trajectories frame the different individual meanings and implications of the current family problems and changes. They frame the different stakes individuals have and stances they adopt on whether their family is to change and, if so, in which directions. Their personal bonds with the family and their feelings of belonging to it differ depending on the position they have reached and the futures they anticipate in their individual life trajectories. Their current family problems and changes, on the other hand, make them face different challenges to reevaluate and change their personal participation in the family life and the composition of their own personal conduct of life and life trajectory. Let me use the two remaining members of the family to illustrate this. The older daughter is caught up in a complex problem situation in a transition period of her life trajectory at the point of leaving public school, starting vocational training, and striking up other kinds of relationships with people of her age. She had been relentlessly harassed and isolated for years and has great trouble presenting and sticking to what she stands for in ways that other young people will recognize. This difficulty spills into her family life when her friends wreck the family's apartment at weekend parties, and the family is threatened by expulsion from their home. The conflict with and between her relations in these two contexts makes her withdraw into isolation in her room at home. She feels let down by her friends, and she feels guilt, but also resentment, toward her parents because they do not recognize her as the "big" person she now considers herself to be; they still regard her as a "small" person who cannot be trusted to handle such things. The problem of being recognized as a "grown-up" is her main concern in relation to the rest of the family. The father wrestles to build a closer relationship with his two daughters with room to unfold mutual recognition and support in spite of acute trouble. At the same time, he renegotiates the relationship with his wife and their anticipated future when their two daughters will soon leave home. Finally, he attempts to change into stating his mind at work at a time when layoffs loom on the horizon.

Fifth, their individual life trajectories, with different individual stakes in the common family life, also frame their different individual stakes in family therapy and its different meaning to them. Against this background, the family therapy sessions are marked by a particular constellation of participation, a particular dynamic of changes, and particular constellations of problems and possibilities. Phenomena such as these lead to the question: In relation to whom or to what mix of members' concerns are family therapy interventions primarily grounded and directed and their effects evaluated?

Sixth, as mentioned briefly at the beginning of this chapter, my analysis calls for research psychotherapy that differs from what is usually done. I consider the present study a preliminary example. We need further studies of the composition of personal participation in complex social practice across times and places. As a corrective, we especially need to study everyday practice and trajectories outside of sessions and to comprehend the role of therapy sessions as seen from there. By contrast, the dominant tradition of research analyzes therapy viewed within the context of sessions and from the position and standpoint of therapists and researchers. The clients' own perspectives are neglected, massively reinterpreted, or abstracted from the contexts of their complex everyday social practice, including the place of therapy in it. While therapy is supposedly conducted for the clients' sake, it is primarily accounted for and researched from the positions and standpoints of the professionals who are hired to conduct and research it. When, in some studies, clients' perspectives do appear, it is their perspectives on their mental states, their sessions, and their therapists. But they rarely appear as experiencing agents outside of their sessions in and across the various contexts of their everyday lives. When a particular study obtains various sorts of data, it mostly only varies its methods of data gathering, but not the position and standpoint of analysis. And when different sources of data are included, they are mostly about the same issue: What goes on in sessions, and what are their alleged impacts on clients' subjective state and personal properties? In addition, the professionals combine the data when they analyze them. In so doing, analysts may easily come to overlook those connections the clients themselves have perceived as they conduct their personal social practice in and across various contexts.

To sum up, therapy is a particular social arrangement. It is a place to go to talk over problems in a peculiar way—with an intimate stranger, in a strange kind of intimacy. Which features of sessions stand out as particularly meaningful and significant vary across participants and over time. But they have to do with those things clients find themselves unable to do on their own accord outside sessions, and so point to the decisive role their everyday social situation plays in determining the meaning of attending therapy and the range and significance of therapeutic change. And they depend on the place of their family and of their therapy in their ongoing life trajectories. Clients configure the meaning of therapy within the structure of their ongoing social practice. Clients' experiences and actions are part of their ongoing complex practice and reach across contexts. This is especially important to notice in a social practice such as therapy, which is directed at promoting change in practice elsewhere and later. In studying client experiences and actions, we must therefore focus on what they can tell us about how changes are brought about or how people may avoid them, as they participate in the interconnected settings of their lives.

PERSONAL SOCIAL PRACTICE AND NARRATIVES

In this final section I shall put forward some general analytic comments on a narrative understanding, especially warning against dimensions that may be bypassed or distorted if one focuses too closely on narrative as it is now commonly understood. There are different narrative positions with which my position overlaps and contrasts in various ways. So to keep this discussion from becoming too complicated and technical, I shall focus on what I hold to be common assumptions. Conceptions of narrative characteristically focus on experience and meaning, which they consider in a dimension of time directed toward a future, ordered from an (imagined) end point and in a way that creates coherence. In some analytic positions all experience has a narrative shape, while in others narrative is a specific practice of storytelling with particular qualities of accounting and cultural and aesthetic dimensions. I do not intend to argue in any detail about these assumptions, which are close to my position and have broadened our understanding of illness and healing. Nor do I claim that one may find no narratives in my materials. I primarily argue that we need a conception that covers a wider range of phenomena and dimensions than a narrative position as now commonly understood. The approach I advocate has not settled the question of the place of narrative in a theory of subjects in social practice—just as there is no consensus among narrative theorists over whether narrative is a specific concept that can be integrated in (other) conceptual frameworks or in and of itself a key concept designating a whole approach.

The concept of narrative orders experiences only in a time dimension and downplays the significance of the dimension of space. However, a spatial dimension to the configuration of experience and meaning is necessary in order to be able to anchor experiences in a robust way in social structure. Experiences in the immediate here-and-now are not only related to the past and future. They are always already located in structures of social practice, and their configuration draws upon this embeddedness as a relevant resource. There is more to relate, order, and create direction, robustness, and generality in our actions and experiences than time, cognitive ordering, symbolic structures, and so on. The structure of times and places of ongoing personal social practice constrains and enables the subjective structuration of actions and experiences. It prevents them, so to speak, from falling apart. In order to work, the subjective "plotting" of ongoing personal practice must rely on these structures. Even the shaping of experiences in "therapeutic time" reaches beyond the present space of time into the subject's life in other places. And what counts as an experience, as well as the meaning of that experience, depends on the particular context in which the subject is presently located.

That everyday life does not take place in one homogeneous location but as participation in and through a structure of diverse social contexts underlines the importance of space. It calls us to highlight the diversity of contextual practices along with the social arrangement of these diverse practices. In order to conduct their lives and pursue their concerns in and across these places in a personally sensible way, subjects must develop personal stances that reach across them. The structuration of personal actions and stances takes place in subjects' participation in and across the structure of their social practice, and subjective meaning is configured as part of this structuration of personal social practice. Concepts of narrative abstract too much from the concrete diversity of social practice and its contradictions. We need to understand concrete, particular situations in their practical, contextual interrelationships and not subsume them too readily in a narrative. Lived experiences are not interrelated only by means of narratives. They are already interrelated in practical terms in the flow and structuring of participation in and across contexts. There is more to the structuration of meaning than the shaping of a coherent narrative.

How central, then, is narrative to the practice of psychotherapy, and what do we gain by adopting it as a key term? Many believe narrative to be central to psychotherapy, especially in light of the crucial role of talk. Still, in a narrow sense of the term, "storied accounts" are not prominent features in the sessions and interviews in the study of family therapy I referred to. These sessions and interviews are mostly structured in question-and-answer sequences. Some would argue that such sequences are part of narratives under construction, which, of course, they might be. Still, in general terms, I doubt that. Sessions may be used to tell and construct stories, but that is not the most important aspect of what takes place in them. And when stories occur, other things frame and drive them than the construal and telling of a story. Indeed, their performative significance is often, say, the situating of a problem or the arguing against an opponent. In this sense, stories rather seem to be means to an end—for example, the pursuit of interests in conflicting relationships—than an end in themselves. In these conflicting relationships other people already are necessary parts in the negotiation of stories because they are characters in the stories. Yet, not only in individual therapies, these "others" include absent others who are not present in the session but are encountered in other times and places. Again we see that narratives reach beyond the present space of time into the structures of personal social practices. And the intersubjective dimension to narrating reminds us that the subjects involved may never reach a consensus on "the story." In my materials there seems to be no end to the divergences of their perspectives. It is, rather, their conflicting stances that fuel the process of therapy and the change of personal perspectives. Particular differences change, but differences remain. What is more, these changes seem not so much to be driven by trying to reach a common story as by challenging the conflicts, ambiguities, and indeterminacies of present points of view, by moving along the lines of the problematic, confused, and contested toward an uncovering of alternative possibilities of handling problematic aspects of personal social practices. The belief that we arrive at "a story" may rather result from the therapists'—

and researchers'—need to interpret what the clients tell them and mis-taking their interpretation for "the client's story."

If we did analyze the practice of psychotherapy with the concept of narrative as now commonly understood, what might we risk losing sight of? Of course, some topics might be included in our analysis just because we find certain phenomena interesting, without their having anything to do with using a concept of narrative. So, to be a little more precise, the question I raise here concerns which topics the concept of narrative does or does not point us toward. Like any other theoretical concept, the role of the concept of narrative is primarily to direct our analytic attention toward some particular features and relations rather than other features and relations. The features and relations of therapeutic practice I shall now briefly mention seem relevant for an analysis of subjective experience and action in relation to psychotherapy, but they seem to be external to the common understanding of narrating.

First, the concept of narrative seems strangely free-floating. It would not make us ask what particular social arrangement for "narrating" psychotherapy really is, and which particular "culture" of narrating might have developed in this arrangement. Psychotherapy would be analyzed just like any other case of narrating. It would not be of theoretical significance for the analysis of psychotherapeutic narratives that psychotherapy is conducted in a particular place with a particular kind of intimate strangers and confidentiality. The concept of narrative does not itself consider the practice of narrating to be a situated practice with particular situated concerns, pursuits, and stakes for the narrator(s). That would, instead, have to be introduced as something external to the very practice of narrating. Even though narrative theory may emphasize the question of the perspective of the narrator, that perspective seems strangely unlocated. The same holds for the question: What particular situated, more or less clearly delimited public does the narrating create, or what particular public constitutes the frame within which people find reasons to narrate in one way rather than another? There certainly might be quite substantial differences between the narratives produced in different kinds of publics with different meanings for the narrating persons.

The strangely unsituated character of the conception of narrative would easily make us overlook the fact that, as I stated earlier, clients have multiple relations with talk in multiple settings, that is, a quite peculiar one in sessions. In fact, the clients I quoted emphasized that they never before talked to each other the way they did in the sessions, and they do not do so in other places. They have quite different grounds for talking and pursue talk and their concerns in quite different ways. What I called "concerted problem talk" remains a peculiarity of their sessions. Even if they were to talk at length and intimately to somebody else about (the problems of) their lives, it seems doubtful to me whether, say, a friend or a lover would hear the same story. Only a concept of situated practice, including situated talking, would make us aware of the relevance of posing the analytic question of how talk or narrating here is related to talk and narrating in other settings.

We would, therefore, also easily lose sight of the fact that psychotherapy works precisely by virtue of being something different from what normally happens at home, in school, at work, and so on. It stands out as a particular experience because it is different and hence may contribute something different. Clients even do something different with these peculiar experiences from sessions when they get home and in other optional future situations.

This leads us to ask how one can understand the practice of narrating across contexts. How does situated narrating relate practices across places? How do subjects relate their local practices of narrating and acting? What kind of interrelationships do they establish between them? How do subjects configure their narratives so that they may be of help in the pursuit of their concerns from other places in the sessions and, at the same time, in their pursuit of future concerns in other places by means of the narrating in the sessions? And how do professionals find a way to be helpful in all these pursuits across contexts of which they take part in only one?

All this boils down to coming to understand the place and role of narrating in personal life trajectories in complex social practices. In fact, the concept of life trajectory is itself an attempt to reconceptualize our common concepts of personality, self, identity, and life history in a way that differs from a narrative approach and builds on the recognition of the social structure of practice and of the social arrangement of people's personal conduct of life in and across a set of diverse social contexts. It takes up the challenge to reflect in theoretical terms the sociohistorical changes and challenges to being a person in complex structures of social practice.

REFERENCES

Dreier, Ole. 1993. Researching psychotherapeutic practice. In *Understanding practice: Perspectives in activity and context,* edited by J. Lave and S. Chaiklin, 104–24. New York: Cambridge University Press.

————. 1994. Personal locations and perspectives: Psychological aspects of social practice. In *Psychological yearbook,* edited by N. Engelsted et al., 1:63–
90. Copenhagen: Museum Tusculanum Press.

————. 1996. Subjectivity and the practice of psychotherapy. In *Problems of
theoretical psychology,* edited by C. Tolman, F. Cherry, R. V. Hezewick, and
I. Lubek, 55–61. York, Canada: Captus Press.

————. 1998. Client perspectives and uses of psychotherapy. *European Journal
of Psychotherapy, Counseling and Health* 1:295–310.

————. In preparation. Trajectories of participation in social practice: Subjects
in psychotherapy and beyond.

Holzkamp, Klaus. 1983. *Grundlegung der Psychologie.* Frankfurt am Main:
Campus Verlag.

————. 1995. Alltägliche Lebensführung als subjektwisenschaftliches Grund-
konzept. *Das Argument* 37:817–46.

Lave, Jean. 1988. Cognition in practice: Mind, mathematics and culture in
everyday life. New York: Cambridge University Press.

————. 1997. On learning. *Forum Kritische Psychologie* 38:120–35.

Lave, Jean, and Etienne Wenger. 1991. *Situated learning: Legitimate peripheral
participation.* New York: Cambridge University Press.

Tolman, Charles. 1994. *Psychology, society, and subjectivity: An introduction
to German critical psychology.* New York: Routledge.

Tolman, Charles, and Wolfgang Maiers, eds. 1991. *Critical psychology: Contributions to an historical science of the subject.* New York: Cambridge University Press.

ELEVEN

Narrative Turns

LINDA C. GARRO and CHERYL MATTINGLY

The original vision behind this collection was to bring together a variety of perspectives to better understand what a focus on narrative offers to an understanding of illness experience and the practices of healing. To that end, we solicited contributions from scholars whose previous writings shed light on the narrative dimensions of illness and healing as well as those who cautioned about the limitations of narrative approaches. It is thus not surprising that this gathering is quite diverse. The chapters differ on many planes—in the questions asked, the evidence considered, the style of analysis, and the value accorded a narrative perspective in addressing the problem posed. In this closing chapter we do not attempt any resolution of the outstanding issues. Rather, by highlighting the claims and concerns put forward in this group of essays, we hope to further an understanding of what narratives are, what they help us to think about, and when they limit our view. Since there are many ways to tell a story, many situations of telling, and many lenses through which a story may be interpreted, we couch our reflections primarily within the universe provided by the essays in this volume. Even when limited to this collection, it is clear that there is no single narrative turn but a number of possible turns. Some of these cultivate a narrative perspective, even going so far as to suggest new ways of conceptualizing and extending narrative analysis, while others seek to contain and bound narrative while pointing out other paths. While the issues do not separate neatly into separate topics, nor are we as comprehensive as our organization

implies, we have placed our comments under three headings: telling narratives in cultural worlds; the narrative turn under scrutiny; and narrative theorizing and lived experience. We seek to strike a balance with the
generally favorable tone of the introductory chapter by orienting two of
the three sections around the questioning and/or skeptical voices in this
volume.

TELLING NARRATIVES IN CULTURAL WORLDS

Across the volume as a whole, the authors share an awareness of the human propensity to endow experience with meaning and the role of stories in this ongoing work of everyday life. Storytelling is also understood
to be a highly selective process. Narrative form requires, as Pollock explains, "that events or episodes be selected from among the vast range
of possibilities in the flow of experience and then be presented in an order
that itself intentionally or unintentionally conveys significance." Pollock
uses the term *narrative referentiality,* although limiting its application to
written autobiography, to characterize the way "an autobiography purports to describe some reality separate from and independent of the
text itself, yet autobiographical 'truth' is often a matter of verisimilitude
rather than of verifiability . . . a function of narrative strategies that convey a kind of basic believability." Nonetheless, in general, stories that
are told of personal experience lay claim to a "basic believability." The
rarely questioned expectation that stories are "experience-near," "close
to the ground," and "in tune with how people experience their own
world, and therefore true to life" (Wikan this volume) is one of the issues that is reviewed in the subsequent sections of this closing chapter.
The relationship between experiences and events, and the stories told
about them, is an important thread that runs through this final chapter.

Another starting point for this collection is the recognition of the
power of narrative to impart a vision of reality and one that is at once
socially positioned and culturally grounded. Text is linked to context,
always grounded in interaction and history. While the perspectives taken
are quite different, the chapters by Good and Good and by Garro illustrate how individual and collective frameworks can be brought to bear
on the interpretation of illness and its care. Good and Good contend
that an important part of becoming a competent physician and entering
the world of medicine is mastery of the narrative practices through
which an illness case is constituted "as a project, a temporal ordering of
illness processes that projected technical interventions as the work of the

physicians." In the medical world, there are agreed upon standards for composing stories that can be relied upon. Accounts from students on the process of learning how to participate in producing such shared constructions convey both their experience of the conventionality of medical practice and their growing sense of professional control through telling "stories that accurately represent physiological reality and provide a basis for effective interventions." Good and Good provide a compelling analysis of how a shared version of reality reproduces itself. In contrast, Garro's chapter situates the creation of an alternative narrative framework in the collective experience of oppressed people. A reality shared by individuals living in a Canadian Anishinaabe community is the ubiquity of maturity-onset diabetes in the present coupled with its nonexistence in the relatively recent past. While the primary biomedical narrative framework used by doctors in the community implicates the individual patient as ultimately accountable for the disease, an alternative narrative framing locates diabetes within the continuing historical context of widespread changes wrought by the coming of white men. Encompassing the emergence of diabetes within a broader disruptive history of relationships with the dominant Canadian society is widely shared within the community, echoing deeply held sentiments and gaining persuasiveness through the reverberation. But it is not a predetermining structure because both of these narrative frameworks coexist and are used differentially by individuals to make sense of the occurrence of diabetes. The "culturally available explanatory frameworks do not shape the construction of illness experience in a deterministic fashion but are flexible and provide relatively wide latitude for constructing a narrative that is both plausible and consistent with individual experience." In according primacy to individual experience, this tailoring process sets the stage for individual variability in dealing with diabetes.

But narratives are more than just reflections on experiences; while narratives may be composed of words, they are words that "do things." One of the things that these narrative constructions do is demarcate the parameters of appropriate responses to deal with illness. In the situations that both Garro and Good and Good describe, they are pragmatic and persuasive while upholding a particular moral world. Storymaking is fashioned to convince others to see and comprehend some part of reality in a particular way so that what happens follows from the way things are portrayed to be. For the medical students studied by Good and Good, it is through experiencing "the efficacy of a well-told story" that they come to adopt such narrative practices as a privileged means for representing material reality. Narratives precede and authorize medical endeavors, with the official story subsuming subsequent developments as either successful or failed technical interventions. Being a good doctor means being able to construct narratives that persuade others of an ordered reality requiring identifiable curative actions.

Stories need not take canonical form to affirm a moral stand. Although a privileged account, the official story is not the only story that can be told by physicians in training. Without seeking to change the structure of clinical life or call into question the legitimacy of sanctioned narrative practices, there are also stories attesting to the moral inadequacy of a purely technical medicine, which serve "in a modest way to protest against dehumanizing aspects of ward culture" (Good and Good this volume). In their autobiographies, physicians in training offer "alternative truths" and a "moral alternative" to "bureaucratized, technologized, dehumanizing forms of practice and patient management" (Pollock this volume). To Pollock, "it appears almost as if a broad lay public had 'authorized' these physicians to provide precisely these kinds of critical accounts of medicine and psychiatry, to construct a moral discourse in which patient welfare and patient rights are central to clinical work, and in which the bureaucratic barriers to care that have plagued patients for years are finally acknowledged and resisted by physicians themselves." Such critical accounts, as Pollock notes, are a relatively recent trend in physician autobiographies, embedding their advent within a broader historical, social, and cultural setting.

Personal stories about illness may also be resourceful improvisations. The essay by Hunt asks us to consider the "strategic implications of illness narratives" and the way in which they "can become potent micropolitical tools, reforging the disrupted identities of patients." Hunt draws attention to narrative as the "practical outcome of people creatively constructing a revised identity." For the cancer sufferers in her study, the use of illness narratives "reflects the practical outcome of people creatively constructing a revised identity" that addresses "their long-standing difficulties with the ideal gender roles of their culture" while "averting the necessity to call for revision of the moral principles underlying those roles." To be persuasive and to achieve pragmatic ends, one must work creatively within cultural bounds.

Without denying the import of narrative in informing and orienting the self, an understanding of the pragmatic, moral, and persuasive dimensions requires attention to the audience in the process of meaning construction. Even when an audience is not physically present during a narrative's composition, as in published texts, the supposed expectations of potential readers may lead authors to fashion their stories around particular themes and events. Thus, for example, Pollock notes that physician autobiographies provide a "rich source of insight into the resonating ways in which the physicians and the public understand medicine and agree to represent it." The presence of an audience can significantly shape a narrative performance, even to the point where distinctions between text, context, narrator, and audience become blurred. By considering what transpired in an interview setting as a "collaborative performance," Riessman draws us close to the intricacies of eliciting and interpreting narrative texts. The multiplicity of possible readings precludes any simple foreclosure on the meaning of the text. She presents several provisional readings, evaluating possible interpretations of what is said in relation to the text as a whole as well as the preexisting concerns or interests and interpretive "precommitments" of the audience while also attending to the broader social, cultural, and historical contexts that inform and enter into the text. Concurring with other authors in this collection, the meaning of the text is situated and dependent on a host of considerations external to the text itself. As Riessman notes, translated texts serve to "make visible interpretive problems that all narrative analysts face," for all stories "have ambiguities and relative indeterminacies. The texts are sparse, there are gaps and uncertainties, and they leave considerable room for reader response." Without tidying up all of the remaining ambiguities and relative indeterminacies, Riessman's analysis of the emerging story is one of a woman's agency in the face of stigma.

Kirmayer's chapter addresses how narratives take form in clinical encounters. At first, rather than something told, narratives are enacted through persuasive contest as patient and clinicians actively "struggle to negotiate meaning with materials given to them by the cultural surround." Narrative possibilities are tendered and may or may not be fully developed. However, once established, "authorized and accepted, a story is retold and so persists, becomes stabilized, and influences future stories."

As all these essays reveal, to understand the persuasive and pragmatic possibilities of narrative, one must go beyond text to examine the social world in which a story is told, or even tellable. This requires developing an analytic gaze that reaches beyond the immediate context of performance; it demands placing the narrative event within a broader range of social, political, and cultural contexts. Narrative meaning is in important ways emergent and situated rather than already given by social and cultural structures.

THE NARRATIVE TURN UNDER SCRUTINY

The very power of narrative is also its potential drawback. It is just these persuasive, pragmatic, and selective possibilities in personal storytelling that concern Wikan and Kirmayer. For them and others raising concerns about the narrative turn, telling stories or eliciting stories from informants is not necessarily a problem in itself. And, most assuredly, Kirmayer and Wikan are very talented and persuasive storytellers. Their ability to tell a good story encourages the reader to adopt the more abstract morals they wish to draw from their examples. Their critique of narrative is directed elsewhere. It has to do with what to make of stories, how they ought to inform our theoretical gaze and our understanding of cultural life. Kirmayer alerts us to the way narrative realities are vulnerable to social influence, most palpably shaped in clinical settings by the authoritative weight of medical interpretations. In practical terms, the clinician is "heavily constrained by the institutional context and the necessity to act based on his reading of the situation." Wikan draws attention to anthropological encounters. One of her points is that the narrator has freedom to construct the story, while it is "the essence of the anthropologist's trade that we should tend to be taken in by what people tell us." And it is especially easy to be taken in when stories are personal and told in a way that invites trust, as Wikan's own story does. Although she does not seek to disabuse our trust, she complicates any simple correspondence by making clear that this is by no means the only way her illness story can be told. Our ability to do things with words complicates matters considerably. Narrative may disguise things, too.

For Wikan, who holds a pragmatic view of meaning, stories are constructed for particular audiences with particular goals in mind, goals in which illness may figure primarily as a means to another end. For an "empathetic anthropologist trained to be attuned to illness and suffering," the "sheer pragmatics of storytelling stand in danger of getting lost." Interactive clues given by the anthropologist (as audience) influence how a story emerges. Through this dynamic, we may miss comprehending the main message of the story, mistaking the story as being about illness when the point lies elsewhere.

Wikan suggests that the heavy analytic weight placed on personal narratives in anthropology seems to reflect an underlying message that "this is as close as we can get" to lived experience. While noting that there are indeed situations in which other kinds of data are not available, she argues that these are truly exceptions and that observation of real-life behavior is "necessary to fill in the picture and understand what a narrative is all about, and that we can indeed get closer to a person's experience that way." Stories offer no "privileged access to lived experience"; they cannot be taken at face value as "authentic."

Wikan, Dreier, and Kirmayer worry that stories have become too important in social theory and that there is more to cultural life than can be encompassed by a narrative vision. In this and other writings, Wikan contests "the place of narrative in much current anthropology, arguing that it has been given a place out of all proportion to the role of stories in real life for many people." Such concerns echo voices of scholars both inside and outside anthropology who have argued that attention to narrative means neglect of other crucially important features of cultural life and human experience.

In Wikan's and Dreier's chapters, narrative is not the primary structure that gives meaning to social action. Wikan entreats us to attend to "lived predicaments" and "compelling concerns" of those we study. Dreier introduces his own framework for the analysis of social practice by contrasting it with a narrative analysis and "warning against limitations and distortions if one focuses too closely on narrative and loses sight of its performative significance and place in people's ongoing personal practice across social contexts." Dreier's concern to understand meaning as organized by contexts is contrasted with the way meaning is commonly construed within a narrative framework. He notes: "Conceptions of narrative characteristically focus on experience and meaning which they consider in a dimension of time directed toward a future, ordered from an (imagined) end point and in a way that creates coherence." His key critique (but others are implicit) is that this is insufficient, and that a "spatial dimension" is needed to "anchor experiences in a robust way in social structure. Experiences in the immediate here-and-now are not only related to the past and future. They are always already located in structures of social practice, and their configuration draws upon this embeddedness as a relevant resource."

And what of meanings conveyed without recourse to language? Talk is not necessarily central to the way meaning is created or shared by social actors, a point made by both Wikan and Dreier. Wikan reminds us of silence, pointing out that there is much that goes unsaid, and perhaps is not even tellable, especially when life circumstances are the most trying. For Dreier, prenarrated or nonnarrated experience is no booming, buzzing confusion, but highly structured and constrained by any number of contextual features. There are sources of form, order, and mean ing that are other than and prior to narrative. Dreier concludes: "We need to understand concrete, particular situations in their practical, contextual interrelationships and not subsume them too readily in a narrative. Lived experiences are not interrelated only by means of narrative. They are already interrelated in practical terms in the flow and structuring of participation in and across contexts." Dreier does not worry that life may lack coherence; rather, in his view, life has plenty of structure and coherence provided by activities and contexts themselves. Narrative is certainly not necessary to lend coherence or form to experience.

With regard to clinical storytelling, Kirmayer argues that the literary analogies guiding the field of medical anthropology obscure essential features of clinical encounters and do not address what he considers to be the "central problems in analyzing illness narratives," namely, the "relationships of narrative to bodily experience and to social power." Medical encounters between patients and clinicians to decipher troubling bodily experiences occur within the context of "larger institutional ideologies and practices that inform and constrain their individual agendas." It is just these "limitations of the metaphor of narrative as text" that led Kirmayer to explore "how clinical narratives come into being."

Yet another concern is that the academic emphasis on narrative establishes and structures the problems we address and the evidence we consider. Analogous to the postmodern claim, reviewed in the introductory chapter, that anthropologists are guided by implicit stories that shape their perception of what is in the world, Dreier asks whether the perceived importance of therapeutic storytelling grows out of similar expectations: "The belief that we arrive at 'a story' may rather result from the therapists'—and researchers'—need to interpret what the clients tell them and mistaking their interpretation for 'the client's story.'" He asks us to consider the activity of narrating as simply another type of "situated practice with particular situated concerns, pursuits, and stakes for the narrator(s)." Chapters by Good and Good and by Kirmayer highlight the active role of clinicians in ordering reality by means of narrative practices. Dreier suggests that we entertain the possibility that that is what scholars are doing as well.

NARRATIVE THEORIZING AND LIVED EXPERIENCE

Continuing a discussion tendered in the preceding section (and first broached in the introductory chapter), the frequent distinction between life as lived and life as narrated takes center stage here. At stake are questions about the power of narrative—often examined in terms of how narrative is treated in contemporary narrative theory—to adequately reveal the nature of lived experience. Does life gain coherence through narrative? Are narrative efforts to express the personal truly experience-near or, does narrative lead *away* from experience rather than toward it?

For Kirmayer, "narrative represents an end point, not a beginning" for we can "articulate our suffering without appeal to elaborate stories of origins, motives, obstacles, and change." He pays particular attention to how "prior to narratization, salient illness experiences are apprehended and extended through metaphors." One's experience—especially during serious illness—may be fractured and lack a sense of continuity, and metaphors admit, but do not determine, "narrative possibilities." Somatic distress in illness is described as "the breaking through into consciousness of nonnarratized, inchoate experience that resists narrative smoothing and containment." Kirmayer shares the wariness of a great many others who are concerned to get at experience and are dubious of those familiar cultural forms, which are supposed to be the expressions of something ineffable or at least a great deal more fragmented than life as portrayed in a story.

From this perspective, narratives may provide a standardized or clinically authorized cultural form imposing order, which is actually far removed from life as lived. "Indeed, in acute illness," Kirmayer writes, "narratives are often fragmentary or undeveloped; where narratives are most coherent, they may also be formulaic and distant from sufferers' experience." In other words, when stories are told, life may appear as far too coherent, full of continuities and connections that are the product of the narrative itself, not of life as it is felt and experienced. If narratives connect the experiential to the cultural, Kirmayer argues that this may be because the experiential is, in fact, sacrificed in order to produce a culturally acceptable account. The powerful force of narrative as a vehicle for both communicating and shaping experience carries a certain danger, Kirmayer points out. If narratives "reshape memories to fit conventions . . . [the] effect can be therapeutic or pernicious according to the psychological and moral consequences of rewriting the past." Kirmayer's critique echoes a host of anthropologists and literary theorists who have contended that narratives are illusory, forcing the unruliness of lived experience into a coherent form with a clear beginning, middle, and end.

From a different angle, Wikan and Mattingly ask to consider whether (some) narrative theory is experience-far. While it is now quite common in anthropology and elsewhere to speak of the *discontinuity* or probable lack of correspondence between experience and narrative, Wikan and Mattingly both challenge this presumption. But they do so in different ways. Wikan claims that the nearness of a story to an experience may have less to do with its authenticity regarding the facts of the case than its aesthetic display of the feeling of events from the perspective of the narrator. Reflecting upon the personal story she tells in her chapter, she is struck that it is "bare to the bone, *thin.*" She notices that she barely mentions some of those closest to her—husband, mother, and son—although actually they were extremely concerned and involved during the time of her illness. "But," she writes, "my *experience* was of being utterly alone in a trauma that shook me out of my life. The structure of my story . . . captures this." Wikan also argues that stories are not nearly so coherent as narrative scholars claim them to be. She says of her own story that it has "a definite beginning (or two), a moderately clear middle, and a muddled, unfinished end." The idea that narratives are composed of a clear beginning, middle, and end is "absurd," she declares. Further, what coherence does exist, exists in life. She writes:

> The coherence I depict is not an artifact of my story, it is the essence of my life. Things cohere, even when they maddeningly jar. I experience my life through my efforts to make sense of events. It is not that experience is formless, languageless. From my first experience of the black dashing shadows, when I didn't have a clue other than "stress" to what they meant, I put words to my experience, I told myself stories to account for them. And yet the literary theorists tell us life does not cohere, only narratives do.

Following Mattingly, Wikan notes that there is a "continuous groping for meaning" that "determines the structure of lived experience."

Mattingly also challenges discontinuity theories and the popular view that coherence is the main thing narrative offers, but she does so through an examination of events rather than narrative texts. It is drama, not coherence, that lies at the heart of the narrative moment, experience worth telling a story about. And narrative moments "arise, in part, because the actors are in search of narrative, in quest of drama." Narrative moments are creative acts and meaningful ones. Mattingly argues that a narrative portrayal of experience is necessarily artificial, since "no life as lived has the congruence of the well-told tale." However, there is a more compelling quality than coherence that links narrative to action and experience. Mattingly contends, "If narrative offers an intimate relation to lived experience, the dominant formal feature that connects the two is not nar-

rative coherence but narrative drama. We follow a narrative suspensefully, always reminded of the fragility of events, for things might have
turned out differently." She agrees with discontinuity theorists that life
is never merely the enactment of prior narrative texts and that stories
told about events necessarily "fictionalize" them by providing a form
and meaning that they lacked when they were lived out. However, she
contends, "one need not abandon the exploration of [the relationship
between narrative and experience] for fear of losing sight of these central points. Although there are strong reasons to claim that action is one
thing but narrative is something else entirely, there are stronger reasons
to recognize their kinship." This does not imply a return to a naive correspondence theory. Rather, she suggests that it requires the simultaneous investigation of narrative discourse *and* of social action. As argued
here and elsewhere, Mattingly contends:

> The opposition between lived experience and narrative discourse registers
> sensibly only by positing a false notion of what prior events are and how they
> are structured. Literary theorists . . . and others whose primary concern is
> written and oral texts have not investigated the structure of lived experience,
> and thus the distinctions between life and art rest on far too simple a view of
> how life in time is experienced. Even anthropologists fascinated with the eth-
> nographer's task of converting field experience into text have been too quick
> to dismiss the narrative structures of social action.

Thus, we come full circle to where we started, namely, with issues of
meaning in social and cultural worlds. We have covered much ground
through these papers, including our introductory and closing chapters,
so much that a straightforward and cogent summary of all the points is
simply not a feasible task. So we simply say that attention to narrative
forces us to confront the problem of meaning and the human affinity to
endow experience with meaning. As we come to a close, we wish only
to add that the issues and questions that make up this book are not limited to those concerned with narrative, or even medical anthropology.
They are relevant to all who study and seek to understand the human
condition.

Contributors

OLE DREIER is Professor of Personality Psychology, Department of Psychology, University of Copenhagen.

LINDA C. GARRO is Professor, Department of Anthropology, University of California, Los Angeles.

BYRON J. GOOD, PH.D., is Professor of Medical Anthropology and Vice Chairman in the Department of Social Medicine, Harvard Medical School, and Lecturer in the Department of Anthropology, Harvard University Faculty of Arts and Sciences.

MARY-JO DELVECCHIO GOOD is Professor of Social Medicine, Department of Social Medicine, Harvard Medical School, and Co-Director of the Center for the Study of Culture and Medicine.

LINDA M. HUNT, PH.D., is Associate Professor, Department of Anthropology and Julian Samora Research Institute at Michigan State University.

LAURENCE J. KIRMAYER, M.D., is Professor and Director, Division of Social and Transcultural Psychiatry, McGill University, and Director, Culture and Mental Health Research Unit, Sir Mortimer B. Davis–Jewish General Hospital, Montreal, Quebec.

CHERYL MATTINGLY is Professor, Department of Anthropology and Occupational Science, University of Southern California.

DONALD POLLOCK, PH.D., is a health care consultant in Washington, D.C., and can be reached at 3119 Lancer Place, Hyattsville, Maryland 20782.

CATHERINE KOHLER RIESSMAN is Research Professor, Department of Sociology at Boston College.

UNNI WIKAN is Professor of Social Anthropology at the University of Oslo.

Index

Text:	10/13 Sabon
Display:	Sabon
Composition:	G&S Typesetters
Printing and binding:	Rose Printing Company, Inc.
Index:	Victoria Baker